615.1
CHA

7-05

D1194825

Buying Rx Drugs Online:
Avoiding a Prescription

for Disaster

Date Due

b.s

BLUE ISLAND PUBLIC LIBRARY
BLUE ISLAND, ILLINOIS

Buying Rx Drugs Online: Avoiding a Prescription for Disaster

Kate J. Chase

THOMSON
———✴———™
COURSE TECHNOLOGY
Professional ■ Trade ■ Reference

A DIVISION OF COURSE TECHNOLOGY

© 2005 by Thomson Course Technology PTR. All rights reserved. No part of this book may be reproduced or transmitted in any form or by any means, electronic or mechanical, including photo-copying, recording, or by any information storage or retrieval system without written permission from Thomson Course Technology PTR, except for the inclusion of brief quotations in a review.

The Thomson Course Technology PTR logo and related trade dress are trademarks of Thomson Course Technology PTR and may not be used without written permission.

SVP, Thomson Course Technology PTR: Andy Shafran
Publisher: Stacy L. Hiquet
Senior Marketing Manager: Sarah O'Donnell
Marketing Manager: Heather Hurley
Manager of Editorial Services: Heather Talbot
Associate Acquisitions Editor: Megan Belanger
Senior Editor: Mark Garvey
Associate Marketing Manager: Kristin Eisenzopf
Marketing Coordinator: Jordan Casey
Project Editor: Jenny Davidson
Technical Reviewer: Benjamin Garvin
PTR Editorial Services Coordinator: Elizabeth Furbish
Copy Editor: Kim Cofer
Interior Layout Tech: Jill Flores
Cover Designer: Nancy Goulet
Indexer: Kelly Talbot

All trademarks are the property of their respective owners.

Important: Thomson Course Technology PTR cannot provide software support. Please contact the appropriate software manufacturer's technical support line or Web site for assistance.

Thomson Course Technology PTR and the author have attempted throughout this book to distinguish proprietary trademarks from descriptive terms by following the capitalization style used by the manufacturer.

Information contained in this book has been obtained by Thomson Course Technology PTR from sources believed to be reliable. However, because of the possibility of human or mechanical error by our sources, Thomson Course Technology PTR, or others, the Publisher does not guarantee the accuracy, adequacy, or completeness of any information and is not responsible for any errors or omissions or the results obtained from use of such information. Readers should be particularly aware of the fact that the Internet is an ever-changing entity. Some facts may have changed since this book went to press.

Educational facilities, companies, and organizations interested in multiple copies or licensing of this book should contact the publisher for quantity discount information. Training manuals, CD-ROMs, and portions of this book are also available individually or can be tailored for specific needs.

ISBN: 1-59200-671-X

Library of Congress Catalog Card Number: 2004114488
Printed in the United States of America

04 05 06 07 08 BH 10 9 8 7 6 5 4 3 2 1

Thomson Course Technology PTR, a division of Thomson Course Technology
25 Thomson Place
Boston, MA 02210
http://www.courseptr.com

This book is dedicated in loving memory of Arnold Brackman, a fine journalist and author, who was also my college journalism professor.

Acknowledgments

First, I want to thank you for picking up this book. I think buying drugs online can be a great way to save time and potentially money, but it also comes with some risks when you happen to use a less than fully standard pharmacy. Reading this means you want to do things right, protecting yourself from the problems that can come from doing something as important as drug shopping without some good old-fashioned research.

Secondly, my great thanks to Course Technology's associate acquisitions editor, Megan Belanger who immediately saw the worth in this project and gave me everything I needed to produce it. Project editor Jenny Davidson was superb, calmly working around missing files from my flaky Internet service to keep the pace moving ever swiftly ahead. They have been invaluable not only in bringing this book to market on an accelerated schedule; they've been a joy to work with as well (and trust me, I do not say that lightly). Copy editor Kim Cofer and this project's extremely helpful technical editor Benjamin Garvin worked deftly and wisely. Also thanks to layout tech Jill Flores and indexer Kelly Talbot.

David Fugate, my agent, deserves praise by doing what an agent does best—helping me to design a proposal for a book that meets its objectives and then presenting it to the right people.

My thanks are also extended to my superb physician, Mark Yorra, M.D. who has perhaps been the best doctor I've ever had. He's one of those wonderful types who understands that doctor-patient communication is vital and always presents choices rather than edicts. If you're one of those shopping online because you're just completely frustrated with trying to find a doctor who listens to you, I'm here to tell you that there seem to be many still around. So find one.

Finally, thanks to the wonderful medical resources online (there are so many, and I've included those I could in the book) as well as the online shoppers who were willing to share their experiences with me. Many were willing to admit mistakes they made in the hope that this information could help you in avoiding them.

About the Author

Kate J. Chase is an author, a journalist, and a Web services professional who has worked for major players in the online industry. She has also authored, coauthored, contributed to, or edited more than 20 books in the last 8 years. Before specializing in online and technical issues, Chase was a general interest and medical writer whose work has appeared in *The New York Times*, *The Hartford Courant*, *The Los Angeles View*, *BBW Magazine*, and others.

Contents at a Glance

Contents

Chapter 5 Patient, Prescribe for Thyself? 85

Introduction

Welcome and congratulations on picking up this book. This book is designed to answer some of the questions and explore some of the many different important issues that people wonder about in light of the new trend of online pharmacies. What I've found over the last year is that the one major factor in keeping people from taking advantage of cyber ordering for drugs are the big questions they can't answer. These questions include:

- ▶ Is it legal?
- ▶ Is it safe?
- ▶ Can I save money?
- ▶ What will I get asked?
- ▶ Will I get exactly what I ordered?
- ▶ Who's watching what I do and who's protecting me from buying bogus or counterfeit medications?
- ▶ Should I buy from Canada even though some U.S. agencies say we shouldn't?
- ▶ What happens if I place an order at a foreign pharmacy and my order gets seized?
- ▶ How can I tell whether my loved ones are using and abusing these easy-order pharmacies?
- ▶ What should I share with my doctor and what do I do if I don't have a primary care physician?

Buying drugs online can be completely safe and legal, and can save you money if you shop carefully. But you have to know what to look for and you need to be prepared to protect your own interests rather than rely entirely on the system of checks and balances to keep you from harm or fraud. This book tries to address all these common questions and provides a great deal more information as well.

You're going to learn that there are major differences between legitimate online drugstores and those who simply sell a cache of pills—real or counterfeit or foreign substitutions—to you without much regard to whether the drug is appropriate for you to take. The differences between the two can make the difference between sound medical care and the start of nasty complications you never counted upon.

Now glance at your watch and note the time. There's a reason, and I'll let you know what it is in a moment.

As a Web and online professional who has developed and led successful Web sites and communities, I believe very much in the wealth, the information, and the overall sense of connectedness the Internet can offer to us all. Yet I also recognize its dangers.

Many of the online risks are presented clearly and loudly to you each and every day in the news: people seeking out children for less than honorable reasons, scams, credit card fraud, and identity theft. But the presence of so many drugstores online offers both the bounty of more choices and some substantial risks that people can go beyond their doctor to obtain and take drugs that may do everything but help them. You've no doubt heard this discussed on the news, too, but this book explores far more background.

Read the Acknowledgments for this book and you'll see the number of people who helped bring this book to you. However, one entity not mentioned there is an illness that landed me in intensive care for a few weeks in the summer of 2003.

Believe it or not, the idea for the book came while surfing the Web by laptop from my ICU bed while listening to the relentless hiss of my oxygen hookup. I was online looking for information about my fairly rare illness as well as learning about the drugs and other forms of treatment I was being given.

Suddenly, I was getting all these unsolicited ads for pain medication promising me I could get it without a prescription. This seemed pretty ironic because medication there in the hospital was very carefully monitored; I couldn't even get an antacid tablet without medical staff double-checking. So I wondered how the heck any online store was trying to sell potent painkillers and sleeping pills without a prior prescription. It also worried me; I've seen the devastation substance abuse can wreak. It genuinely concerns me how many people are using the online ease of the less legitimate online drug mills to self-medicate themselves. Like many Americans, I've had periods of depression, of uncontrolled pain, and sickness that I've sometimes treated myself—and very ineffectively.

Once I was finally freed from the hospital, I went home on a battery of drugs only to have friends and colleagues say, "Why aren't you filling these prescriptions in Canada or Mexico? It's much cheaper there."

This phenomenon also amazed me because it had never occurred to me that I—or they—would feel the need to leave the country, physically or by modem, to obtain basic medical needs. Yet apparently people were tapping into these resources, and were surprised that I was not.

Ding! Look at your watch again. In the time it took for you to read less than two full pages, I located an online pharmacy I've never visited before, picked a drug, clicked the Order button, filled out a brief medical information form, and requested a powerful medicine without any prior prescription, with my order confirmation shown below. So can you, your children, your parents, and those you work with. That's how widespread the nature of illegal prescriptions online has become.

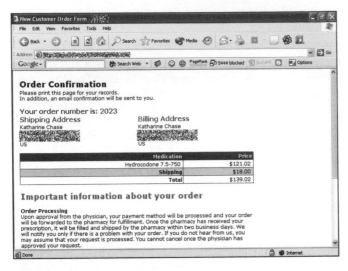

Pretty easy? Oh yes. But it's also not legal, despite what the online drug vendor may tell you. Nor is it ethical for an online pharmacy—which is what this site calls itself—to fill. But aside from law and ethics, this drug can be a bad match for my condition, can create the beginning of a drug dependence or addiction, create powerful and unwanted side effects, and it can perhaps even kill me.

But because it's easy and accessible, many people are choosing to do it despite the risks. Some call ordering their own drugs an effort to take control of their own medical care. Professionals call it self medication.

Yet there is a distinct and drastic difference between becoming a partner in your wellness and health and trying to prescribe medication for yourself. As you'll read in this book, particularly in Chapter 4, good doctors are often reticent to treat themselves for a variety of reasons. If they need to weigh many factors, we certainly need to stop and think because we don't have the breadth of knowledge on medicine, chemistry, and body function that they possess. There's also the very nasty reality of something called drug dependence that, once we develop, can be a bear to break since that very dependence can have us dreaming up nifty excuses to keep us taking our drug of choice.

Yes, health care in this country is some of the very best in the world. Yes, there's a looming crisis as medical prices rise and more Americans face either extremely high health insurance premiums or going completely without. Yes, many people with chronic pain and illness are not getting good symptom management, at least in part because of rules in place that can affect what your doctor does to treat your condition. And yes, this can lead us to desperately search for relief in non-standard means.

The path you take when you order drugs through "no prescription needed" sites can be dangerous to your health on so many different levels: You may not have the precautions in place to keep you from wrong doses, from harmful drug interactions, to be sure you aren't getting bogus or counterfeit medications, and to watch your response to these medications.

Nor do you just need to worry about yourself. Studies and anecdotal stories tell us that "pharming," the practice where kids experiment with drugs found on the shelves of the local drugstore and in the family medicine cabinet, is on the rise. With access to cash and credit and/or debit cards, kids or their schoolmates are going online and purchasing potent drugs to add to their "fun." Increasingly, older Americans are availing themselves of easy-to-obtain online drugs to combat depression, loneliness, and the very real pains of aging. Your spouse or your friend may also be abusing these pharmaceuticals because it's fairly anonymous and simple to do so.

It's probably no simple coincidence that the Internet's less reputable sources have come together to offer a whole medicine cabinet full of prescription drugs at this time. A number of factors come into play here, including:

1. The Desperation Factor

People are losing health insurance or the great coverage they once enjoyed, so they're more prone to self-treatment even if they have to pay more for their prescriptions.

2. The Embarrassment or Hassle Factor

If you can just go online and buy a drug much like you purchase a book or a pair of shoes, some people wonder why they should bother going to the hassle of seeing a doctor. This is especially true for so-called high embarrassment drugs such as erectile dysfunction medications, antidepressants, diet pills, and herpes treatments.

3. Convenience

We're working or otherwise away from home for record numbers of hours each week. It can be harder and harder to find the time to see your doctor and to run down to the corner pharmacy to fill an order. The beauty of the Internet is that you can set your own fill-refill schedule.

4. Bargain Hunters

Looking for better prices? With some legitimate pharmacies, shopping around can save you money even if you don't go outside the country to purchase them.

5. General Anxiety

Today, we're involved in a global War on Terror, we're watching the job outlook here erode, and suffering from a depressed economy. Studies show us that since 9/11/01 with the attacks on Washington, D.C. and New York—people are taking antidepressants and anti-anxiety drugs at a record pace.

6. Overall Social Acceptance

For the last few decades, drug names like Xanax are dropped in movies we watch, books we read, and in discussions with friends. While we might keep our use of certain drugs quiet, hearing about others we respect or work with who use psychotropic drugs like antidepressants or anti-anxiety medication tends to bolster our justification for taking it ourselves.

7. Doctor Scrutiny

Doctors are finding themselves under increased scrutiny by the federal government in what they prescribe, making them almost have to battle policies to treat their patients effectively. The latter is particularly true when it comes to chronic pain management—with chronic pain likely to strike nearly one in six of us each year—where each prescription for a potent controlled painkiller can be monitored and reported as suspicious.

8. People Trying to Avoid Feeling Like Patients

This one is often underrated, at least until you talk with some of the people who are shopping for medications online. Some people are really irritated at the idea of having to go through a doctor to "get permission" to take a particular drug. Chronic pain patients often report feeling as if they're treated like children asking for candy when all they want is more effective relief of their discomfort. For wise and not-so-smart reasons, they're going online to replace or supplement what they get from their physicians.

But easy-access online drug mills can represent every bit as much danger as they offer convenience.

Information in this book is organized into the various issues surrounding this major topic:

Chapter 1: "Enter the Digital Drugstore"

This first chapter offers an overview of the types of online drugstores available with a look at the primary distinctions between them. Here, too, you get an introduction to some of the other online shops kids and adults are using both to learn more about their own health care but also to experiment recreationally with prescription drugs, chemicals, and herbs.

Chapter 2: "Big Brother Watches, But How Much?"

The federal government along with the private sector—including shipping companies, pharmaceutical manufacturers, and pharmacy boards—have measures in place to try to keep potentially harmful legal prescription medications as well as illicit drugs from getting in the wrong hands. But some of the guidelines seem to conflict with compassionate care and not all the safeguards are strictly observed, resulting in many ways drugs are becoming more accessible to those without a legitimate, documented need to use them.

Chapter 3: "The Electronic Drugstore Shopper"

Who's shopping online? Let them tell you themselves, sharing some of their blunders and solutions.

Chapter 4: "When and If Your Doctor Says No"

We get so conditioned to drug ads that suggest we talk with our doctor about getting a particular drug that few of us think about exactly why a physician refuses to write a prescription for a medication we think we need. Every decision a doctor makes has to be the right one and right not just in the sense of making you momentarily happy or relieved.

This chapter examines some of the many issues such as your weight, your current physical condition and overall health, and your past medical history that a doctor must consider before agreeing to place you on a particular drug.

Chapter 5: "Patient, Prescribe for Thyself?"

Have any idea of how many years of training a pharmacist goes through? Training can come close to matching that of a physician. This chapter examines some of the education and experience that is needed to make sound judgments about appropriate treatment, a foundation most of us laypeople can't have.

But the chapter also presents you with some resources so you can learn more, ask better questions of your physician, and become a stronger partner in your care without resorting to self medication.

Chapter 6: "The Drugs You Want and Need"

The spotlight here is on the most popularly prescribed and Internet-available drugs on the market, differentiating between the standard range of drugs offered through more traditional pharmacies and the more limited but targeted marketing of diet pills, antidepressants, and male potency drugs on the "no prescription needed" sites. You also get a better understanding of the serious issues that can result from misuse of your dosages or mixing certain drugs in combination.

Chapter 7: "Finding Good Stores Online"

Rather than offer you a list of "best 10 online pharmacies," I show you how you can determine which online pharmacies are legitimate and which you should avoid.

Chapter 8: "Placing Your Order Online"

This chapter steps you through the actual online order process, from locating cyber pharmacies through recommendations and Web search engines, as well as through the many consumer health information sites online such as WebMD and DrKoop.com.

Chapter 9: "The Price You Pay"

All too often, we have no idea what the going price of our medications are until the cash register—real or virtual—rings them up and presents us with the unpleasant news. But the best way to save money with online drug shopping starts with knowing what other pharmacies charge for the same drug. I'll show you how to find the price before you start shopping.

Chapter 10: "Identifying What You Really Get"

Whether you're getting your drugs from the local pharmacy or through an online vendor you've never used before, you have to be sure that what you ordered is what you get. Mistakes happen but you don't want errors in something as important as your prescription medicine.

Thankfully, a number of online resources make it possible for you to look up your pills and capsules before you take them so you can identify the right from the wrong and possibly even the legitimate from the counterfeit ripoffs. Yet more sites let you find out about potential drug interactions, proper doses, possible side effects, and what you should watch for.

Chapter 11: "Getting Refills and Transferring Prescriptions"

The two very standard procedures of obtaining refills on your medications or transferring them from one pharmacy to another often helps you identify the legitimate online drugstores from the fly-by-night drug sellers.

Chapter 12: "Are Your Kids Pharming?"

If you don't know what pharming is, you should, especially if you make a habit of leaving drugs around in family medicine cabinets where they may be pilfered by teens and other loved ones. This chapter presents vital information on how the ease with which we can now order drugs online is making them more accessible to teens and other vulnerable people, and shows you some common sense ways of trying to watch for the warning signs.

Chapter 13: "Avoiding a Prescription for Disaster"

This chapter rolls all the key details together into a checklist to help you be sure that you're covering all the important bases before you place your prescription order online.

Chapter 14: "Border Skirmishes: Special Issues in Drug Importation and More"

We keep hearing the federal authorities tell us that drugs from Canada and other nations may not be as safe as American drugs. But why?

This chapter looks at the phenomenon of cheaper drugs across the border, the Canadian system and proposed changes in it that may potentially affect U.S. citizens ordering from them, as well as examine what it means that so many of us are crossing the border by vehicle or modem to shop there. Then it goes beyond to deal with conflicting government policies and what may be in store in the short-term future.

With so much to cover, let's get started.

Kate J. Chase

South Woodbury, Vermont

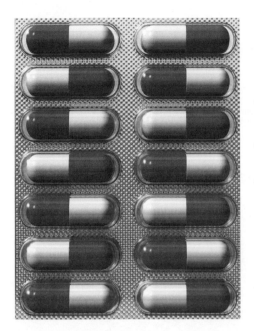

Part I

The Good, the Bad, the Legal, and the Illicit

It's very likely your favorite pharmacy has a Web site these days, a site where you can get answers to questions, check drug prices, and even place orders as well as refill or transfer prescriptions. But there's so much more out there, including a number of places that operate outside the boundaries of the laws and your safety.

This part looks at your available options, the regulatory and other systems in place to try to protect your interests, and who's taking advantage of the Internet revolution to move their medication shopping online.

Chapter 1
Enter the Digital Drugstore

Among the many huge changes in American society over the past generation or two is how we receive our health care.

Doctors' house calls and affordable hospital bills became extinct first. Then many of us moved from the friendly family physician and the corner apothecary shop to a world of Health Maintenance Organizations (HMOs), specialists, and a ream of forms we can't begin to understand. Terms like co-pay, preferred provider, diagnosis eligibility, required pre-admission verification, and pre-existing condition have crept into our vocabulary—if not in daily use, then in trying to make sense of our health insurance manuals that get thicker with each passing year.

There have been more recent and less fortunate developments as well. Health care benefits, once a near-certainty as one of the standard incentives with any good job, have been scaled back severely. Medical costs and health insurance premiums are skyrocketing. Universal health coverage never seems to move beyond the debate stage. Right now, between 40 and 50 million Americans are without any health insurance whatsoever, and that figure may climb dramatically in the next few years.

But being without health insurance doesn't necessarily mean you qualify for low-cost or no-cost aid. While the emergency rooms of hospitals that take federal aid usually can't turn someone away because they can't pay, many of the Americans without health insurance are working, meaning they may make enough to disqualify them for assistance even though they cannot afford the bill.

With all these changes also comes a big shift in our medications as well. There have never been more different types of drugs available to treat thousands of conditions and diseases. We've also moved from a time where nearly all our medications were name brands with little competition into a world where most of us know that generic versions of the same drugs can save us money.

Added to that is a fundamental expansion of how we buy our drugs. Gone is the corner drugstore where our parents often had a sandwich and a milkshake at the lunch counter while they waited for their order to be filled. It has largely been replaced by chain drugstores and mega med shops that take up an acre or more of real estate, and are filled with regular department store merchandise.

Now there's another evolution. People are beginning to move away from a process that involves calling the doctor, who calls the pharmacy, which packs up your prescription awaiting your pickup. The new pharmacies deliver, by way of UPS, FedEx, and snail mail. It's a system where you may never see your pharmacist. It offers convenience, although sometimes at a high cost, and there are some pitfalls as well.

An Overview of the Online Explosion

Just five years ago, everyone with a product to sell was still debating whether American consumers would ever feel comfortable shopping online for anything. Before the year 2000, most of those taking advantage of electronic shopping were pretty much limited to early adopters of the Internet.

This changed, but the speed accelerated sharply, aided in no small measure by the terror attacks on the United Stated on September 11th, 2001. Soon after, there were threats that terrorists would hit shopping malls and other public places. Suddenly, people who had never even browsed an online store did most or all of their holiday shopping on the Internet by the end of 2001. A critical threshold was crossed, opening up huge new audiences to the speed and convenience of virtual shopping carts.

Yet one thing few could envision was a time when we would take our health care to the Web. Sure, in the foreword to the revision of Alvin Toffler's *Future Shock*, former Speaker of the House Newt Gingrich talked about a consultation console where we will one day get a complete medical workup and diagnosis from the comfort of our own homes. But when Mr. Gingrich wrote that, we had not yet witnessed the full hemorrhage of health care benefits in the workplace.

Beginning in 1999, the first pharmacies opened online, spurred to some degree by the initial success of health-oriented Web sites like WebMD.com (see Figure 1.1) and DrKoop.com. These sites swiftly began to attract patients and caregivers who often went online to research illnesses and symptoms. Whole online communities were formed around people offering or seeking support and advice for medical conditions. This continues today, with a great rise in the number of participants.

Of these virtual drugstores, the biggest and best known still in business is Drugstore.com (see Figure 1.2). In fact, today many pharmacies and pharmacy chains such as Rite Aid (see Figure 1.3) use a partnership with Drugstore.com to service their Web customers.

Figure 1.1
WebMD.com is one of hundreds of different sites where patients and caregivers come together to do research, ask questions, and receive both answers and support for dealing with a host of different illnesses and diseases such as diabetes, cancer, and arthritis.

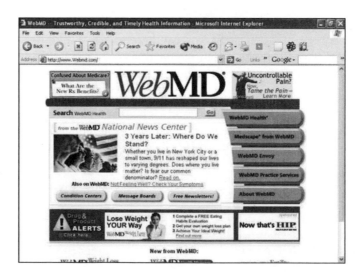

Figure 1.2
Drugstore.com is one of the oldest and best known of the Internet-only pharmacies, providing service to customers and to other pharmacies.

Figure 1.3
The busy drugstore chain Rite Aid is one of several that partner with Drugstore.com to service some of their online customers.

What early business adoptees of virtual pharmacies found, however, was that the majority of people were not yet eager to go online for their prescriptions. Some of this reticence had to do with security. During 2000–2001, the media frequently reported stories of hackers obtaining confidential credit card and personal customer information because some Web sites exercised poor data security.

But the growing importance of medical information sites has helped people become more comfortable with the concept of finding and using online pharmacies. Slowly but steadily, corresponding to the overall rise in online shopping of all types, people are changing their minds and using online pharmacies.

It's estimated that to date about 6 million U.S. customers have placed orders through legitimate online drugstores. Even if they don't use them to place orders, they use them to check drug information—Web sites tend to offer a rich mine of details that are harder to find in a traditional drugstore—and pricing.

If you need proof that the trend is moving toward online drugstores, just look in your email box. Unless you use an extremely good filter, you're likely inundated by spam offering you a cornucopia of different medications, with our without a prescription. Figure 1.4 shows one of an average 125 messages I get every day offering prescription drugs with no prescription required.

These are similar in some respects to the TV ads that flood in during dinner hour and the evening news, with promises to treat depression, weight gain, insomnia, hair loss, and sexual dysfunction. All urge you to talk with your doctor, all offer convenient Web site addresses to let you get more information, and most promise you discounts or a free month's sample to get you to try them.

Why Online Drugstores Are Attractive

Convenience plays a huge role in the rising popularity of online drugstores. Not everyone has easy access to their local pharmacy or the patience or time to wait between 10 minutes and an hour for a prescription to be filled.

To some degree, too, our traditional pharmacies have primed the pump. They took advantage of the big Web revolution that began with the explosion of personal computers and Internet access in the mid-to-late 1990s—along with the increasing adoption of online shopping by consumers—to set up their own sites. They frequently advertise such sites and encourage customers to check prices and order their refills online to be picked up at their usual pharmacy counter. As you'll see later in this chapter, your preferred local pharmacy often makes it easy to "click" a refill rather than making a call or waiting in line.

Yet these aren't the only reasons online drug shopping is now a hot commodity. Some employers and municipalities are moving subscriber prescriptions entirely online to take advantage of bulk purchasing. Some other organizations, too, now encourage members to shop

Figure 1.4
Drug-based spam sent through email accounts for between 20% and 60% of all unsolicited ads sent to U.S. consumers, according to Internet service providers.

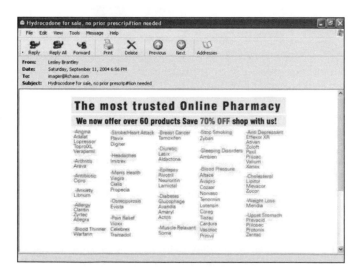

for their needed drugs through special sites they've set up. Also, you may not live close to a border with Canada and Mexico, two countries that usually have much more attractive drug prices than the U.S., yet have different standards than we do. It's a lot easier to travel with your mouse than it is to take a long trip, through customs, to place international orders.

Privacy, anonymity, and access to a wider selection or better pricing play factors, too. So does the phenomenon of a patient self-treating certain conditions. As you'll also learn, a number of drug shopping sites make it all too easy to prescribe for yourself. These same sites, however, will not be there to help if you run into a problem.

Privacy is prized among many consumers regardless of what they buy. With medications, this seems to have extra importance.

Some people feel uncomfortable or embarrassed with having their local pharmacist, who may be a friend or neighbor, know that they take a particular drug. Contraceptives and sex-related medications, psychotropic drugs such as antidepressants and tranquilizers, and sleeping pills number among the prescriptions that some feel carry a degree of social stigma. Chapter 3, "The Electronic Drugstore Shopper," explores some nuances of the privacy issue that can affect us all.

Anonymity is a factor, too, but this is something of a red herring. A virtual pharmacy may not know you like the staff at your local bricks-and-mortar drugstore does, but you do have to provide your name, mailing address, and credit card information.

WHO IS A DOCTOR TO GIVE ME PERMISSION?

In talking with people who have ordered drugs online, many brought up a specific issue about right of access that you don't see documented everywhere. A number of people said that they don't feel, as adults, that they should have to acquire their physician's approval to take a drug they feel they need. Part of the reason many of them choose to shop online, they indicated, is because it gives them the ability to choose what they wish to take.

"My doctor's great but why do I need a permission slip from him?" said one woman who has been shopping online for diet and anti-wrinkle prescriptions for more than a year. "The only restriction on any drug should be keeping them away from children. Doctors, pharmacies, and the FDA (U.S. Food and Drug Administration) don't have to treat us all like kids to do that."

Beyond these reasons, online venues may offer the following:

- ▶ Easy ability to check prices before ordering
- ▶ A streamlined system that can make it much simpler for your doctor to authorize a prescription
- ▶ More choice in pricing and access to more types of generic medications than a typical bricks-and-mortar pharmacy has in stock
- ▶ An automated process so that you can automatically schedule refills to arrive before your current supply is exhausted
- ▶ Delivery of the product through a variety of different services, and to your home or office, depending on which is better for you

There Are Drawbacks, Too

Naturally, not everything about shopping online is wonderful. A big drawback can be time. If you need a prescription fast, this can be a lot harder to achieve online without incurring extra cost. Even today, unless you pay premium prices for overnight shipping, it can take an average of three to seven business days from placing your order to delivery of your medication. As you will learn, it's best to plan ahead when shopping for meds in this way so you don't run out of the drug while you wait.

Another issue is just the simple logistics of what you have to do if there's a problem with your order. Perhaps it gets lost in transit or you happen to receive the wrong order. In the latter situation, you need to repackage the erroneous shipment and send it back. Either situation tends to add time onto the wait for your proper order. It also becomes a bit harder to deal with should you receive the wrong count or need to check your order when you receive a different brand than you're accustomed to getting. Later chapters will show you how to deal with that.

NO RETURNS

U.S. law prevents pharmacies from accepting medication returned by customers. Before you place any orders, make sure you know what you are ordering and what you expect to get. Check the online store's policies regarding problem orders, too.

You'll find that some sites only take credit cards for payment, although not everyone has or chooses to use plastic. The good news is that you can usually find an online shop that takes alternative payment methods, such as:

▶ Checks or money orders to be sent before shipment of the medication

▶ PayPal accounts where you can deposit money that can be applied against online purchases

▶ Cash on delivery (COD)

There's also the matter of health insurance pharmacy co-pays. If you use the online site for your regular pharmacy or chain, it's likely that your health insurance information is already entered into its system so the price you pay reflects the price after insurance reimbursement. Others may require you to pay the full fee upfront and then seek reimbursement from your insurance company after the fact. It's also possible that some of these online pharmacies may be considered mail order by your insurer which could mean that you need to pay no more than two months worth of co-pay payments on a medication that will last you three months. Check your policy.

Types of Services

Not every online pharmacy is the same. Different pharmacies offer various levels of service and assortment of products offered. Some, too, may have different rules. This is particularly true when you're dealing with pharmacies not based in the U.S., but even within the U.S. you'll see variations in store policies.

Which type of service and pharmacy you're dealing with when you order may not be obvious. In this section, you'll learn about the major types, but later, you'll discover some of the ways you can try to better assure yourself that you're dealing with a legitimate pharmacy rather than a quick-sell drug mill.

The four major types we'll cover in this section fall into these basic categories:

▶ Internet-only pharmacies that follow the same rules as standard pharmacies

▶ Traditional pharmacies that allow you to order refills from their Web site

▶ Online drugstores that provide an online consultation prior to initiating a new prescription

▶ Virtual pharmacies where you click and buy with little or no medical consultation

Nearly all of these types of services offer both prescription and non-prescription products.

You will also see that there are places on the Internet to obtain drugs that are *not* drugstores in any traditional sense of the term. This can be of special concern if you have children or have a loved one who you suspect may be using drugs that are not prescription-based.

Major Points of Difference

No legitimate pharmacy allows you to go behind the counter into the controlled drug inventory, select the type you want, and buy it without a prescription. Yet many online drugstores exist that allow you to do just that, sometimes with few if any questions asked. This presents a real risk. Your doctor, for example, knows that most sleeping pills are meant for only short-term use. Do you? Used long term, they can actually impair your natural sleep process and create a physical and/or psychological dependence.

But the difference amounts to more than ethics and access. Which type of service you use can have a big effect on the following:

▶ Price

▶ Whether you will be reimbursed by private insurance or Medicare

▶ The quality of medication as well as quality control in making certain you get the right drug in the right dose with the correct instructions

▶ Whether someone checks to be sure that a medication you've ordered will not conflict with other medications you tell them you're taking

▶ Overall customer service

The type of service can also impact whether you will have problems receiving your order, since some of the less legitimate sites seem to play fast and loose with U.S. drug distribution and import laws. Should you happen to order from a place that simply sends you pills with no valid prescription, mere possession of them may be illegal (this depends on the drug involved).

Before we get into specifics of each type of service, let's look at some major points of difference between these services as well as why over-the-counter medications you can obtain aren't necessarily safer because no prescription is required.

QUALITY CONCERNS

One issue you often hear mentioned in the media regarding drugs imported from other countries is product quality. FDA officials and others say they don't want drugs from elsewhere imported because they have no control over the quality of the products.

Yet there is no hard-and-fast rule that guarantees that a product manufactured in the United States is better than a similar product manufactured in India, Ireland, or the Netherlands. Many factors come into play: production standards, quality of materials, and variations in formula. In fact, some of the drugs you can receive from Canada or England may turn out to be manufactured in the U.S. but sold elsewhere at a significantly lower price.

Yet counterfeit drugs can be a problem everywhere. In other countries, the counterfeit rate may be quite high. In the U.S., it's a growing problem but has not yet reached the level seen in some other countries.

Chapter 2, "Big Brother Watches, But How Much?" gives you some interesting results from some of the test orders I did from a number of "no prescription needed" sites.

Over-the-Counter Versus Prescription Meds

Your body doesn't know the difference between prescription and non-prescription drugs. Instead, it responds to the ingestion of any drug. By definition, many of the drugs we consume aren't bought at a drugstore per se. Coffee and alcohol, for example, are both drugs and both alter our body chemistry at least temporarily. Chocolate and sugar are considered by some to also act as drugs on our bodies.

Let's look specifically, however, at the differences—and similarities—between the types of drugs you can obtain in a drugstore, looking at both prescription and over-the-counter preparations.

Without seeing a pharmacist, you know that today's pharmacy shelves are packed with products. Everything from arthritis pain relievers to migraine pills to cold medicines, along with a number of herbal or "all natural" substitutes, can be found there. Yet just because a product is sold without a prescription does not make it completely safe for your consumption.

Why Over the Counter Isn't Always Safe

One key—and ultimately, quite dangerous—misconception is that while some prescription drugs may be dangerous, virtually anything we can buy over the counter without a doctor's prescription can be used safely. While this is often true, it's not always the case. Also, our risk can rise significantly when we choose to ignore product labels.

Even when used strictly by the dosage instructions printed on the label, some tiny number of people (sometimes one percent, sometimes three to five) will have an adverse reaction to just about any over-the-counter medication. This is true with just about any drug and extends to prescription pharmaceuticals.

Some of these bad reactions can be anticipated from cautions placed on the product package. For example, many cough and cold medications bear warnings to consumers who may suffer from various breathing disorders. Those with emphysema or some form of chronic obstructive pulmonary disease (COPD) who choose to use an over-the-counter cough syrup with such a warning could experience increased difficulty in breathing.

Over-the-counter medications may also affect the overall usefulness of other medications—prescription and non-prescription—that we take. For example, recent studies show that herbal remedies like St. John's Wort, often taken to promote overall well-being and as an herbal anti-depressant, can interfere with the effectiveness of some prescription medications. Other studies suggest that those who take both aspirin to reduce heart attack risk along with the anti-inflammatory drug ibuprofen to treat muscle aches may see a reduction in the usefulness of the aspirin. This is another strong reason why you need to consult your medical professional.

But not all adverse side effects can be predicted. You might take a medication containing either an active ingredient or filler you've never taken before, so you don't realize you have an allergy to it. Or the medication may have an ingredient that is a bad mix with something else you may be taking.

WHAT IS FILLER?

The term *filler* with respect to medication refers to additional material added to a drug as it's packaged into pill or capsule form. This filler may be something as simple as starch or may be a material added to either increase the medication delivery or reduce the initial effects of the medication.

There's another issue. Unfortunately, as consumers, studies show we're not always careful about heeding those warnings and dosage instructions. We seem to be especially sloppy with regard to drugs we can buy without prescription. When I was younger, I used to think that if two Excedrin would eventually stop a nagging headache, three or four would do the job faster and more effectively. I had only myself to blame when later, I felt edgy from the caffeine in the pills or had an upset stomach from the excessive dose.

Exactly what differentiates a prescription-only drug from one you can purchase in just about any store sometimes has little to do with a drug's relative safety. Some drugs move quickly from prescription-only to over-the-counter simply because the drug seems to work well and has few problems associated with it. Examples of this are Claritin, used to fight allergies, and Nexium, for acid reflux. Others join the fast track to over-the-counter status because of political pressure exercised by advocacy groups.

But consumer and advocacy groups argue that many other drugs that also seem safe retain their prescription-only status just to profit the drug companies. Once a drug makes the move from prescription to regular store shelf, most health insurance policies with pharmacy discounts no longer cover all or part of the cost to patients. The price often changes, too, because there is less overhead involved in providing the product because it's already gone through testing and approval to become an approved prescription drug.

Some Specific Examples of Over-the-Counter Concern

The misconception that over-the-counter drugs are always much safer than prescription drugs probably accounts for many unnecessary deaths. A number of factors go into this. One is the issue already discussed, our belief that we don't need to closely follow product directions. But another danger comes when we may fail to tell our doctors about over-the-counter medications we take when we're asked to identify all the medications we use.

Look closer at the labels on your over-the-counter products and you will see that most advise you to take the product for no more than a few days or weeks. Something as simple as a laxative can be abused to the point where it upsets the delicate balance of body chemistry. Repeated excessive use can stop our body's natural process of removing waste.

Take some of the most common over-the-counter drugs as an example: aspirin and Tylenol. Every day in the U.S., thousands of people—both adults and children—take large amounts of either aspirin or Tylenol. This is usually done as a desperate bid for attention: trying to get others to pay attention to their depression or upset, they take a deliberate overdose of these drugs in the mistaken belief that these medications are less dangerous than a similar quantity of sleeping pills.

Unfortunately, the results can be tragic. Taking either of these medications in large volume can be very dangerous. Some people quickly lapse into comas from which they do not return, whereas others suffer irreversible liver or kidney damage.

Think of drug abuse among teenagers and your mind jumps to illegal drugs like marijuana and heroin. However, more and more, teenagers are using another over-the-counter drug: "night time" cold formulas. In some it produces sleep, whereas in others it can produce a sense of euphoria.

Long-term use of these sedative-style cold formulas, even when taken in normal dosages, is not advised. Yet some of the stories related by teenagers and young adults who abuse this type of drug indicate they may take between 10 and dozens of these capsules in a single night. Some repeat this experience several times a week for weeks and months at a time. Many pharmacists and pharmacy managers say that such cold capsules are among the most frequently shoplifted items in their stores.

Direct ingestion isn't the only way this type of drug is abused, either. Cold formulas are one of the ingredients used in methamphetamines, a synthetic drug frequently manufactured in home-based labs (called "meth" labs) from a number of different easily-obtained components.

Because of both situations, many communities and states have outlawed the sale of such cold medication to minors, both on and offline. In brick-and-mortar stores, some require you to specifically ask a clerk or pharmacist for it. Additionally, some law enforcement agencies request or require that stores (virtual and physical) report anyone purchasing more than three packages of the drug at a time.

The Virtual Drugstore Bonanza

When you first go online to explore the availability and choices among online pharmacies, you may see that many look very similar. At least, that is, until you take a closer look.

It's that closer look that gives you the ability to begin to distinguish some of the differences that point you to whether you're dealing with the online sales component of a regular pharmacy, one that is just providing refill and/or discount drug services for existing prescriptions, and those that are willing to sell you any drug in their stock with or without an existing doctor's order.

Let's look at the major categories of online stores available. Then, before you move to the next chapter, you'll learn about an additional venue for obtaining drugs—popular with kids and adults like—that is *not* a drugstore at all.

Refill Orders through Regular Pharmacy Sites

Most people first shopping online for medications will use the Web sites sponsored by their regular pharmacy or pharmacy chain. CVS, Duane Reade (see Figure 1.5), Kinney Drugs, Rite Aid, and Walgreens are just a few of the standard pharmacy chains offering their customers a way to shop via the Web.

What you'll usually find on such sites are features such as the following:

▶ A refill tool that allows you to place a refill order for your current medication for later pickup (some also provide delivery services)

▶ Information about transferring an existing prescription from a different pharmacy

▶ Articles about the new Medicare services including the drug discount card

▶ Medical appliances such as blood pressure monitors and thermometers, first aid supplies, and standard over-the-counter medications

▶ Additional resource articles about a variety of health issues

▶ Specifics about local events (health fairs, community health programs, and others) that you can usually search for by typing in your zip code; you can also locate your nearest member pharmacy this way

Figure 1.5
Duane Reade drugstores, found throughout New York, has set up shop to allow customers to order refills, identify their pills and capsules, and buy related health items.

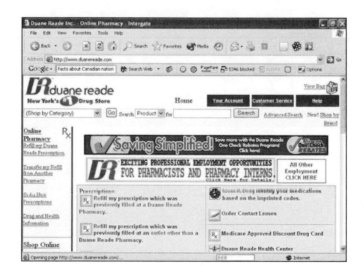

CHAPTER 1

Here's an example. I'm located more than 20 miles from my closest pharmacy, so I like to be sure my drug refills are waiting when I arrive. Although I can call the pharmacy's automated refill line, it can take several retries before I get past a busy signal.

To avoid the hassle:

1. I go to my pharmacy's (Kinney Drugs) online site.
2. I click on the Refill page, which is part of a secured site, meaning my financial and personal data should be protected.
3. Referring back to my prescription bottle, I locate and type in the Prescription #, pharmacy phone number, and my last name using the instructions on the page (see Figure 1.6).
4. I choose the time and day when I expect to pick up my order at the pharmacy.
5. Once the site verifies my information, I can go ahead and provide information for additional refills, as needed.

With this done, I can simply go pick up my order at the appointed time. Since my health insurance information is on file there, my discount is already applied and I can pay by cash or credit card just like with any other order.

With other pharmacies and sites, I could also pay for the order online and have it delivered, either through a local delivery service or even by mail or other package carrier.

REFILLS

If you really need the prescription ready when you arrive, you may want to double-check by calling the pharmacy to be sure they received the refill order through the Web site. In two years of handling refills this way, I've only had one delay. But mistakes happen everywhere.

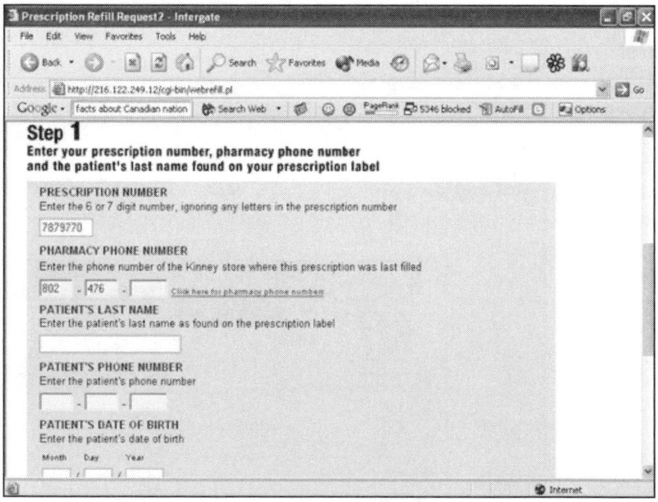

Figure 1.6
Instructions on the site guide me in finding the necessary information on my pill bottle so I can fill in the necessary details.

Place Orders through Online-Only Recognized Pharmacy Sites

Certain pharmacies exist only on the Internet. Drugstore.com is an example of this.

Such online drugstores allow you to use a new prescription provided by your doctor to begin your account there or transfer an existing prescription from another pharmacy. This category of pharmacy, however, will not originate a prescription for you, so it's up to you to request the prescription from your doctor ahead of time. They behave just like a traditional pharmacy in this regard, except you can't pick up your order. They will deliver it to you and you can choose the delivery service or style you want to use.

Using Drugstore.com as our test site, here's the process:

1. Go to Drugstore.com and search for the drug you want using the site's alphabetical index.

2. Check the options available for this drug (the number the doctor has approved), the brand or generic name, and the price.

3. If you find the match you want, click Add to Cart to place the product into your virtual shopping cart (see Figure 1.7).

4. Assuming you have no additional prescriptions to shop for, click Checkout.

5. You are asked to confirm your order. Be sure that the quantity, drug, and dosage are correct. Then click Continue.

6. Where directed, type in your email address. Click to specify whether this is a new account or whether you have an existing one. Assuming you're new, select new customer, and then fill out a user name and password to create an account.

7. You are then asked for personal information (your name, address, and credit card number) as well as information about your doctor (name and contact number).

Figure 1.7
When you add a product to your shopping cart, you can then move on to make additional selections or choose to Checkout.

8. Next, you're prompted to indicate the way you want to provide the doctor's prescription to them (see Figure 1.8). You can choose from these options:

    ▶ Mail or fax the prescription sheet to them at the address provided to you

    ▶ Have the doctor call the prescription into a number they provide

    ▶ Have them contact your doctor directly (they'll use your doctor's contact information to call and confirm the order)

    ▶ Transfer an existing prescription from another pharmacy

9. You will receive an order confirmation and a way to track your order. If you have opted to send the prescription to them, do this immediately to prevent any delay in receiving your order.

If you opt to transfer your prescription from another pharmacy, you will get the option to provide details about the other pharmacy so that Drugstore.com can take care of the transfer for you. Many standard pharmacies with online sites also offer this option.

Depending on variations in your order, such as how the prescription is provided to Drugstore.com and which shipping method you selected, your order should arrive in 3–10 working days. For this reason, it may be wise to at least initiate a new prescription through a standard pharmacy and then later transfer it online, if desired, so that you don't have to wait a period of time to start your new medication.

Figure 1.8

A separate page on the Drugstore.com Web site thoroughly explains your different options for getting your prescription to them for processing. Choose the best match for you.

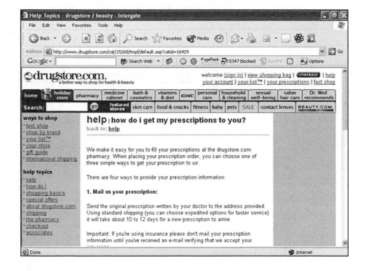

Get an Online-Only Prescription

If you're wondering how any pharmacy could fill an order without a prescription from an attending physician, you're smart to question.

Federal guidelines were redrafted in the past few years to try to reduce this practice, since there are risks involved in writing any prescription and these can be increased when the doctor writing the prescription only has information you provide upon which to base his or her decision. These new guidelines state that an online-only consultation is an insufficient medical review to do this.

Regardless of that, many pharmacies in this category continue to use an online consultation as the sole basis for a contracted doctor to approve or reject an order. But there's some variation here.

In our research, the process for most sites goes something like this:

1. Locate the medication you want to obtain and then select the product based on quantity (this can run from as little as 10 to as much as 180).

2. Place the product in your online shopping cart.

3. When finished, click Checkout.

4. You are asked to provide a basic medical form that includes your age, height, weight, existing medical conditions, any drugs you are currently taking, what surgeries you have had, the name and contact details for your primary care physician, whether you have ever taken the same drug in the past and whether you had a negative reaction to it, and any drug allergies you have.

5. You then choose your payment method and fill out your name, address, credit card, and telephone number. Confirm and finalize your order.

6. You get an order number to allow you to track the progress of your order right through to delivery.

Exactly how the pharmacy gets a doctor's approval to authorize a prescription can vary dramatically. Some of the methods offered include:

▶ A doctor under contract by the online pharmacy reviews only the answers you provide on your online consultation form and then writes a virtual prescription so that the pharmacy can process it or reject the order.

▶ Most orders for non-controlled drugs can be filled using the preceding method, but you may be notified that those for pain killers and sleeping pills require additional consultation and/or an in-person examination by a physician chosen by the pharmacy.

▶ The pharmacy submits your medical history and other details to a physician who then contacts your primary physician before making a determination about whether to write the new prescription.

▶ A doctor contacts you by phone—or sometimes online via special chat software—and discusses the information you've previously provided along with your symptoms before making a decision on whether to authorize the prescription.

▶ You may be asked to supply paper copies of your most recent medical examination and lab results to substantiate your request.

Who are these doctors writing prescriptions for the pharmacy? These are usually physicians located in whatever state or country the pharmacy site is based. In some cases, U.S. patients may have their prescriptions authorized by a doctor in a completely different country, such as India or the Netherlands. This can present a real drawback since certain ethnic groups may be prone to certain diseases or conditions not seen in others. Doctors not watching for these differences could prescribe something inappropriate.

But the arrangements between the pharmacy and the doctors also differ widely. Some physicians work exclusively for such online pharmacies, receiving a salary. Others get a set contracted amount each week or each month to review patient histories and perform phone or other consultations as needed. Yet others, and this practice can cause more concern, pay physicians a set fee (anywhere from $2 or $5 to quite a bit more) for every order they approve. The problem with this method is that physicians have a financial advantage for writing a prescription but a disadvantage (no fee) if they do not. An unethical doctor might be inclined to approve prescriptions because of this.

Using this type of pharmacy often costs quite a bit more than the more standard pharmacies discussed earlier. You not only pay more for the drugs themselves, but you may be subject to a physician fee that often ranges between $25 and $150 (U.S.). Some tack on additional fees as well, and not all advise you of extra fees before you confirm your order. Only when you receive your confirmation email or, in some cases, your credit card bill, will you see that your $35 prescription ultimately cost you $150. In this case, the added fees might come close to the price you would pay to see your own physician, which is likely a much better choice.

Another nasty phenomenon with this type of pharmacy as well as the next one listed is that some of these sites are "fly-by-night" operations. They open one day, advertise like mad to get a huge volume of orders, only to close again before authorities can find them and shut them down. But they may reappear again a day or two later under a different—or even the same—name and Web address.

Finally, many of these sites operate multiple online drugstores simultaneously. Interestingly enough, although the Web sites can look identical and offer the same exact drugs, the prices and policies can be quite different. For example, on one group of sites, you might be charged $99 for 50 tablets of a muscle relaxant, whereas on another version of the site, the cost for the same pill in the same quantity may run you $139. Ouch!

Order Prescription Drugs with No Prescription

In the previous section, you learned about some of the sites that make it possible to obtain a prescription for a drug through an "online consultation" without the need to visit your doctor. Yet there are others that streamline the process even more, some not even going through the pretense of soliciting your medical history to be reviewed by a doctor.

In these cases, you're ordering a drug just like you would order a book or a box of candy online: select your products, click Checkout, fill in your credit card and shipping information, and your order arrives a few days to a few weeks later.

Although such sites are fairly rare, they do exist. In the test orders done for research for this book (and reported in Chapter 2), we found a half dozen sites that allowed you to place an order without any questions asked. Also, like the previous category of pharmacies, these often open and close rapidly. This makes it very difficult to establish a long-term relationship so that you can safely assume you can reorder your drugs through them.

The Drugs That Aren't Sold as Drugs

Finally, let's look at two other types of online stores selling drugs: chemical and herb suppliers.

Go to either of these types of businesses online, found easily through a Web search engine such as Google.com or AskJeeves.com, and it's clear that these are legitimate companies selling products that are both legal for distribution and in demand.

Yet both offer products that can be exploited by people who know enough pharmacology to transform what they buy into by-products that are illegal, lethal, or both. As you'll see, the information needed to do this is no harder to find than the chemicals and herbs themselves.

Many substances that can be used and abused by people are not classified as drugs per se but as chemical compounds. As such, they can often be ordered by individuals through chemical supply companies that regularly sell to manufacturers, research groups, and just about any school with a chemistry lab. The cost can be a lot cheaper through such a venue than it would be to buy the end-result drug on a pharmacy store shelf (if available that way) or on the street.

Some of the sought-after chemicals are restricted-use so they can't be easily purchased from a legitimate U.S. firm without proper credentials or filling out special forms. Yet there are ways around this, such as ordering from a Canadian or Mexican chemical supplier.

Before you dismiss this idea as just something serious drug addicts would do, think again. Even strictly casual, recreational drug experimenters—kids among them—find out what they need and how to prepare or consume it.

A little bit of research through your Web browser can turn up a virtual mountain of resources for this, no degree in biochemistry required. The resources take the form of general Web sites, Web-based message boards, Web logs (called blogs), and Internet chat rooms where people trade information (and misinformation) about obtaining and using chemicals—either in a raw state or already part of a preparation—to achieve a particular result. Often enough, the desired result is getting high or achieving some other form of mind-altering state. One of these sites is shown in Figure 1.9.

There are exceptions to this, of course. Some exchange information to try to alter body chemistry to reduce the risk of cancer or increase responsiveness to a particular treatment regime. Also, many resources are started by those doing serious academic or commercial research into chemical effects.

The same—legitimate and not—holds true for herbs, herb suppliers, and online resources. This makes sense when you consider that our first medicines as well as the first documented cases of drug abuse came not from pills and potions (those have been developed relatively recently), but from plants.

Figure 1.9
Many Web sites and Internet resources abound that are devoted to discussion and research regarding non-traditional use of chemicals and herbs, where the purpose or focus is not always strictly therapeutic.

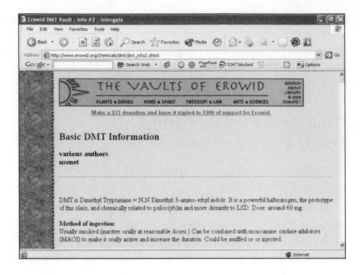

Humans early on started using plants that grew wild in their location not just for food but also to cure or relieve ailments. Eventually, as humans began to move from one area to another, we began to learn about herbs found in one area that we could cultivate into our own to benefit from their medicinal or recreational properties.

Think of the poppy, the discovery of opium from it, and how we still use it as the basis for critical pain relievers. Hops is an herb used in the production of beer to prevent bacterial action that also has strong psychoactive effects.

Just as people learned how to take advantage of these plants, they've found ways to use and abuse many others that they can either grow themselves or order through an herb or plant supplier. The Internet simply makes the dissemination of this type of information much more global.

For example, it took me just over eight minutes using the Yahoo search engine and a few careful search phrases to learn what I needed to obtain to form the basic recipe for Ecstasy, a wildly popular "club" drug among teens and young adults often used to enhance the music and reduce social inhibitions. On another night, about 15 minutes of reading showed me how people are using combinations of cold medicines to achieve hours of a trance-like state through a chemical called dextromethoraphane (DXM). Who knew?

A short stint on a third night introduced me to a chemical you can order quite cheaply and legally that many use in place of LSD, which is illegal to possess. Using information I found in the search, I checked a few recommended chemical companies, where I was asked for my MasterCard or Visa details but not my age.

Folks posting at such resource sites are not only asking questions, some seem to be experts who point out flaws in so-called "trip recipes." Here's an example: when one message poster said he planned to take 12 to 16 caplets of a popular cold medicine to achieve the best results from the chemical DXM (dextromethoraphane), someone else immediately chimed in to say, "No! Doing that will give you a toxic level of [another substance]. Here's a different, safer, cheaper way." Figure 1.10 shows one of these message bases.

Figure 1.10
Beyond regular drugstore sites, the Internet offers a multitude of ways for people to research alternative uses for chemicals and herbs as well as combinations of existing medications.

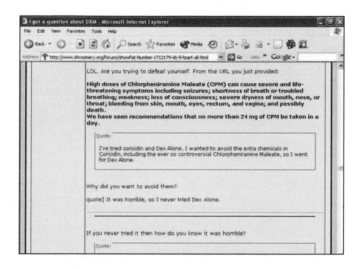

There's often nothing very complicated here. Any person from age 10 to 112 who can figure out the requirements for making a peanut butter-and-jelly sandwich can use these Web sites to make a drug. None of the sites of this type I found asked for an ID or age check. Because of this, parents and caregivers should be concerned. Not all drugs come in a pill vial or in a baggie sold on the street.

You may be wondering how some of these less legitimate Web sites continue to operate and to deliver drugs when they're skirting some of the federal requirements. Some operate outside the U.S. where it may be tougher to close them down. Others are fly-by-night operations. Many of these sites are shut down only to reappear under a slightly different name and Web address just days or even hours later.

In the next chapter, you'll learn about some of the safeguards that are in place to try to protect you as a medical drug consumer. You will also see how you can report a problem online pharmacy.

Chapter 2
Big Brother Watches, But How Much?

In talking with people in preparation for this book, one of the most common misconceptions repeated by consumers again and again is that anything you can get on the Web—particularly something as important as pharmaceuticals—must be legitimate. Otherwise, as many asked, "How could they get away with selling it? The government would close them down."

At best, this viewpoint may be selective naiveté. After all, most of us know that Internet scams are perpetrated on people each and every day. We've heard about swindlers advertising useless or phantom products on eBay, people soliciting money for bogus causes, and even people trying to sell body organs.

But this misconception about legitimacy with all drugs purchased online is a dangerous one. It's one fueled by ads in our email boxes promoting "all FDA approved drugs" and proclaiming to "save big bucks." It's also boosted by drugstore Web sites insisting that even though you can purchase products such as morphine (a potent opiate-based painkiller) and U.S.-banned diet drugs without a prescription, it's all perfectly legal (it's not legal and it's not safe, however). Some of the most blatantly illegitimate sites will actually link you back to the FDA Web site that talks about using Internet pharmacies.

This is the big difference between a traditional pharmacy model applied to an Internet drugstore and one that offers to originate a prescription for you. With the latter, some of the prescription medications are not presented in a strictly legal fashion. Some of their products are not legal for sale in the U.S. at all (for example, you can buy diet drugs through them that you can no longer get from a regular pharmacy because the FDA has banned their sale).

However, if you think the government (or as some people refer to it, Big Brother) will protect every aspect of drug sales online and prevent you from being taken or exposed to improper medications, think again. In Chapter 1, you learned that many illegitimate drugstores run multiple sites simultaneously, and can always open up shop somewhere else if they're closed down in one place. Many of them come online just long enough to advertise, grab enough sales, and then disappear only to pop up again at another time. Nor is this the only problem "the system" has in trying to stop such illegal sites and sales.

This chapter looks at some of the many issues and entities that come into play with the current online pharmacy boom, starting with federal organizations such as the Food and Drug Administration (FDA) and U.S. Customs Authority and going through to others like pharmacy organizations, pharmaceutical companies, credit card companies, health insurance providers, and shipping services. One thread that runs common among them all is that everyone has at least some policy in place to try to prevent illegal sales and shipment. Yet the illegal sites and sales continue.

Coping with a Very Complicated and Often Contradictory System

When you need to get a prescription from your doctor, you probably aren't aware of an entire huge system that stands behind it hidden from your view. This system, largely regulatory in nature, can affect every aspect of the process, from which medications ever make it to market all the way through to the point you get the medication. Price, availability, how well the effects of the drugs have been studied before and after government approval, how many pills a doctor can prescribe for you at any one time, and which versions of a drug are reimbursable by different health insurance plans are just some of the details that come into play.

No single chapter, and perhaps not even one book, could do justice to all the aspects of the system. Yet because many of these aspects can factor into the process by which we obtain medicine and medical care, it seems necessary to discuss them briefly here.

Since the federal government is charged with protecting us, and its laws are the ones on which everything else is based because compliance with federal law is mandatory, let's start there, focusing in on how the government monitors and controls our access to drugs.

As you go, think about how complicated tax code is. There are specialists who do nothing but examine tax code to try to figure out how to leverage it for, rather than against, the taxpayer. Now picture consuming a pill that has not been looked over. What if it leads to adverse reactions due to lack of testing? Not pretty, eh?

Well, if you think tax code is almost hopelessly difficult to master, wait until you discover the intricacies of federal drug law, combined with how those drugs are approved (or rejected), which drugs your insurance company will cover (if you're fortunate enough to have coverage and it includes drug benefits), and how federal law enforcement agencies such as the Drug Enforcement Agency (DEA) operate. In a later chapter, you'll see, too, that doctors are often pressured by certain manufacturers to prescribe a specific drug over one that may be best or cheapest for you. Add to that not-quite-legal online store vendors who want to make a profit and you've got quite a maze to pass through.

Just as it does not take a real tax cheat to get in trouble with the Internal Revenue Service, it doesn't take a drug abuser to run afoul of some of the conflicting drug laws currently in existence.

The end result is that consumers—just trying to look for a cheap product that helps their health—can get caught in the middle. As I mentioned in the introduction, that's a big reason this book is being written: to try to help you navigate through the system so that you can get the help you need without risk to your health, medical and otherwise.

How the Government Watches Drugs

Read some of the material posted on government Web sites related to the (re)importation of drugs into the United States from Canada and sometimes Mexico, combined with interviews that have been given by officials, and you come away with at least two impressions.

One is that it's not very easy to understand whether you can safely go to Canada to buy your drugs less expensively than here. The other, more subtle, conclusion is that it's not altogether clear that federal authorities distinguish between the kind of sale from an illegal site where you can obtain morphine, hydrocodone, or Viagra without a prescription, and what many consumers do now in purchasing lower-cost medications from across the border.

That's a big problem, and not just because it seems confusing. After all, how can you compare someone who can't afford heart medication getting it from Canada with someone buying large quantities of painkillers to sell to others at a mass markup? That doesn't seem fair.

Complicating this is that many municipalities, states, and even private employers are encouraging people to save money by buying their drugs elsewhere. They've ignored federal requests to stop doing that. States such as Vermont are actually suing the government to make them stop treating drugs from Canada as illegal imports.

In 2003, Capitol Hill passed a drug import law that made it legal for people to buy small supplies of medication for personal use to bring across the border from Canada or across the Atlantic from England. In fact, the 2003 law just reinforced one dating back from 1954 that basically promised consumers the right to obtain small quantities of drugs for personal use. For example, if you go to Canada or overseas on business or vacation, you might happen to pick up a headache remedy there that isn't available here. Canada and England, for instance, allow over-the-counter medicines to contain small amounts of codeine, an opiate-based pain reliever, and other substances that the FDA does not permit here. If you happen to have one of these drugs when you drive back over the border from Canada or come through Customs as you fly back into the U.S., you're probably going to be able to keep your bottle of pills but this can be open to interpretation by the agents handling you. There are legal issues involved in the very way certain drugs, especially narcotics, are transported. If the medication is not in a prescription bottle with the usual prescription details on it, you could be in for a grilling.

Although these laws may make it sound like it solves the problem of getting the drugs you want or need, it doesn't. The FDA does not want you to purchase your drugs outside the country and bring them back in (you'll see their reasons elsewhere in this section).

At the same time, the U.S. Customs Service has the ability to stop shipments coming into this country that contain banned substances (you can find a list of the rules in the Food and Drug Administration section of this chapter). They catch thousands of orders each year, although that may be just a fraction of the actual drug shipments. Beyond the ones they simply don't spot as drug shipments, there are thousands more they knowingly pass through because of that 2003 drug import law.

Which orders go through versus which ones do not may amount to the luck of the draw, according to a few current and former Customs workers I spoke with. They said that different offices and inspectors have their own interpretation of the rules. One order might get seized because it contains a drug completely outlawed in the U.S. or because there were much larger quantities than "personal use" would imply, whereas a similar order might go through normally.

When an order is seized, the drugs within it are ultimately destroyed or sent back to the company that sent them. In some cases (although it's unclear how many), the intended recipient of the order will get a "tsk tsk, do not do this again" letter from the federal authorities. This is supposed to occur in all cases where a shipment is intercepted, but several people sharing personal experiences for this book stated they did not always receive such a warning when an order (they presume) was seized. Such seizures happen often enough that you will see a few overseas and Canadian pharmacies actually guarantee delivery of your order, promising that if your order is seized by Customs, they'll send you a fresh order.

Is your head buzzing yet? The short version of this is that even though one law gives you the right to go place your order, other laws discourage importation of drugs, so your Canadian or other foreign order may not reach you on the first try. There are also very specific rules about certain categories of drugs. You'll find, for example, that most Canadian pharmacies do not sell controlled-access medications such as heavy-duty painkillers, sleeping pills, and anti-anxiety medications. Many others do not sell Ritalin or drugs like it used to treat hyperactivity.

Here's another head-shaker. For the most part, so far, the government has not shown much interest in prosecuting individuals who buy legal drugs for legitimate personal use that are imported against federal desire. You've no doubt heard of the caravans of senior citizens who ride buses up to Canada to fill their orders at regular pharmacies; the feds also haven't been inclined to arrest them at the border. Wait, we're not quite at the head-shaker part, which is that at any point they wanted, federal authorities could change that policy and go after individuals. This places people who shop across the border—by bus or by Web browser—at some potential for risk. The federal authorities usually leave it to the states to prosecute patient-oriented crimes such as doctor shopping, as discussed in Chapter 3.

We see some of this schizophrenic approach to what gets enforced and what doesn't in situations where some communities and even whole states have opted to legalize marijuana for compassionate medicinal use. While marijuana is almost never a prescription drug (there are a very few exceptions made through a federal supply program), it's being more and more looked at by American voters as a treatment for certain illnesses. The federal authorities have challenged this by bringing growers, sellers, and even patient/users to trial because the federal government makes marijuana cultivation, possession, and distribution illegal. Other states, while not outright legalizing medical marijuana use, allow medical need as a defense if you're caught with the medication. But just because the local or state authorities may not prosecute a case doesn't mean the feds will be so tolerant. It's a catch-22 that can trap seriously ill people, along with those trying to help them, under federal scrutiny.

Here's another thing to consider. Just because the government, through its various federal agencies, hasn't arrested huge numbers of people importing drugs under the "personal use" allowance does not mean they aren't keeping records of the names of patients, the types of drugs, and the people or stores supplying them. Part of the broad law enforcement initiative known as the U.S. Patriot Act passed in late 2001 gives the government much greater powers to collect information and share it between agencies.

A subsequent and controversial program was developed called "Total Information Awareness" to mine databases of credit card, bank, and other records looking for patterns of purchases and even who gets packages from foreign countries. When word of the monitoring reached the public, the program itself was scrapped. However, components of the program were broken down into separate units and placed in other bills—some having little or nothing to do with the Homeland Security Department—which were subsequently passed.

The short version of this is that we know the government has new abilities to mine incredible details from our private records, but because they're doing it as part of the anti-terrorism effort, we have no idea what they're looking at. The intent here is not to sound paranoid, but to let you know the potential exists that much of what we do privately through our Web browsers and with our credit cards may not be very confidential at all. Some of the people interviewed for this book cited these concerns as one of the reasons they don't shop online more.

The Food and Drug Administration (FDA)

Considering that the FDA exercises control over most foods and drugs available for sale in the U.S., its job and its scope is not exactly unimportant. New prescription drugs must be reviewed and approved by the FDA before they can be prescribed for use by doctors, although some drugs are approved ahead of general release for special studies.

Yet not everything you could classify as a drug comes directly under the rules and enforcement of the FDA. Some are made available to the general market before it's determined that their use should be more limited. One example of this is the "club" drug Ecstasy, which has only been made illegal within the past few years because of deaths and side effects associated with its use.

Herbal remedies and some food and medication supplements are other examples. Although there is discussion of placing all of these under the jurisdiction of the FDA, most are sold without any major control whatsoever. You may remember that the herbal preparation called Ephedra caused a lot of controversy once it was associated with deaths and illnesses among its users.

The FDA and Your Prescriptions

Earlier in this chapter, you learned about some of the conflicting rules regarding prescription drugs and importation that can lead to confusion about what you can legally order through online Web sites, especially those that ship to the U.S. from a different country.

FDA rules specify the following guidelines (posted on its Web site) about drugs coming to you

GUESS WHO IMPORTS THE GREATEST QUANTITY OF FOREIGN DRUGS?

If you guessed the U.S. government, give yourself a bubblegum cigar. According to figures from the federal General Accounting Office (GAO) and other sources, the single largest importer of foreign drugs to the United States is our government.

Most of these drugs are ordered by the Department of Defense. It obtains them for research and analysis. But it also purchases them to reduce the costs of providing medical care to the men and women in the military as well as veterans served by government-sponsored programs including veterans' hospitals. Beyond the DoD, the U.S. sometimes buys drugs through foreign sources to provide to other countries as humanitarian aid.

This seems to fly in the face of all the warnings the government gives to consumers about buying drugs from foreign sources.

through shipment or that you physically carry over the border:

▶ If a bag or package arouses suspicion, Customs will set it aside and contact the nearest office of the FDA or the Drug Enforcement Agency for advice on whether to release or detain the drug product.

▶ Even though your bag may not be checked, it is against the law to not properly declare imported medications to Customs. Failure to declare products could result in penalties.

▶ Possession of certain medications without a prescription from a licensed physician may violate federal, state, and local laws.

▶ Prescription drugs should be stored in their original containers, and you should have a copy of your doctor's prescription or letter of instruction.

▶ If a drug is detained, the FDA is required by law to send you a written notice asking whether you can show that the product meets legal requirements. If you can't, the drug could be destroyed or returned to the sender.

In general, the FDA cites the following six issues as major potential risks with imported drugs:

▶ Quality assurance

▶ Potential for counterfeit drugs

▶ Presence of untested substances (either the active drug or some inactive ingredient or filler material contained within it)

▶ Heightened risk with unsupervised use

▶ Labeling and language issues (no distinct prescription presented or the information about the drug and usage is offered only in non-English)

▶ Overall lack of information (harmful side effects not listed)

FDA: Are Foreign Drugs Less Safe and/or Potential Terror Targets?

Some of the FDA's positions on importing foreign drugs are understandable when you realize that the FDA can only control drugs manufactured within this country. The agency has no power to monitor or regulate those products made outside this country except where a foreign manufacturer specifically states it wants to sell its drugs largely within the U.S. In such cases, the FDA can require inspection of the manufacturing facility overseas.

But there is some controversy here, too. For one, the FDA has made a number of statements questioning the purity of foreign drugs as a whole. Not only does this fly somewhat in the face of the fact that the government is the largest purchaser of foreign drugs, but there are also some legitimate issues about the origin of some of these drugs.

For example, some of the drugs Americans routinely import from Canada or Mexico are actually the exact same drugs made in the same factories that produce the standard U.S. supply. In other words, we're just re-importing our own drugs. The difference with this type is usually in cost: American consumers pay a much higher price for many of the same drugs sold for far less in other countries (from media reports and research conducted for this book, the average savings from Canada can be anywhere from 10% to 70%). This has led to charges that American pharmaceutical companies are overcharging us, either because the pharmaceutical lobby has so much power among elected officials that the government chooses not to stop this, or that we're subsidizing the lower prices for poorer nations. Drug companies say that is not true, although they admit U.S. consumers tend to bear the brunt of the costs of product research and development.

Aside from that, there appears to be no hard-and-fast evidence that proves foreign-manufactured drugs are always of inferior quality to U.S.-manufactured drugs. In some select cases, other countries may actually have more stringent standards. In others, the water supply or variations in prescription formula may make a significant difference in quality and performance. Regrettably, consumers generally have no access to this information to make an informed choice. This leaves you shooting into the dark when you buy from a shop that doesn't disclose to you the source of your medication ahead of time. Many of the online pharmacies claiming "all FDA approved drugs" are selling drugs that are not FDA approved because they are at best foreign versions of approved drugs and at worst, these drugs could be just about anything.

Recently, too, some officials from the FDA have voiced concern that terrorists could try to attack Americans by intercepting drug shipments from Canada to lace them or substitute them with harmful substances. While that is a possibility, it may be no more likely than others.

NOTE

From an article posted on the FDA Web site: "The Medicine Equity and Drug Safety Act (MEDS), enacted in 2000, would have allowed prescription drugs manufactured in the United States and exported to certain foreign countries to be re-imported from those countries for sale to American consumers. Supporters of the bill hoped that lower drug pricing in other countries would be passed along to consumers. But Health and Human Services Secretary Tommy G. Thompson responded by saying that, while he believed strongly in access to affordable drugs, he could not implement the act because it would sacrifice public safety by opening up the closed distribution system in the United States.

Though the law was enacted in 2000, before the bill can take effect, one provision requires that the HHS secretary determine whether adequate safety could be maintained and whether costs could be reduced significantly. Both Thompson and his predecessor, Donna Shalala, concluded that these conditions could not be guaranteed."

The FDA and Controlled Substances/Restricted Prescriptions

With regard to drugs, the FDA assigns certain medications that it judges to have specific dangers (overdose, side effects, or addiction potential) to what they call schedules. Any drug assigned to a schedule category usually is subject to more monitoring than non-schedule drugs. The lower the schedule number, the stronger and more dangerous the drug is considered to be. The major drug schedules are shown in Table 2.1.

Within most individual schedules are subcategories. These subcategories usually correspond to a drug's potential for abuse, whether or not the drug has an "accepted" (as defined by the FDA) use in U.S. medical treatment, and its probability of creating a physical and/or psychological dependence in those who use it. For example, in Schedule I, you see drugs the FDA considers to be without any currently accepted medical use (subcategory b) and which lack accepted safety for use of the drug under medical supervision (subcategory c).

CHAPTER 2

Reporting Illegal Drugs or Pharmacies to the FDA

In 2003, as the number of online vendors selling drugs began to skyrocket, the FDA and the DEA set up a joint task force to deal with concerns about illegal sites and those dispensing drugs that are specifically controlled.

NOTE

Knowing drug schedules can be important if you're a chronic pain sufferer, for example, who needs narcotics to control pain. The FDA does not permit people to import narcotics or others of the more serious categories of controlled schedule drugs. It also seriously frowns upon anyone ordering them without a proper prescription from U.S.-based pharmacies.

TABLE 2.1 FDA SCHEDULE OF DRUGS

Schedule	Category	Type of Drug	Example Medications Included
Schedule I	a	Opiates	Pure forms of morphine
	b	Opium derivatives	Heroin and codeine-N-Oxide
	c	Hallucinogenics	Marijuana, LSD, and mescaline
Schedule II	a	Opium	Poppies, cocaine
	b	Opium derivatives	Fentanyl and methadone
	c	Methamphetamines	
Schedule III	a	Stimulants	Amphetamines
	b	Depressants	Barbiturates
	c	Nalorphine	
	d	Narcotics	Vicodin, Percodan, hydrocodone, of higher dosage than Schedule IV and V
	e	Anabolic steroids	Used by some athletes to build muscle and speed
Schedule IV		Lower level barbiturates	Many sleeping pills and anti-anxiety drugs
Schedule V		Narcotics mixed with non-Narcotics	Those of lower dosage than Schedule III narcotics with higher dosages of non-narcotics such as acetaminophen, paracemetol, aspirin, or ibuprofen added

As part of this, the FDA solicits help from online consumers. It provides a Web form to report sites you believe are open illegally (shown in Figure 2.1) and available at **http://www.fda.gov/oc/ buyonline/buyonlineform.htm**.

However, concern exists that the FDA only has the manpower to go after just so many shady online vendors, and little recourse to combat the flood of sites that appear to be based in the

U.S. but are actually businesses established in Trinidad, Argentina, India, and the Netherlands.

The FDA and Foreign Pharmacies

One of the problems you hear about again and again surrounding the FDA is the lack of manpower relative to investigations and inspections. For example, the FDA can monitor only a tiny fraction of the meat that is imported into this country every day.

The rise in availability of foreign drugs to U.S. citizens through the Internet has overburdened the agency even more. Its system seems better able to respond to reports of problems after the fact (for example, when you report a serious problem with a drug you received) than to be able to catch the drugs before they make it into consumers' medicine cabinets.

Although the FDA has no hard-and-fast authority outside of the United States, it does utilize agents outside the U.S. along with agents from other federal agencies based overseas who work with other countries to try to stop the flow of illegal or counterfeit drugs before they reach the U.S. In some cases, they can get other countries to shut down illegal drug sites. In others, they may be able to intercept large shipments or track and prosecute outlets in the U.S. that are set up to receive such shipments.

U.S. Customs Service

The U.S. Customs Service is empowered with stopping contraband and unsafe materials from entering this country. This can range from plants and animals that are illegal or subject to long

TIP

Besides specific controlled substances being banned from import from other countries, federal law prohibits the shipment of drugs that have been designated as illegal by the FDA.

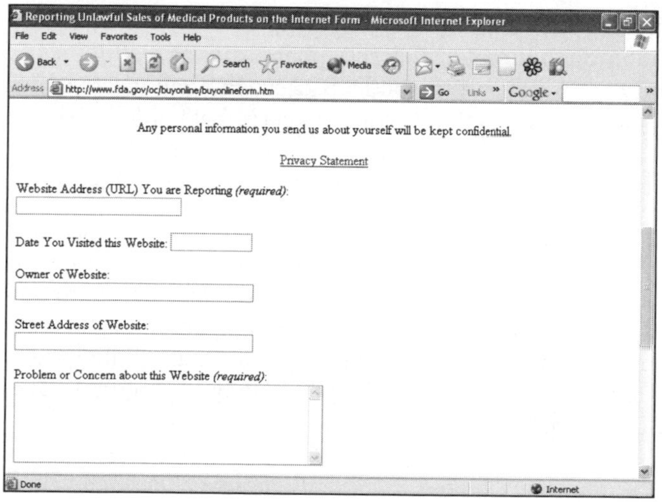

Figure 2.1
Simply fill out the form if you want to report an online pharmacy that you believe is not following the rules.

CHAPTER 2

quarantine periods, to guns and other potentially life-threatening devices, to drugs of all types. As such, it works with a number of different federal authorities, including the FDA, in trying to limit products deemed harmful from reaching U.S. citizens.

According to the government, there is no way to estimate how many packages come in containing "questionable" foreign drugs that would be subject to seizure. The most recent information supplied by the government involves a 2001 pilot study the FDA conducted with the help of the U.S. Customs Service. They examined 1,908 packages of drugs and drug products that arrived at a Carson, California facility over a five-week period. Of these, 721 packages were seized and recipients notified that the products "appeared to violate" the federal Food, Drug, and Cosmetics (FD&C) Act. However, they estimated that if they had sufficient resources, a total of at least 16,500 packages from this facility alone for just those five weeks would likely have been seized for the same concerns.

Like most federal agencies, however, Customs is particularly overworked since the terrorist attacks of September 11, 2001 on U.S. targets. Most authorities acknowledge that Customs can check only a tiny percentage of incoming shipments—sent by standard mail and parcel shippers, as well as those arriving on container ships and cargo planes.

For more information about what U.S. Customs allows into the country, you can visit its Web site at **www.customs.ustreas.gov**.

The Rules and Issues with Shipping Companies

No legitimate shipping company will receive or deliver illegal drugs of any kind. Each of them, from the United States Postal Service to FedEx to United Parcel Service (UPS) and beyond, has very specific policies about what they allow to move through their system for delivery. They employ specialists who try to monitor their shipments to make sure what they handle meets federal guidelines and often work with authorities when there is a suspicion that a sender or a recipient is abusing the system.

Yet the reality is that "illegal" drug shipping happens each and every day, both for prescription medications sold through illegal or overseas pharmacies as well for so-called street drugs such as marijuana and heroin. When you send a package through most venues, you may be asked for the value of the package or whether it contains glass that could break or fluid that might seep out and present a hazard or safety concern. But we wouldn't like it very much if every shipper required us to show them exactly what we're sending or receiving.

Your greatest concern is probably with the U.S. Postal Service if you knowingly break the rules of what can be shipped—either by you or to you—with regard to drugs you obtain for even personal use. The USPS, as part of the federal government, has more powerful leverage to come after you should it choose to do so. This is possible if you order the types of drugs mentioned earlier that are not allowed to pass over state lines, such as opiate-based painkillers. Also, while your drugs may start out in a foreign mail system, they are generally passed to the USPS once they arrive at a U.S. port.

Credit Card Companies

Your credit card company isn't in the business of making "value judgments" about what you order. Its basic responsibility is to verify and authorize transactions sent to it by vendors from whom you either place orders or make direct purchases—oh, yes, and collect your money each month for doing that.

As a consumer, your credit card company may be able to offer you some degree of protection should you not receive your order or receive the wrong order, only to find you can't get the issuing pharmacy to make good on the mistake. Because of this, it may be the wisest course to pay by credit card since you have some degree of protection over cash-on-delivery or a personal check for payment.

Also, watch your credit card statements carefully once you have placed an order. A few of the less legitimate pharmacies may "sign" you up for special discount services or try to automatically refill your order without your authorization. The only way you may catch these is by reviewing your statements and questioning any charges you do not understand.

With one of the test orders, for example, my order from the pharmacy itself was declined for no stated reason, but without approval they signed me up for a $19.99 per month "discount drugs" service. I immediately contacted them saying I did not want this service, but sure enough, the charge appeared on my next Visa bill.

Big Pharma

"Big Pharma" is the label often given to the pharmaceutical industry, based at least in part on the acronym "PHRMA," used to refer to the Pharmaceutical Research and Manufacturers Association, the main Washington lobbying group for the industry. The members Pharma represents include all the major drug manufacturers.

Regardless of whether people love them or hate them, everyone agrees that Pharma wields an incredible amount of influence among politicians, and with it, influence on laws that affect how consumers buy their medications. As an industry, they are very generous contributors to political campaigns.

The pharmaceutical lobby—just as with any other type of lobbying organization—tries to be sure its members' interests are properly represented in any federal or state initiative that may affect the way they do business. For example, Pharma was represented at the drawing board when the government came up with the new Medicare overhaul in 2004, which includes a prescription drug benefit.

Having that kind of participation makes sense because experts working in the industry have unique information to share. But it also raises concern among consumer groups. Critics of the plan argue that the government made big concessions to the pharmaceutical lobby that will result in ever-rising prices with no structure for keeping such prices in check. Some of the people involved in the development of the plan who worked for the federal government and the Medicare program were offered positions with the industry immediately thereafter. Although this isn't illegal—in fact, it's almost common practice in Washington—it leaves at least the impression of a conflict of interest.

However, only parts of the new Medicare program are in effect at the time this book is being written. It's too early to fairly assess whether or not the majority of seniors will truly benefit from the changes. What we do know from early figures released by the government and the media is that seniors are very confused about whether this is a good idea for them. So far, there doesn't appear to be any reduction in seniors looking to Canada for cheaper prices.

The Canadian Connection

Although the practice of U.S. shoppers going across the border to Canada to obtain cheaper prescriptions is not entirely new, publicity about it has grown exponentially. People organize bus trips and even bus caravans to take U.S. citizens to a Canadian pharmacy to fill their orders, and some have reported that a single Canadian bus excursion has saved its participants as much as $19,000 over those same drugs purchased in the U.S.

Add to that the increase in the number of Canadian pharmacies that are now serving U.S. customers via the Web, such as that shown in Figure 2.2. Canadian pharmacies, like their U.S. counterparts, need to follow the rules and regulations for their own country, and when shipping products into the U.S., they cannot ignore specific laws in the U.S. As noted before, most Canadian pharmacies are very careful about not selling controlled substances such as painkillers or Ritalin to U.S. customers because it would violate U.S. law.

But Canada pays a price by aiding U.S. citizens in obtaining less expensive medicines. First, there's the issue of a strain on the country's medical system, which really wasn't designed to extend across the border. Canada has implemented a more universal-access type of health care system. This is part of the reason for its lower drug pricing. Offering pharmaceuticals to U.S. consumers represents a burden to its system, and Canada now has more "fly-by-night" pharmacies open there that it needs to watch.

The United States, by comparison, uses a what-the-market-will-bear system. Although there is probably more interest today for a U.S. universal health care plan than ever before, not all of the

Figure 2.2
Many Canadian pharmacies widely announce their welcome mat to U.S. customers.

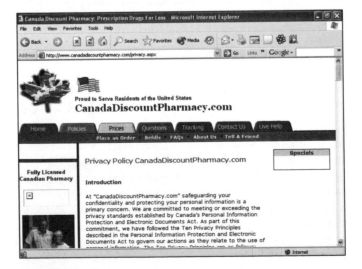

country is in agreement. So one of the ways we're getting around instituting our own universal health access is to piggy-back on Canada's. How long this will remain a workable short-term solution is unclear.

Pressure is being exerted on Canada to end the practice. Drug companies have stated they may either raise their prices to Canada—perhaps bringing them more in line with U.S. pricing—or limit the drugs the country receives unless it stops selling to U.S. citizens. While different U.S. states and municipalities are embracing the cheaper prices, the U.S. federal government is displeased, as you have already learned. U.S. authorities are also very concerned because Canada has passed laws that reduce the criminalization of marijuana and make it easier for people to get it and use it for medical need. They don't consider the idea that U.S. customers might start ordering pot over the Internet a joke.

In response to the pressures, some Canadian pharmacies have banded together to stop selling drugs to U.S. citizens either in-store or over the Internet. Right now, this does not appear to have a huge effect on the availability. This could change, however.

Pharmacies and Pharmacy Associations

Most pharmacies in the United States belong to one or more pharmacy associations, groups that not just represent the overall interests of its member pharmacies but also usually provide some type of standards by which pharmacies must operate to be recognized as a member. You'll learn more about pharmacy regulation in the next section.

With the advent of online drug sales in the late 1990s came great concern over how consumers can tell an American pharmacy from a foreign one, or a "legitimate" pharmacy from one that just manages to have a supply of drugs it's willing to send you. Most of the efforts to separate the wheat from the chaff have been done through state regulation as well as pharmacy association self-regulation.

Pharmacy Regulation

Most pharmacies don't just make up their own rules, although each store or chain of stores will have its own individual policies for how customers can pay and other similar issues. Instead, pharmacies operate under various types of regulation. Some of this regulation is directly affected by American drug laws, but not all.

Pharmacies not only must comply with federal law, but they also must meet licensing standards within the states in which they operate as well as comply with overall state law. Local communities may have their own laws, too, which may affect everything from the minimum number of hours a pharmacy must be open to prohibiting specific drugs from being sold within the boundaries of that community. But as you read earlier, many pharmacies belong to associations that often have some rules for how their members must do business in order to be part of that association.

In most if not all states, pharmacies are primarily regulated by each state's pharmacy board. Also, most if not all pharmacies must seek approval from that board just to open for business and sell prescription drugs. Each state is beholden to make sure its pharmacies meet federal guidelines and comply with federal law, although the federal government itself does not license or approve pharmacies directly.

One of the chief ways different states' pharmacy boards stay in touch with one another and try to offer some uniformity throughout the country is through an organization called the National Association of Boards of Pharmacy (NABP). This group's members include groups from all 50 states as well as U.S.-controlled holdings like Puerto Rico, the District of Columbia, Guam, and the Virgin Islands. It also includes eight Canadian provinces, two Australian states, and the countries of New Zealand and South Africa. The NABP operates the best-known certification program for online pharmacies known as VIPPS (see "The VIPPS Program" later in the chapter for more details).

The NABP provides resources to consumers trying to find good online pharmacies. Visit the NABP site at **http://www.nabp.net** (see Figure 2.3) and click on the link "What you need to know about Internet Pharmacies". There you can get answers to some of the most frequently asked questions about using online pharmacies, as shown in Figure 2.4.

Legitimate online pharmacies that open for business in a particular state also need to meet state licensing and other regulations. Even though the Internet is a global network, the place where a Web site is registered is usually considered its primary site of operations. There's a problem there, however. You can register a Web site just about anywhere in the world. The actual base of operations could be dozens, hundreds, or even thousands of miles away, in a completely different country.

TIP

Beware of any online drugstore which states that it is FDA approved. The Food and Drug Administration approves drugs to allow them to enter the marketplace. The FDA does not approve pharmacies and it does not approve the exact way drugs are sold in every drugstore.

Figure 2.3
New information is added to the NABP site regularly; check back for additional alerts or tips.

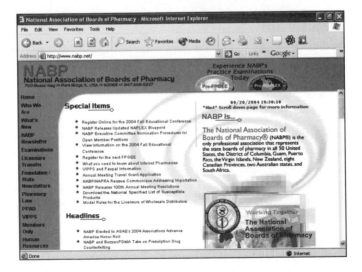

Figure 2.4
This NAPB site page offers specific details about its member program and how to verify that an online pharmacy is part of a network of recognized pharmacies meeting specific standards.

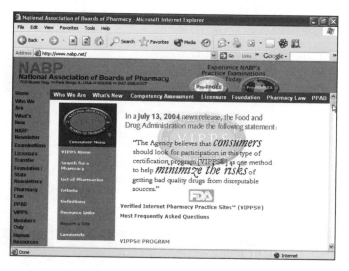

The VIPPS Program

The Verified Internet Pharmacy Practice Sites, usually referred to as VIPPS, is the primary association regulatory program that specifically oversees how its member pharmacies do business on the Web. It's part of the National Association of Boards of Pharmacy. It was started in the late 1990s to address the rising numbers of online pharmacies and to try to distinguish established pharmacies with an online presence from those merely selling drugs.

One of the things to look for when shopping online for medicine is the VIPPS seal, usually prominently displayed on participating member pharmacy sites. Figure 2.5 shows the VIPPS seal on a member online pharmacy. Click on the link, and you jump to information about VIPPS (see Figure 2.6). From there, you can check and verify that the online pharmacy linking to it is a member in good standing.

Figure 2.5
Look for the VIPPS seal when you're seeking an online pharmacy that pledges to observe all laws and business practices that relate to the sale of safe, legal medications.

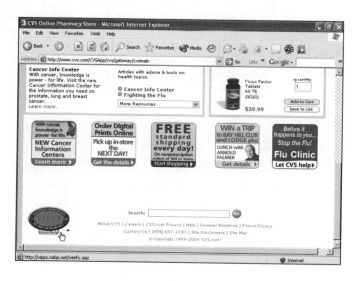

Figure 2.6
The VIPPS official site.

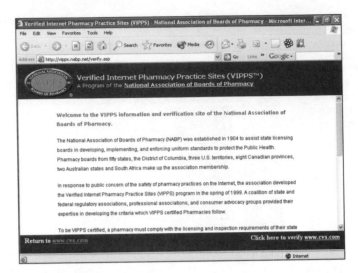

A July 13, 2004 press release from the FDA states, "This agency recommends that consumers should look for participation in this type of certification program (VIPPS) as one method to help minimize the risks of getting bad quality drugs from disreputable sources."

However, even the VIPPS site could potentially have a problem. Nor are all the risks from strictly online shops. Just as this book was being written, authorities announced an investigation into reports in the greater New York area that counterfeit drugs were sold to a number of regional brick-and-mortar pharmacies. So it's still possible that a good pharmacy could inadvertently sell drugs of inferior quality or obtained from less-than-ideal distributors.

TIP

To learn more about VIPPS, you can either click the VIPPS logo on a participating Web site or visit the VIPPS site yourself at **http://vipps.nabp.net/**. One thing to note is that the site has an option for reporting pharmacies that do not appear to be following the rules. You can also reach this reporting form (shown in Figure 2.7) directly by visiting **http://www.nabp.net/vipps/consumer/report.asp**. Certain information is required, but providing your name and identifying details is optional.

NOTE

Chapter 10, "Identifying What You Really Get," provides information on verifying the identifying information often found on medications, such as the drug imprint code on a tablet or the markings on a capsule. It's a smart practice to verify the count and identity of any drugs you buy, regardless of whether you buy them in a traditional pharmacy or online.

Figure 2.7
The VIPPS reporting form allows you to report suspicious Internet-based pharmacies, which the association then passes on to the proper authorities.

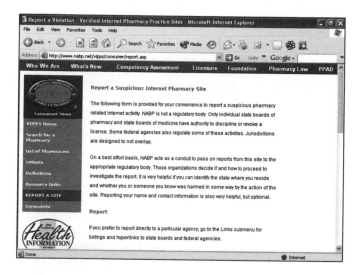

Questions About Other Programs

You'll see that some online sites, even those offering controlled substances without a valid prescription, may have a logo and statement that they belong to some approval, association, or accreditation program. But if it's not VIPPS or another notable one, click on the link for the organization to read about it.

I've seen a few different programs listed on some of the more questionable "no prescription required" sites. Reading the information contained in the link usually tells you very little. For example, if it only states something like, "This seal tells you that this pharmacy meets our criteria for acceptance in our program," consider this a warning sign. Which standards and what program? Before you order from this site, you might try to find out more about this certifying group. If it doesn't seem legitimate, perhaps its members aren't either.

TIP
If you're relatively unfamiliar with the Internet and don't know much about links, all you need to do is locate and click the logo image itself or the hyperlinked text, which is usually in a different color or underlined to set it apart from other text.

The Differences in "No Prescription Needed" Pharmacies

Walk into your corner pharmacy, go up to the counter, and say to the pharmacist on duty, "I'd like 60 penicillin tablets, please."

The pharmacist is either going to laugh and explain the facts of life to you, or he or she will simply ask you for your doctor's prescription, which is needed to honor your request. That's how a legitimate pharmacy usually does business.

This is also the major difference between a legitimate pharmacy as defined here and one that is simply selling prescription drugs. Stop and think. Most pharmacies do not have a doctor behind the counter who is ready to write a prescription for you strictly on the basis of your request for a particular drug. There are good reasons why, too.

Writing a useful prescription is usually based on a number of factors, including:

▶ Knowledge of your medical history and other drugs you may be taking (prescription and non-prescription)

▶ Evidence of your current physical condition including but not limited to your age, height, and weight (all three of which can affect proper dosage)

▶ Any drug or chemical allergies you've reported

▶ Other medication that has worked well (or poorly) for you before

If a staff doctor at a pharmacy could write you a fast prescription without this kind of information and experience with you, the potential is much higher that whatever he or she prescribes could be a bad choice for you. Few pharmacies would survive the malpractice insurance rates or the court cases that could result from that kind of risk. You might not like it much either.

Yet when you walk into "no prescription needed" online drugstores using your Web browser, many promise you that there is indeed a doctor behind the virtual counter waiting to write you that prescription. Most of them work like this from your point of view as the customer:

1. You browse their list of drugs

2. Select one or more different drugs

3. Place them in your shopping cart

4. Choose "checkout" when you're finished

5. Answer an online consultation form

6. Provide your mailing address and credit card information (some may allow you to pay with alternative means such as cash on delivery or personal check)

7. Review your information and finalize your order

8. Receive a summary of your order to the email address you provided during your order; sometimes, you will be asked to confirm that you indeed want to place the order before the order filling process begins

9. Use a customer or order number provided to you to check the status of the order and then to track the shipment and delivery

That's it, at least from your standpoint. Now, there can be some variations here. For example, the doctor or someone from the pharmacy may phone to do a follow-up consultation before the order is approved. Others may require that you provide them with the name, address, and phone number of your primary physician so that they can approve the order with your doctor before the order is filled.

You may also see that some sites tell you they will check to be sure you have not filled any other prescriptions through other pharmacies for this or other drugs in the past 30 days. This is done, most state, to prevent situations in which people are simply self-treating or abusing drugs. Still others may say that they will later ask for some type of verification of age to keep kids from ordering.

This makes it sound like every site, to at least some degree, tries to be sure they are acting responsibly. Yet, as you will read next, these checks and balances that some sites add to the process are not always verified.

Results from Test Orders

Many online pharmacies build a system of checks into the process to be sure they are filling legitimate orders for legitimate needs. As you read earlier, some sites require you to provide the name and contact information for your primary physician, for example, as well as follow up with you, as the patient, by phone before an order is filled.

As part of my research for the book, I placed more than fifteen test orders. (Figure 2.8 shows one of the test orders received.) The study was not a scientific one, but designed to try to test some of the checks and balances that are (or should be) in place to protect customers. Except in one case, I used different online drugstores for each order. These orders were placed between December 2003 and May 2004.

I requested various medications. Each drug was selected because it met one or more of the following criteria:

▶ Drugs that I've never been prescribed in the past or for which I have no current prescription

▶ Those that I had no legitimate need for at the time the order was placed

▶ Drugs for which I have a documented allergy (for example, if I take penicillin, I may experience anaphylactic shock, which means I stop breathing)

▶ Those that represent a specific danger of overdose or complication if not used as directed or used in combination with other drugs ordered in the tests

▶ Drugs that might be contraindicated based on my height, weight, gender, age, and overall physical health

▶ Medications that are often categorized as those with strong addiction or abuse potential, many of which are classified as "controlled substances" by the U.S. government

CHAPTER 2

Figure 2.8
A prescription for hydrocodone, a potent painkiller, that arrives with directions but no identifying prescription information such as issuing pharmacy or doctor.

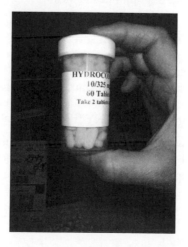

Certain information (such as symptoms or the height, weight, or age I reported in my consultation detail) was deliberately varied with each order. However, my name, delivery address, email address, and telephone number was the same for each and every order placed. I chose to keep this information identical to make it easier for a site to determine that I had placed other orders.

The drugs I requested in the test orders were:

▶ Cipro, an antibiotic that became well-known during the anthrax scare that occurred after anthrax-laced letters were sent to U.S. senators, media outlets, and others in September and October 2001

▶ Penicillin, another antibiotic (remember, I have a really bad allergy to this and noted the allergy when I placed my order)

▶ Xanax, a powerful and potentially addicting anti-anxiety drug

▶ Ativan, another anti-anxiety drug, also tied to addiction

▶ Carisoprodol (also known by its brand name, Soma), a strong muscle relaxant sometimes used for sleep

▶ Cyclobenzaprine (also known by the major brand name Flexeril), a muscle relaxant

▶ Glucophage, used by some diabetics

▶ Darvon and Hydrocodone (known also as Vicodin), both strong, controlled-access painkillers

▶ Ritalin, a drug often used to treat hyperactivity in children

▶ Cialis, used to treat erectile dysfunction, almost exclusively prescribed for men

▶ Ortho Novum, a contraceptive (not a good match for me since I have a family history of breast cancer and blood clots plus I suffer from bouts of high blood pressure)

▶ Amitriptyline, a tricyclic antidepressant (a really poor choice with drugs like Xanax, Ativan, and Carisoprodol)

▶ Imitrex, a drug used to treat migraine headaches

In all cases, I tried to restrict orders to sites that said or implied they were U.S.-based pharmacies. However, subsequent research showed that several were actually operated or registered outside the U.S. Strangely, though, several of these sites delivered orders from pharmacies located in Florida, Pennsylvania, and Wisconsin. Others delivered them in non-prescription form (the kind of blister pack of pills or capsules you might get in physician samples), with no prescription documentation provided, and sent from non-descript addresses such as a wholesale warehouse in Flushing Meadows, NY (see Figure 2.9).

These tests included a few situations in which I placed back-to-back orders at different pharmacies. This was to test the system by which some of these pharmacies promised to check customer information to eliminate those patients ordering large amounts of drugs from multiple venues in a short period of time.

Figure 2.9
What you get from some of the "no prescription needed" pharmacies are prescription pills packaged like doctor's samples.

In the sample test orders conducted for this book, pharmacies that required customers to give them a primary physician's name and address often would reject the order if a doctor's name was not provided. However, test orders for which a bogus doctor's name and number was given were approved. Where bogus information was given, the phone number used was a working one with an answering machine to receive calls. But no calls or messages were received from any of the drugstores to verify or authorize the patient information.

Of the orders placed, only three were rejected. Two rejected my order for failing to supply a physician's name (two others accepted and processed the order without the required information, three others accepted a bogus physician's name), and one rejected the order without giving a reason (although they charged my credit card as if the order had been processed). In a fourth case, the order stayed open as if being processed for a period of time, with no change in status. My credit card was never charged and the order was never delivered.

Of these, very few responded to any contact from me regarding my order. Those that did used form letters to respond, whether or not that form letter applied to the question I asked. For example, when I received one prescription from one pharmacy in Florida and another from a different-named pharmacy in Wisconsin, with both bearing the exact same doctor's name, I wrote the online drugstores to ask how that was possible. None replied.

Here are some other interesting results from the tests:

▶ Pill counts were often inaccurate (one order for 30 pills sent 28, whereas another order for 90 pills sent 97); only three orders arrived with the exact number of pills or capsules ordered

▶ One site offering 10 mg hydrocodone (with 500 mg acetaminophen) sent instead codeine (with 500 paracemetol); codeine is a much cheaper drug, with one-sixth the effectiveness of hydrocodone

▶ The order for Cialis arrived with no prescription label, just a sticker stating, "Take as directed" but without any directions

▶ The orders that had to pass through U.S. Customs all went through easily, even when one package clearly indicated that it was sent by a Netherlands pharmacy

▶ Of all the drugs, only four could be traced to foreign manufacturers, specifically Pakistan, Thailand, the Netherlands, and Mexico

▶ Only one drug, one of the muscle relaxants, arrived with any warning labels advising against taking the drug with alcohol or other drugs that might cause sedation effect

▶ Orders from Canada passed into the U.S. mail and were delivered with no incident

▶ Darvon arrived not quite as ordered, substituted with Darvin, an equivalent product made in Lahore, Pakistan

▶ Except for the codeine substituted for Hydrocodone and the Darvon/Darvin noted before, every single order was for exactly the drug ordered, which I verified through a service available at Rxlist.com; from this, however, I only know they match appearance (counterfeit drugs sometimes do as well)

▶ Several orders offered overnight delivery but were often shipped via cheaper methods (2-day or U.S. priority mail)

▶ Some services contacted me as early as 10–14 days after the first order was placed encouraging me to buy a refill, even in cases where I had purchased what would be a 2–3 month supply

Insurance Companies

Before you order any drugs online—and this really extends to those you obtain from a bricks-and-mortar drugstore as well—look through the booklets or documentation that came with the pharmacy portion of your health insurance.

Depending on the type of coverage you have, you may be stuck paying for any out-of-pocket drug costs that are not ordered through the insurer's preferred provider network. Others require you to submit invoices, proof of need, and other details for them to review before they make any decision whatsoever.

One thing you will find, too, with some of the less legitimate pharmacies is that they will not accept drug coverage insurance at all to defer part of your up-front costs. Check each online pharmacy's FAQ (frequently asked questions) and policy pages before you place orders.

So who exactly is ordering drugs online? You may be surprised. Chapter 3 explores some of the diverse groups of people using these services, and offers you some feedback from those who have shared their experience.

Chapter 3
The Electronic Drugstore Shopper

There isn't just one type of consumer taking advantage of the Internet both for health information and to order prescription medications. Web-based shopping has been accepted to some degree by most age and demographic groups. Even those who don't have credit cards can usually find alternative methods to pay for orders.

This chapter looks at some of the types of people shopping for drugs online and the feedback on the kinds of experiences people have encountered. With this, you discover that some find bargains while others pay more, and some others are shopping online because they feel it's their best alternative.

Who's Shopping Online?

Ask around among friends, family members, and co-workers. When you do, you may be surprised to see how many have at least considered, if not purchased, their prescriptions online. Although most of the shoppers seem to be of median age, many are Web-savvy senior citizens and some, perhaps a bit too young.

Here, I've divided Web drug shoppers into major categories, although you'll discover that many actually fit in more than one category. For example, I've used my local pharmacy's online shopping option to order refills because my home is actually more than 20 miles from my drugstore, which makes me a rural customer with limited pharmacy options. But I'm also a very busy professional who doesn't usually have the time to go shopping around for the best prices, so I tend to look for what I need on the Web. I know lots of other people who shop this way who fall into multiple categories as well.

These categories include:

- ▶ The bargain shopper
- ▶ The rural or limited-access shopper
- ▶ The frequent traveler and/or busy professional
- ▶ The private shopper
- ▶ People without health insurance or a regular doctor
- ▶ People choosing their own course of therapy
- ▶ Those using programs that require online ordering

> ▶ People with addictions
> ▶ Kids and young adults buying medications for specific effect

The Bargain Shopper

Few of us pass up the chance to obtain what we want at a bargain price. That extends to prescription medications, especially in situations where we must use a particular drug daily.

For those on a fixed or otherwise limited income, the need for a bargain can become acute because a savings in price can make the difference between being able to take a drug as prescribed or not. For example, many senior citizens and others on limited income—at least before some began to cross the border into Canada or shop foreign pharmacies through the Web—have been known to split their prescribed dosage in half trying to extend the period before they need to purchase the drug again.

In some respects, the Internet as a pharmacy has been a bit of a disappointment to bargain shoppers. While many pharmacies advertise "lowest prices," many seem to provide the same drug at a comparable or somewhat higher price than a traditional bricks-and-mortar pharmacy (and some wildly inflate). This isn't always because of price-gouging; rising fuel costs have raised most shipping costs. You may encounter situations in which the per-dose drug cost through a legitimate Internet pharmacy is lower than you pay now, at least until you factor in shipping costs. Likewise, those that offer free shipping may have higher drug prices.

The truth is that you usually can find some bargains online. But as you'll see in subsequent chapters (especially Chapter 9), you need to know the going price for your medication before you go shopping. If you don't, you may pay a much steeper price than is necessary because the price range between one online pharmacy and another can be dramatic.

Price alone, however, probably should not be the only factor in any decision you make about how to buy your drugs. You want to obtain them through a reputable source that tries to be sure it isn't accidentally selling counterfeit versions of your medication, that ensures care will be placed in preparing your order, and that has enough information about you to be sure you aren't at risk from conflicts between a drug you're ordering now and other medications you may be taking. In fact, good pharmacists catch potential drug interaction issues every day that even a primary care physician may miss. Software used by many pharmacies today makes it even easier to spot potential drug interactions.

NOTE

This chapter offers profiles of individuals who responded to my request to share their experiences with purchasing drugs online. Some provided just basic information, some were kind enough to answer a detailed questionnaire, and others chatted with me online. Because of the sensitive nature of this material—particularly in some cases—no one was asked to supply their real name or address.

PROFILE: A FAMILY IN SEARCH OF COST CUTTING

Jon and Debbie are a young couple with three kids who operate a farm in New England. With money extremely tight, Debbie began looking for ways to save money.

Visiting family in the Midwest last year, she noticed that filling a particular prescription there cost less than it did back home. Back from vacation, Jon and Debbie began looking around to see if they could shave some costs associated with regular medications that each of them takes. Jon has acid reflux disease and a skin condition for which he takes pills and uses a prescription cream, while Debbie uses prescription-only eye drops and a non-insulin medication for diabetes. She also takes a particular drug for dysmenorrhea (highly symptomatic menstrual periods).

Debbie discovered that through regular research (see Figure 3.1) and including paying shipping fees, they could save anywhere from 8%–25% by ordering online. Their doctors understand the situation and are willing to issue a new prescription for a different pharmacy when an existing one can't be easily transferred.

However, she notes that she must re-check prices regularly rather than simply reorder a medication automatically. If she doesn't, she said the price that began low at one online pharmacy may climb beyond that charged at another. She also warned that some pharmacies charge special fees that, when added onto a lower price-per-pill, obliterate the bargain.

This works well for them, although they usually avoid going online for their kids' prescriptions. "With the kids, it's usually something I need to get faster than I can with an online order unless I pay extra for overnight delivery. But if one of the kids needed to get the same medication regularly, I'd probably add something like that to my online order." She also prefers the opportunity to speak with a local pharmacist concerning her kids' prescriptions because she feels a pharmacist can offer additional details the pediatrician may not discuss.

Figure 3.1
The CVS pharmacy chain is one of many that allow you to check prices on at least their most frequently ordered drugs before you place your order.

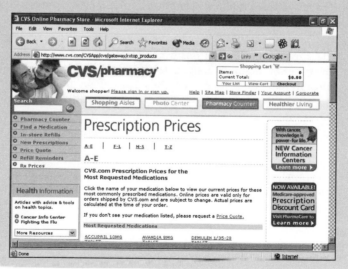

The Rural or Limited-Access Shopper

While more than 60% of the U.S. population lives close enough to major shopping venues to allow for real choices in where to shop for drugs and other necessities, this means that nearly 40% do not. Some communities have just a single pharmacy, whereas others may not have one at all.

But even within busy metropolitan areas, many people have neither access to a car nor public transportation. Others may be house-bound by illness (theirs or a loved one's). Still others may have a physical infirmity that may allow them to be ambulatory, but can make it very difficult to run all over town looking for the best prices.

Among some contingents of rural and limited-access shoppers, online ordering has become the difference between obtaining what they want or having to settle for what they can more easily get. Even with shipping costs applied, some find it more price efficient to shop online than to expend a lot of gas to drive round-trip to buy a needed item. Slowly, drug shopping has joined the other products such people seek out online.

PROFILE: AN OLDER COUPLE WHO CAN NO LONGER MAKE THE DRIVE TO CANADA TO PICK UP CHEAPER PRESCRIPTIONS

Donald and his wife are both in their late sixties and retired now, living on a fixed income in central Montana. Both also have chronic medical conditions that require them to take an average of seven different drugs every day (Donald has asthma and early emphysema, and his wife is a diabetic who also must take a blood thinner and high blood pressure medication).

When Donald retired, he was able to continue his health insurance benefits through his former employer. But when that employer went into bankruptcy, retirement benefits were cut. Hearing about the lower prices in Canada, the couple began to make bi-monthly 400-mile round trips to stock up on cheaper prescriptions.

By early 2004, however, complications from diabetes had decreased his wife's vision so that she could no longer help him on the long drive. Donald found it too difficult to drive these distances himself. Skeptical that the new Medicare program then being passed would significantly help their drug costs, yet unable to find an alternative way to get to Canada to get their cheaper drugs, Donald turned to the Web.

Now, the couple continues to use mostly Canadian pharmacies (see Figure 3.2), but without the drive. Their doctor prepares a written prescription for each drug, which is then faxed to whatever pharmacy offers the best price. The Canadian pharmacy verifies the U.S.-originated prescriptions and has a Canada-licensed doctor review and approve the order. Then the pharmacy fills the order, which is shipped to the couple. Buying in volume (enough of every drug to last 60 or 90 days) helps the couple shave costs further.

Continued

Donald reports no problems in receiving his shipments but notes that he really has to plan ahead since it can take more than a week for an order to arrive. When a new medication gets added, he asks his doctor for two prescriptions: one for a short-term supply he can get locally the same day and another to order through the Web to arrive before the short supply is exhausted.

He believes they save between 10% and 15%, or about $40–$60 per month over using local pharmacies. They're waiting to see whether they will continue to need to use Canadian pharmacies now that the new Medicare drug discount cards are available.

Figure 3.2
One of the many Canadian pharmacies that allow U.S. residents to order their drugs for shipment to their homes or offices.

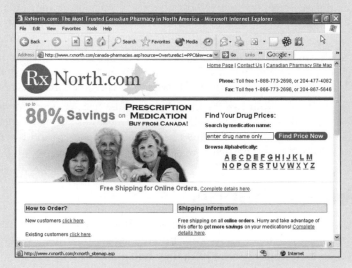

The Frequent Traveler and Busy Professional

Many of us work far more than 40 hours a week, especially when you factor in all the extras we must do as part of daily life. Some of us, too, must travel frequently and may not have access or time to spend on weekends to catch up on our errands, such as obtaining drug refills.

In this category, you also find people who have their prescriptions delivered to the office rather than home. This is helpful either when no one is home to receive the order, or parents with children at home do not want to leave such packages lying about. Others, through special arrangement, can get their drugs shipped to alternative locations such as a remote work site or a hotel where they are temporarily staying.

CHAPTER 3

PROFILE: "I'M RARELY IN THE SAME PLACE FOR MORE THAN THREE DAYS"

Yasmin is a senior field service engineer for a major data services company who must travel to as many as three different cities in a single week dealing with emergencies. She says she's rarely home for more than 72 hours at a time and really has no time to run simple errands. A single woman living on her own, there's also no one at home who can take care of these details for her.

However, she suffers from irritable bowel syndrome as well as a thyroid condition. These require her to take at least four different prescriptions on a daily basis. She says she's had health emergencies when she's run out of her required drugs because she's stuck with a client or gets home on a holiday weekend when local pharmacies may be closed. This sometimes resulted in her needing to go to an emergency room in a strange city or consult with a hotel doctor.

Starting in late 2001, when increased security and surveillance post-9/11/01 made easy travel more difficult, she found it much tougher to be sure she always had an adequate supply of medications with her. Her health suffered. Then Yasmin's doctor suggested she consider using online pharmacies to get her medications when she couldn't connect with her pharmacy at home.

She reports that she didn't like the experience at first because she sometimes paid more than was necessary. Now she's learned which online drugstores she can depend upon and now uses one online pharmacy exclusively. She likes the level of service and it will deliver to her hotel or remote work site when needed.

The Private Shopper

As you learned in the previous chapters, many choose to shop using Internet-based pharmacies simply because they don't want to walk into the corner pharmacy where everyone knows them to pick up a prescription for something they find embarrassing.

Beyond that, however, are people who feel they don't even need or want to involve their own primary care physician in the process of obtaining prescriptions for certain medications. Some of the reasons they cite include:

> ▶ A desire to keep a particular drug off their permanent medical record, which could find its way back to an insurance company or an employer

> ▶ Those using drugs that may be frowned upon by other members of the community, particularly in close-knit religious or conservative communities (for example, one woman cited the need to go online for birth control medications because her physician, a family doctor who belongs to the same Roman Catholic church as her parents, has advised her not to take them on religious grounds)

> ▶ Those who feel they do not need a doctor to "give them permission" to take a drug they feel they need or want to use

Viagra, Cialis, and diet pills are just some of the medications advertised at sites, such as that shown in Figure 3.3, that allow people to obtain a variety of drugs without a physical examination, without notification to the primary care physician, and without a prior prescription. The people I spoke with who use services like this say they know the risks but feel their privacy outweighs any potential for danger, even though the practice is illegal and fraught with dangers

Figure 3.3
All too often, people are turning to the Web to order drugs they find it too difficult to ask their own doctors to prescribe. But without a full checkup, this is a dangerous practice.

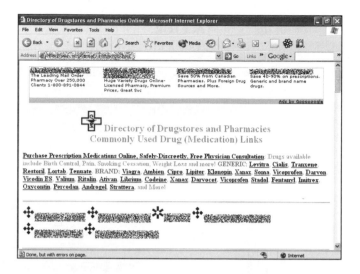

PROFILE: "IT'S NOBODY'S BUSINESS BUT MINE"

Here's a good example of someone who explored the easy route and then took a more sensible road.

Carl found he had a tough time going to his doctor when he felt he needed medication to treat erectile dysfunction. When he did, he felt the doctor assumed the problem was more in his head than with his body and would not prescribe what Carl wanted. It took a third doctor to issue a no-refill prescription for Viagra. When he got the medication filled, Carl says the pharmacy clerk joked that he must have a big weekend planned.

Describing himself as a very private person who normally does not take so much as an aspirin, he was unhappy with the whole experience. He thought it was more invasive than necessary and the process treated him like a teenager looking for a good time.

After what he calls a great deal of consideration, Carl decided to go online to place orders for the drug. At first, he used pharmacies that provided the medication with just an online consultation but felt he was paying too high a price (about three-to-four times that charged at a traditional pharmacy). His health insurance gave him a hassle when he submitted the drug receipts for reimbursement.

So he found a new doctor willing to write the prescription, which he mails in to an online pharmacy. Each written prescription allows him to fill the medication and obtain two refills automatically before he must get an updated prescription. Using this method, he says the cost is now comparable to what he would pay at his local pharmacy but without the potential embarrassment if he picked it up in person.

ContinuedHe

follows up with new his doctor to be sure he has not developed any risk factors for taking the drug and says he would not go back to the traditional system. In fact, when he needed to start taking a second drug to treat a skin condition, he again chose to use his online pharmacy. Because he's using an authorized pharmacy (unlike the one pictured in Figure 3.4), his health insurance does reimburse him now.

Figure 3.4
Just because a site offers certain drugs without a prescription does not mean it is safe to use them or that the drugs are real rather than counterfeit.

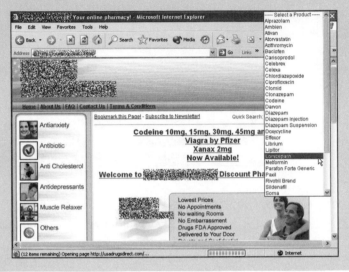

People Without Insurance or a Regular Doctor

Not everyone today feels they have a choice about their medical care. There are those who struggle just to pay their very basic bills. Some have health insurance but can't afford the high out-of-pocket deductibles they may face before treatment is covered. Others are without health insurance altogether.

Yet there's another group: those without a regular doctor. Some may be people who don't like doctors or resist seeing them for other reasons. Others may have difficulty finding one altogether. This can be especially true in rural areas or even more populated ones where there is a scarcity of doctors.

In my case, I found that when I moved from the tri-state New York region to rural Vermont, it became nearly impossible to find new doctors in our area. The number of doctors with practices here is relatively limited and those doctors tend to work long hours trying to cover their current patient load, so they don't take new patients.

When my significant other developed a badly swollen knee soon after our move, it took more than two dozen phone calls to find a doctor willing to see him. The first open appointment was in late August, which was a problem because the swollen knee occurred in early June. With no other option, we scheduled the appointment but had to seek initial treatment through a medical center emergency room. Then he received a referral to a great orthopedic surgeon who helped resolve the medical emergency.

Later, I hit a similar situation when I developed back pain and a fever that would not go away. I dismissed the symptoms at first, and then began taking aspirin. I tried calling doctors, but again, found I could not locate one willing to take a new patient without a prolonged wait. One suggested I try yoga for stress relief to reduce my pain; another said that if I was well enough to make the call, I probably didn't need to go to the hospital. That's a big problem with trying to diagnose a condition and prescribe a treatment regimen without seeing a patient.

Unfortunately, I'm one of those people who tend to resist going to the doctor and I frown on the practice of going to an emergency room unless there is a legitimate emergency. Even when my symptoms rapidly developed to the point where I could not breathe or move without severe pain, I would not go to the E.R. Instead, we kept making calls trying to locate a doctor who would see me.

Finally, when I did go to the E.R. because there was no other option, they took one look at me and rushed me into treatment. The back pain turned out to be pneumonia—a severe form— which quickly progressed into both lungs. Two days after admission, I was transferred to Intensive Care because the pneumonia had developed into acute respiratory distress syndrome, or ARDS, a very serious condition with a high mortality rate. It took three weeks of ICU care and more than $60,000 in bills to get me to the point where I was well enough to return home.

I was very fortunate because not only did I survive (many with ARDS die or require longer hospitalizations and must undergo a drug-induced coma while they are placed on a ventilator for a few weeks), but I got an excellent doctor to follow up with me. There is no doubt in my mind that if I had failed to seek treatment when I did, I would not be alive to write this book. Without the follow-up care from my doctor, a subsequent lung mass would not have been detected and treated.

Even when it's difficult to find and pay for medical care, you really need to investigate what options are available to you. Some communities offer clinics that give people with little money access to at least some types of screening, care, and follow-up. Some hospitals, too, have special funds they can apply to patients who either don't have health care coverage or have what is called a catastrophic illness (like my ARDS) that would not be covered under a normal policy. Also, many doctors are willing to work out a system of payments rather than let patients go without care.

Understand, too, that even doctors, with their knowledge and training, can have extreme difficulty finding the right treatment regimen to help each patient, so self-treatment is not advised. Ignoring the symptoms is bad, too.

Let's look at some other people who have shared their experience.

PROFILE: "I'M ALLERGIC TO DOCTORS"

My friend "Tim" is generally a very healthy man, which is a good thing because he has an almost pathological fear of doctors and hospitals. He likes to joke that the only time he has been in a hospital was when he was admitted while unconscious following a car accident.

Tim, a robust eater, is also an outdoor enthusiast, at least during the summer months when he can spend hours in the pool. But every winter, he tends to put on 15 to 25 pounds he then labors to lose before swim suit season.

For the last few years, Tim has been ordering diet pills online each spring to help him drop the extra weight. He reports that he actually went to his wife's doctor first to ask for a prescription, but the doctor instead placed him on a diet Tim felt he could not follow. Rather than find a different doctor, he began to order the pills himself through a site that just required him to fill out a medical history form. Figure 3.5 shows a site that sells, among other drugs, diet drugs without a prior prescription.

He acknowledges the risk in what he's doing, but feels he reduces the risk potential by only taking it as prescribed and then for just four-to-six weeks each year. He also makes sure his wife, a nurse, knows when he's taking it and if there is a medical emergency, she could let the attending physician know.

His wife, however, is not very happy with the practice. She feels he needs to get a regular checkup and worries whenever he's taking the diet medication. "Doing this without medical supervision is just plain dumb. I've watched too many people come into the hospital because they self-treated themselves into much worse shape than they were before," she adds.

Figure 3.5
Some recent diet drugs have produced some very disturbing side effects or resulting conditions, making them a poor choice for consumption without adequate medical supervision.

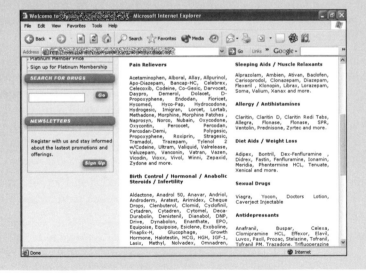

Here's another example of someone who used Web sites to self-treat a known medical condition. In his case, there were repercussions that only medical professionals could identify and treat.

PROFILE: HIGH CHOLESTEROL, NO INSURANCE, AND LITTLE CASH

Keith says he had health insurance through his job when a doctor first diagnosed him with high cholesterol that diet and exercise failed to reduce to safe levels. He has a family history of coronary disease. His physician prescribed a statin drug called Lipitor (atorvastatin) to try to cut his cholesterol level. This was successful and with his doctor's OK, he stopped taking the drug.

Unfortunately, since then, Keith lost his job and with it, his health benefits. He's working now for a temporary employment agency that does not offer any health care.

Recently, through a local health fair, he had his cholesterol checked and found it was once again high. He was told that he should see a doctor as soon as possible.

Unable to pay for both a doctor's visit and follow-up care as well as the statin drug, which can easily run more than $100 per month, he decided to gamble with self-treatment. Using his credit card (so he could spread out payments while he continues to look for a permanent job with health benefits), Keith found he could order Lipitor online through a drugstore where he filled out a form and talked with someone ("presumably a doctor") over the phone. Figure 3.6 shows one of the outlets for obtaining Lipitor without a current prescription. He paid about 38% more than he did through a traditional pharmacy, plus a one-time handling fee of $25.

Three days later, his Lipitor arrived and he began taking it as prescribed. A month later, he used another low-cost cholesterol screening to check his levels. He was disturbed to find that he wasn't seeing the good results he had before.

Still, it wasn't until after he ordered his first refill of the medication that he began to notice muscle cramping and other problems that finally forced him back into the doctor's office. He isn't sure that the higher dosage the online pharmacy had given him had anything to do with the symptoms, but his doctor switched him to a lower dose of a different statin drug, which finally has his cholesterol back under control.

Further tests showed that Keith had probably suffered some low-level form of heart attack sometime between his last doctor's visit and his return. He also needed treatment for newly diagnosed high blood pressure. None of these additional issues could have been diagnosed just through using an online "no prescription needed" drugstore or the by-phone consultation he used to obtain his later prescription.

"I don't think I'd try to go the self medication route again," Keith says now. "It's like playing Russian roulette."

Continued

He notes that he believes he was lucky he was able to stop the practice before he suffered more serious consequences. However, he feels that many others may find themselves in the same predicament he was in: no health insurance and desperate to continue necessary treatment even when they can't afford a doctor's exam.

Figure 3.6
Another site that allows you to order a range of drugs such as Lipitor, Viagra, and powerful painkillers without a current prescription.

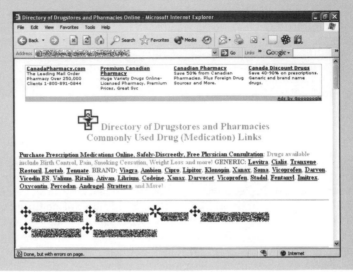

People Choosing Their Own Course of Therapy

There are those of us who see our doctors and try to do everything they tell us to do. There are others who consult with their doctors but may or may not follow their recommendations to the letter (often enough, just because we forget to take our pills or don't like a diet plan). Yet not quite everyone falls into these two broad categories.

Starting in the 1980s, we began to hear how important it is to think of ourselves less as patients and more as savvy medical consumers. Who, after all, knows our bodies as well as we do, at least from an "owner's" perspective? With changes in how medical care is delivered, our doctors may not know us as well as family care practitioners once did. Also, many people now have more than one doctor, making it necessary to try to coordinate information between them. If one doctor isn't aware of a change another doctor has made in treatment, problems can develop. We can't just assume everyone has the same information.

One of the results of this change is that the past few decades have brought a rise in the number of people who make a conscious choice to control their own medical care rather than just following doctor's orders. These people tend to cite one or more of the following factors in making this decision:

▶ Disillusionment with traditional medical care

▶ A need to explore alternative treatments because standard treatment failed or produced nasty side effects

▶ Interest in a specific treatment plan not immediately available through the local medical community

▶ A desire to be better informed about their overall health and the potential effects of any treatment

Exactly how people go about taking charge can differ widely. Just because you make the choice to call your own shots does not always mean you'll make the smartest choice. Professionals can't always anticipate our responses to certain medications, so it's much harder for us to do so.

Yet there are some similarities in how the people who report the highest degree of satisfaction proceed. They usually do this both by doing as much additional research as they can to become knowledgeable about their illnesses and different treatment regimens as well as through consultation with medical professionals. Both parts are needed, they feel, because doctors, pharmacists, and other professionals have a great deal more knowledge about overall human health and drug responsiveness than we have as lay people.

After doing their legwork, some of them are taking advantage of the global accessibility to different medications that Web-based pharmacies offer. One woman I talked with was researching alternative treatments for a sister with sclera derma; through the Web, she found information about a European study with good symptom relief with a particular drug. A doctor in Europe then was able to connect her with an Internet pharmacy in Europe where she could obtain a trial supply of the drug, which had not yet been submitted to the FDA for approval. Technically, the transaction may not be a legitimate one because the FDA—through Customs— could seize the drug when it enters the country. But for this woman and her sister, they were willing to take the calculated risk to prolong the ill sister's quality of life.

Another person who was seeking his own way to end a long-time heroin-then-methadone addiction traveled to Amsterdam by way of the Web to obtain a medication that supposedly acts by blocking brain receptors that respond to opiates. He says the drug has allowed him to break a long cycle of drug addiction, adding that he talked to doctors and researched for a few months trying to find a program in this country offering the same drug. Only when he could find nothing like that here did he go the self-treatment route.

Figure 3.7
While many online drugstores of various types offer "forums" and help with selecting drugs and alternative treatment sources, don't rely on just one source, and certainly avoid situations in which you're buying from the only source advocating it.

PROFILE: SHE WANTS FEWER SIDE EFFECTS AND LESS-EXPENSIVE RESULTS

Mary says she is no stranger to the health care system. Now in her early 60s, she has survived Stage II breast cancer, two minor heart attacks, and a series of problems created by fluctuation of various hormones. For many years, she has also battled with hypoglycemia, recurrent stomach ulcers, and a compromised circulatory system that means she sometimes sees her foot or leg swell with edema. Her high cholesterol levels have only been marginally reduced through diet, exercise, and statin drugs. Recently, she had to stop her treatment regime for post-menopausal symptoms because there was some concern it increased her risk of another heart attack.

At the height of her health issues, Mary claims she was taking 14 different medications on a daily basis and regularly saw five different physicians. She found this situation difficult to manage because not all doctors communicated well with others. More than once, she says, she would take a new prescription to the pharmacy only to have her pharmacist tell her there was a conflict with something else she was taking. She also reported situations in which one doctor would give her advice that totally contradicted that offered by another doctor.

In 2002, when she found herself stuck between decreasing health care benefits through work and not yet ready to apply for Medicare and Social Security, Mary began looking more into less traditional therapies. She dropped a couple of her specialists in favor of a single primary care physician plus a homeopathic doctor and told them both that she wanted to take less prescription medication in favor of more natural alternatives.

With their help, combined with the hours she says she spends online doing research, Mary reports she has achieved some good results. For example, she now uses a common kitchen spice in liquid concentration form to reduce her high cholesterol to the point where her primary care physician has agreed to let her stop her statin drug. She does, however, undergo frequent cholesterol screenings as a precaution. A careful selection of herb tea has helped her cut her body's fluid retention, she says, while changing her diet again has improved her low blood sugar and ulcers.

But she cautions people not to proceed without support from medical professionals, adding that she made some mistakes early on in the process that could have been dangerous had she not gotten medical follow-up.

Issues in Chronic Pain Management

Unlike blood pressure or your cholesterol level, which can be documented, pain can be a very individual experience. Some people have a high degree of tolerance for pain while others do not. A condition that causes pain that can completely incapacitate one person may not do the same to others.

As a culture, we seem to be fairly concerned with the issue of pain. This makes a great deal of sense when you consider how debilitating pain can be and how much of an impact it can have on both our own day-to-day lives as well as those of the people who live with, care for, or work with us. Those who have chronic pain lose untold hours of work, family time, and simple enjoyment each year.

When you focus just on one aspect like lost work time, you're also bringing with it the cost to society as a whole. Absence or reduced performance at work affects productivity, with the burden transferred to other employees, higher benefits such as sick time and additional medical costs (with associated higher health insurance premiums), and a greater risk that someone with chronic pain may not be able to continue to work.

It's difficult to peg just how many people in the U.S. alone suffer from pain for long periods of time. Depending upon how that pain is defined (chronic versus acute, its degree based on how greatly it affects the quality of one's life, and how long the pain must last before it is classified as chronic), some studies suggest that as many as 1 in 10 to as "few" as 1 in 50 adults fit the label of "chronic pain patients." It's also nearly impossible to document how many people commit suicide each year that is attributable to the effects of uncontrolled chronic pain.

Yet as often as we discuss the subject and as little as any of us like to feel pain, we as a country also have a rather schizophrenic history of dealing with chronic pain. One of the most common examples of this was cited in Chapter 2. Some cities and states have adopted laws allowing the medicinal use of marijuana for pain and appetite stimulation in those with terminal or long-term debilitating illnesses. At the same time, the federal government has stepped up efforts to prevent anyone from possessing or using marijuana who is not part of an extremely limited federal treatment program.

Because of the high abuse potential combined with the overall risk of complications with drugs commonly used to treat pain, we make potent painkillers more difficult to obtain. You've no doubt heard some terrible stories about celebrities and others who had access to huge amounts of painkillers who then did something outrageous, or were involved in overdoses or accidents that can be attributed to those medications. Such cases make you think restriction is very wise.

However, you've also probably heard or read about patients with terminal cancer who reported that they cannot get the levels of pain medication they need to control their pain. The hospice movement in both England and the United States was in part brought about by medical professionals and caregivers who wanted to be sure that symptoms like pain could be better handled in the final months of a patient's life.

In the past several years, the government at all levels has often adopted stronger laws to try to prevent people from obtaining painkillers unlawfully. For example, if you happen to be stopped by a police officer and found to have a controlled substance such as the painkiller hydrocodone, but cannot prove that you have a valid prescription for it, you can be arrested. Also, if you have a valid prescription for a painkiller but allow someone else to take any of your pills, you risk arrest because this violates federal law.

NOTE

Don't transfer your medications out of their prescription bottles when you're planning to travel. You never know when it may be necessary to prove what the drugs are, and that you have a valid prescription for them. While this is mainly an issue with controlled substance prescriptions such as painkillers and sedatives, you sometimes see police officers and other law enforcement agents mistake another drug for one of those.

We have also instituted programs to monitor doctors and both the quantity and frequency of drugs they prescribe to try to reduce the amount of abuse. Part of the idea here is to weed out doctors who use their DEA-authorized (the federal Drug Enforcement Agency) license to write prescriptions for which there is no legitimate need.

Unfortunately, the result of this say many who advocate for chronic pain patients, is that the government is making it very tough for doctors to prescribe adequate levels of pain medications to those who truly need that relief. They claim that doctors sympathetic to chronic pain sufferers risk being threatened with long investigations as well as possible loss of their prescription-writing privileges and even their license to practice medicine. The potential for extra scrutiny alone is enough to discourage some doctors from prescribing painkillers for anyone or limit the prescriptions to a low dose for a very short period of time.

Faced with a situation in which they don't feel like they can get proper medical assistance, many appear willing to self-treat. One of the ways to do that is through someone trying to supplement his or her regularly prescribed pain medications with those they can order over the Web (such as those featured in a drug location site like the one shown in Figure 3.8), using the simple online doctor's consultation.

It's probably no accident that some of the less legitimate online pharmacies offer heavy-duty painkillers. They've got a guaranteed audience of those who are in legitimate physical pain but feel they cannot obtain the amount of medication they need from their doctor, and those who no longer need them for physical pain but have developed an addiction to the euphoria these drugs sometimes produce.

Figure 3.8
Sites like this offer free patient forums, but there's always the possibility they exist just to sell a particular product (one of theirs).

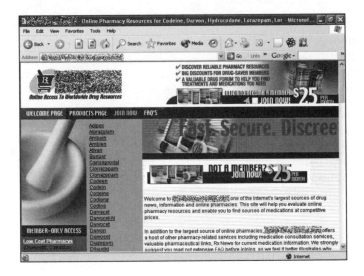

NOTE

If you look around the pharmacy spam in your email box, you'll see many pitch "We now have Vicodin!" or "Hurry, hydrocodone supplies are limited." There's a reason for doing that. For one, they know that those interested in obtaining painkillers are more apt to look at the spam and check their site. But some people might think that any site offering potent painkillers must be a legitimate site. Thus, maybe they'll visit to see what else they have.

In truth, these notices are usually just teasers. Only a fraction of the sites that advertise painkillers offer them. Many that do offer them will advertise something like Vicodin, but the drug you actually order is a lesser-potency codeine compound with high amounts of acetaminophen or other non-narcotic pain reliever added to it.

PROFILE: A CHRONIC PAIN SUFFERER TRYING TO FIND SYMPTOM RELIEF

"Sugar Mom" has suffered with painful rheumatoid arthritis since her late teens (she's now in her fifties). She also had a bad back injury more than a dozen years ago for which surgery and physical therapy offered very little improvement in her pain level. She reports that her pain wakes her from sleep several times a week.

Although she's still a busy and active woman in spite of the pain, "Sugar Mom" changed doctors several times looking for one that would understand the ill effects her discomfort was having on her life. She says she lost weight, did acupuncture, yoga, exercises, and medication as alternatives to try to relieve her pain, but none have worked for her. Despite not being able to locate a suitable alternative, she claims the doctors she's seen have been very resistant to offering her the level of pain medication she feels she needs to continue working. One doctor sent her to a chronic pain management clinic where a specialist there increased her pain medications, but once she returned to her own doctor, he did not want to continue her at the same level. She said he voiced concern not with her ability to handle the painkillers but with potential federal and insurance scrutiny.

Sometimes active on a few Web site message boards where chronic pain sufferers exchange support and suggestions, "Sugar Mom" decided to begin shopping online with drugstores that provide an online consultation. Through them, she's been able to order the same treatment regimen she used before and with good results.

"Before, I was losing days at work. Now, the pain's more manageable," she reports. She notes that she pays more for the ability to get her codeine-based pain reliever online than she would through her local pharmacy, but she believes it's worth it to have the pain under better control.

She says she keeps her primary doctor informed of all the prescriptions she takes, including the ones she orders online. In fact, the online stores she uses have usually contacted her doctor before filling the orders.

CHAPTER 3

Those Using Programs that Require Online Ordering

One of the ways that some labor unions and communities have tried to cope with the rising cost of providing health care benefits to their workers is by purchasing drugs in bulk. However, what they do does not involve pre-purchasing large quantities of common drugs.

Rather, some groups are experimenting with or have already enabled their members to order drugs by mail or over the Internet through a single source (either the organization's own site or through a designated pharmacy provider). In this way, they can obtain better pricing by pooling multiple orders for various drugs instead of picking up the costs for these orders on an individual basis.

People with Addictions: Taking the Doctor out of Doctor Shopping

Certain types of drugs have a built-in high potential for abuse. But it's not just the drugs that drive that potential. Our very brains play a role in the formation of an addiction potential because certain receptors located within the human brain trigger a response that we may not even realize.

Beyond that, experts tell us that people with a family history of drug abuse and/or dependence, whether it's to a social drug such as alcohol or something else, stand a much higher statistical likelihood of developing a physical and/or psychological dependence on other types of drugs, including prescription medications. Yet this type of family history is only one indicator. Too many people do not realize they have developed such a dependence until they find it impossible to function normally without using the drug.

Painkillers, sleeping pills, and anti-anxiety medications are the drugs we most often think of when we consider prescriptions with an addiction potential. But other drugs and the way we use them can trigger dependence as well, including laxatives, the "buzz" effect some experience with certain types of diet drugs and Ritalin, sexual performance drugs, and even sinus/allergy formulas.

Traditionally, people who developed an addiction had three basic options available to them to obtain a drug they felt dependent upon:

- ▶ One doctor willing to provide them with prescriptions
- ▶ Multiple doctors who provide them with a supply, often with the doctors not knowing that the patient was obtaining the same drugs elsewhere (this practice is known as doctor shopping)
- ▶ Through "street" sources such as drug dealers and even venues like flea markets, and foreign specialty stores that import drugs from other countries that are illegal in the U.S.

Increased federal and state scrutiny has made it much more difficult for physicians to provide a patient with countless refills of drugs that may have no therapeutic value to them. Different law enforcement initiatives have tried to reduce the sales available through "street" sources. Also, citizens have occasionally been prosecuted—or at least ordered by courts into treatment programs—for engaging in doctor shopping.

Yet the "no prescription needed" online drugstores are now providing people with addictions another avenue for obtaining what they want. Or at least, such customers may think they're getting a product such as Hydrocodone, Viagra, or Ambien when all they really receive are counterfeit pills that may be little more than sugar, starch, and artificial coloring. Unfortunately, there are even a few sites that tell you how to create a fake "drug imprint code" (the identifying information stamped onto many pills and capsules to uniquely identify them).

PROFILE: WHEN ACCESS TO CERTAIN DRUGS IS TOO EASY

A woman from Delaware wrote in not about herself but her sister, a woman in her mid thirties who has struggled for several years with anxiety and depression.

According to the sister, "Carol" has been under the care of different doctors and clinics over the years who have prescribed various medications, including anti-anxiety drugs such as Xanax and Ativan, antidepressants like Prozac, and pills to treat her insomnia. In addition, Carol also uses marijuana and herbal sleep aids such as Valerian root.

What concerns her sister is that whenever Carol gets very depressed or begins having panic attacks, she's often most resistant to seeing a doctor. When Carol does see a doctor, she often refuses to see him or her again if he refuses to prescribe one of the drugs she prefers. She's also been known to use multiple doctors to try to keep her in the medications she feels she needs since one doctor is unlikely to prescribe more than one drug at a time.

Recently, her sister says Carol has been self-treating by ordering Xanax, Ativan, and a popular muscle relaxant sometimes used as a sleep aid sold as Soma and Carisoprodol through online stores like the one shown in Figure 3.9. One month, she says Carol reported spending nearly $450 to obtain these drugs using "no prescription needed" sites for supplies that lasted just a few weeks.

Her sister finds this all very scary, worried that Carol could get arrested for having a drug without a valid prescription, overdose, or a experience bad reaction from mixing drugs. She also thinks Carol pays much more to obtain these drugs than she would normally and worries that there's no monitor to prevent Carol from "pharmacy shopping" the way she once doctor-shopped.

Figure 3.9
While some online "drug" shops make it very easy to buy pills such as Xanax (alprazolam), Ativan (lorazepam), and Valium (diazepam), drug treatment centers are filled with people who have developed a dependence upon them.

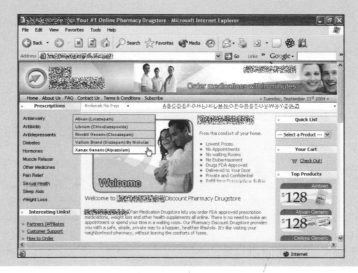

Kids (and Others) Buying for Recreational Purposes

With many kids and young adults having easy access to debit cards, quantities of cash, and either their own or their parents' credit cards, combined with some less legitimate sites' willingness to sell drugs without a prescription and without age verification, some young people find it all too simple to go online to obtain pharmaceuticals, herbs, and chemicals for strictly recreational purposes.

This topic is covered in depth in Chapter 12, "Are Your Kids Pharming?"

NOTE

According to government studies, more than 1 in every 5 young adults between the ages of 18 and 25 regularly abuse prescription painkillers. OxyContin and Hydrocodone are the drugs most cited. Often, their painkiller use is combined with abuse of other drugs, including alcohol, anti-anxiety pills such as Xanax, and illicit drugs like marijuana and heroin, as well as the use of erectile dysfunction medications that include Viagra and Cialis.

In the next part of this book, you move beyond some of the obvious facts and availability covered in Part I to look at issues you need to consider before making choices about your health care. In the next chapter, you'll learn some of the reasons your doctor may say no even when you're certain you need a particular drug.

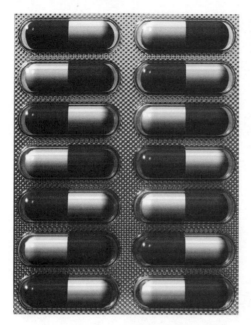

Part II

Getting Beyond the Obvious

There's so much more to getting a prescription medication than asking your doctor and taking the pill. This section of the book looks at critical questions and issues surrounding subjects like self-medication and treatment and the many possible reasons why your doctor may not want to prescribe a particular drug for you.

Chapter 4
When and If Your Doctor Says No

Every day, newspaper and magazine ads along with TV commercials suggest we need a drug and recommend that we talk to our doctors to get it. If you were to jot down each drug name you hear over the course of just a month, you would need to sit with your doctor for an hour or more just reviewing your list.

Yet your doctor isn't there just to dispense medication. Drugs represent just one of various treatments they can offer. Nor are most doctors inclined to write prescriptions on a whim, much less your whim. They usually require that

> ▶ You have a legitimate need or rationale.
> ▶ You are a good candidate for the medication (you don't have any other conditions or illnesses that could be negatively affected by use of the drug).
> ▶ You agree to take it as directed.

This chapter examines some of the reasons why a physician may decline to prescribe a drug for you. I'll take you through some of the many things a doctor has to consider in making a decision on whether to prescribe. Where applicable, I'll tell you about options you can and should investigate before you make the big leap to try to order a drug online without a prescription, an approach I cannot recommend.

You will notice a fair amount of discussion about pain medication and management in this chapter. This is because pain relievers account for one of the most frequently sought online prescriptions and because as many as one American in every six experiences long-term pain. It's also a category of drugs that is not only abused, but often under-prescribed out of fear of addiction or abuse.

Importance of Consulting a Medical Professional

Your doctor isn't there just for medical emergencies. He or she is there to keep you well. Even if you want to be in the driver's seat with respect to your medical care, it's still very important that you see your doctor on a fairly regular basis and consult that physician whenever you plan to add, change, or stop taking a medication, prescription or not.

This is especially true if you're sick or in pain. Remember that pain is usually a symptom of a problem. Most pain medication acts primarily to relieve the pain without addressing its cause. It's unwise to mask the pain without investigating its exact cause.

If you don't have a doctor, get one. Waiting until you have a medical emergency and then trying to work through emergency rooms or clinics does not give you the consistency of care and follow-up that a regular physician can. Your doctor should be aware of your current situation and your past medical history as well as all the medications—prescription, over the counter, and herbal—you regularly take.

NOTE

If you're skimming through this chapter having already decided to go online and get a prescription medication at one of the sites that makes them available without a traditional doctor's order, I strongly recommend you read both this chapter and Chapter 5 before you do so. There are simply too many factors that can go against you. Even experienced physicians may have to monitor the use of a new drug and be ready to adjust the dosage or drug type as needed just to be sure you're getting the desired results with no nasty side effects.

THE MANY MASKS OF A HEART ATTACK

One of the reasons it's so important to consult a medical professional is that there are so many serious conditions and illnesses that may be present with symptoms you do not expect. Each year, for example, many people develop far more dangerous forms of pneumonia simply because their symptoms didn't seem consistent with the illness itself.

An even better example is seen with heart disease and heart attacks. We all know that we should seek help when we experience stabbing chest pain. We also are aware that minutes matter in getting that help and that delay can be costly against our ability to recover. Yet a heart attack's first symptoms in some people may be nausea, back or jaw pain, an ache in the arm, or heartburn that doesn't get better with antacids.

If you're prone to nausea or heartburn or muscular aches, you might just assume the discomfort is more of the same and never give thought to calling your doctor. If you decide to self-treat, it's possible that the aspirin you take for an ache could help, but it's just as likely that you're raising your risk with every passing moment.

Reasons a Doctor May Not Write the 'Script You Want

As patients, we tend to be fairly deferential toward our doctors. It's not just that we recognize the doctor is a person with many extra years of schooling and a certain position in the community. Normally, we simply don't want to pester them with a host of questions because we know that every good physician is also one that is probably overworked.

This section takes a look at some of the many factors that go into the decision-making process when a doctor offers or refuses a prescription. But as you read, understand that it's perfectly acceptable to ask your doctor exactly why he or she has declined your request. One of the flaws in the ease with which you can get prescriptions on the Internet is that you can go order whatever it is the doctor wouldn't. Take the time to ask and understand why the doctor said no, however, and you can learn a great deal.

Your Current State of Health

Doctors are far more apt to feel comfortable in prescribing a medication if they can evaluate your current physical condition, something that is very difficult to do over the phone. Thus, a doctor—especially one who hasn't seen you in person before or has not examined you recently—may resist your request for a drug unless you trundle into the office.

Once there, understand that your blood pressure, weight, temperature, pulse, how you're breathing, and how your heart sounds along with gross physical symptoms can all play into the doctor's treatment decision. This is important because some medication can be a very bad match for someone with high blood pressure, with difficulty breathing, with a fast or erratic pulse, and certain other issues a doctor can only spot by seeing you in person.

Your Own Medical History

A good doctor often does some of the same things a detective does in trying to form a picture out of bits of information you supply as he or she quizzes you about your prior medical history. While you don't have to go in to see the doctor with a 10-page list, it often helps if you can be as direct as possible in presenting relevant details. Don't assume an issue isn't important; mention it and let the doctor decide whether it's useful or not.

A history of respiratory infections may indicate an as-yet-undiagnosed respiratory weakness or a depressed immune system that might make you a poor candidate for certain drugs that can strain your breathing even more or negatively affect your immune system. Likewise, a past diagnosis of asthma, even if you haven't had an attack in years, can influence a doctor's decision about what drugs to prescribe.

Your doctor may ask—and if not, you should mention—any medication you've taken in the past that belongs in the same general category as a drug you believe you now need. This prior experience can be helpful in a doctor's analysis. If you've had negative results with a particular class of medicine, he or she may be able to recommend something quite different for the same condition. A positive prior experience may mean you're a good candidate for getting the same drug again, depending on your current physical health and the symptoms you're reporting.

Roots in Your Family Medical History

That medical history you provide your doctor where you have to scrape up details of the kinds of illnesses your parents, grandparents, or siblings have had can be a powerful tool for a doctor. It gives a physician a frame of reference about your medical situation in relation to those around you.

Your doctor doesn't necessarily choose a treatment plan for you strictly based on your current condition. Instead, the doctor may take a longer view, trying to anticipate the types of genetic conditions that may play a role in your future health. Heart and circulatory system disease, lung problems, and certain types of cancer are just a few of the illnesses and conditions that can be passed down from generation to generation. Outside of strong genetic links, you also see obesity, dependence on tobacco and alcohol, and other life-threatening situations that cycle through families.

Here's an example. You come to see your doctor because you want a contraceptive drug. As he or she takes your medical history, you mention that there is heart disease in your family and that many relatives have suffered from high blood pressure. When the doctor performs your physical, your blood pressure is slightly elevated. All of us can get small spikes in our blood pressure, so it's not something immediately worrisome. Yet your doctor may not want to give you the contraceptive you want (maybe the one you've seen advertised or that your friends take) because of that family history of hypertension. Certain contraceptives, when taken by women with elevated blood pressure—or who could develop it during the time they take the contraceptive—may place them at greater risk for stroke.

Unavailability

The Internet is like the Great Library of Alexandria, at least before that great repository of knowledge was destroyed. Among the countless number of topics explored on the Net are health and medicine. You've already seen some of this in earlier chapters and you'll learn far more before we're done.

Because the Internet is global, you can research different treatment options used around the various parts of the world for myriad health issues. This is a huge benefit for anyone who wants to learn more about diets, treatment plans, illnesses, and even specific drugs.

But as part of this, it's possible that you'll find a particular drug mentioned in Canada or Asia or South Africa that your doctor cannot prescribe for you here. The availability of prescription-needed drugs not approved by the FDA is often tightly restricted to research programs and other special-supervised-use situations.

Legally speaking, doctors aren't supposed to write prescriptions for unapproved drugs and even if they do, such drugs probably won't be on the shelf at most pharmacies. Is it legal for you to order drugs from other countries when it's not approved, or worse, actually banned when the government deems the medication as having no legitimate medical use? Usually not, even though you may be able to both place and receive your order.

TIP

If you decide to try to order a foreign drug not approved for use here, talk to your doctor about it before you place the order. The doctor may be able to suggest research programs or groups that can give you information about any medical studies for which you can apply as a guinea pig to get access to the drug legally. However, it's important to understand that most drug research studies give a certain percentage of its participants a placebo or a fake drug that you're led to believe is the real deal. Placebos help researchers filter out actual benefits and side effects from those the participants expect to experience. But as part of the study, you won't know which one you receive.

Possible Complications

A doctor is responsible for anticipating the range of reactions you may experience while taking a drug or combination of drugs as part of a treatment plan. While I'll show you how to check Web-based resources like that shown in Figure 4.1 to learn about side effects, complications, and drug interactions in Chapter 10, your doctor, along with your pharmacist, is much better positioned to let you know what you may face.

When you're in a situation in which you need to take multiple medications, getting the right balance is very important. For example, a doctor is going to try to avoid a scenario where you have a condition that may be exacerbated by a drug you're taking for another illness or disease.

Blood pressure is a good example because hypertension is so common. Several types of drugs can raise blood pressure at least in short spikes, which has the potential for creating problems for those without blood pressure issues but can be especially dangerous for those with documented hypertension.

The doctor needs to juggle which health problems present the most risk to the individual and how each issue can be treated effectively. It's not always an easy balancing act even for a doctor with years of training and he or she may schedule close follow-up of a patient at special risk.

Interaction with Other Medications You May Take

The Hippocratic oath that doctors take has a very important tenet built into it: "do no harm." Since interaction between two or more drugs is a distinct possibility, doctors—with pharmacists there to back them up—try to be sure this doesn't happen. These interactions may do no more than make you a little nauseated or sleepy, but they can also balloon up into a medical crisis.

In talking with others in preparation for this book, I was amazed—and maybe a little appalled—at how many intelligent people admitted they sometimes deliberately fail to tell one physician what another doctor has prescribed for them. Reasons ranged from "It's really none of their business" to "if I told him about *that* he wouldn't have prescribed *this*."

Figure 4.1
One of the many Web-based resources for checking drug interactions and potential side effects and danger signals.

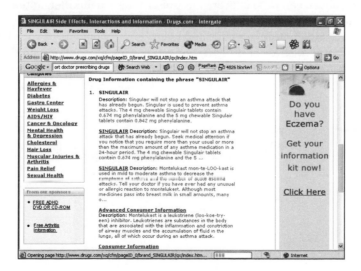

Yes, it can influence a doctor's decision if he or she knows you're taking a drug that's incompatible with something he or she has planned to use. But you risk playing Russian roulette if you get medicines, however non-related they seem, from multiple doctors without letting each know what the other(s) gave you.

Addiction Potential

By definition, addiction refers to a compulsive need for a specific thing. Where prescription medication is concerned, this usually means a high dependence on habit-forming drugs such as you see with codeine and opiod-type painkillers, sedatives, diet pills, stimulants, and others. Addiction is a multi-layered subject with many different components that a whole book cannot begin to do justice.

Since addiction threatens both health and quality of life, a doctor must consider the potential for addiction when starting you on a course of treatment with a habit-forming drug that must be taken for longer than a week or two. As mentioned before, your past experience with drugs combined with your family history of alcohol or drug abuse may be weighed as part of the overall addiction risk.

While we tend to think of narcotic pain relievers, sedatives, diet pills, and stimulants as addictive, experts say that some people can develop at least one type of dependence or addiction to a host of different medications.

If you have a past history of drug or alcohol problems, this is relevant information and should be shared with your doctor or an online pharmacy where you're asking for a prescription. Likewise, if you have a poor track record in remembering to take other medications you're prescribed, you should tell your doctor about that as well. The goal is to keep you healthy, and your doctor is going to be limited if he or she isn't aware of your particular experience.

The aforementioned family medical history can also factor into a doctor's decision about a treatment plan where potentially addictive drugs are concerned. A family history strong in alcohol or drug abuse can raise concerns in prescribing a painkiller, anti-anxiety, or sleeping pill for anything more than a short, monitored period of time. This makes sense since we often first learn our coping skills within our childhood families. If members of your family have a tendency to respond to stress or difficulty by consuming alcohol or using either prescription or illicit drugs, there's a stronger likelihood that you may as well, just as you're more apt to respond with anger or depression or overeating if that's what you've learned to do.

TIP
You'll learn more about physical versus psychological addiction in Chapter 5.

The Addiction That Isn't... or Is It?

There is also something known among pain professionals as "pseudo addiction," which has some similarities to normal addiction but with some important differences.

Because of the stigma many pain patients feel over taking narcotic painkillers, they may begin to consider themselves addicts even though actual cessation or diminishment of pain is all they seek. They may feel this belief is justified because their lives revolve around being able to make it through to the next scheduled time to take their medication. However, the need to relieve pain is a very basic human instinct that comes hand-in-hand with the arrival of the pain itself.

Just wanting to relieve pain does not mean you're an addict. Instead, it can mean you're currently under-treated or don't have the right drug or drug combination to do the job. For example, pain management specialists often approach pain with two different drugs:

> ▶ A primary medication, such as one that acts on a timed-release basis to keep someone comfortable most of the time during the hours or days the drug's effectiveness is designed to last (Fentanyl patches, for example, work for up to 72 hours)

> ▶ A second drug used on an as-needed basis for bursts of pain—called breakthrough pain—not resolved by the primary medication

Many medical and government groups recognize pseudo addiction as a real phenomenon because it can make untreated or under-treated patients with documented pain engage in the same types of behavior addicts would: hording pills, shopping for new doctors who will supply them, and using outlets like the prescription-less pharmacies to obtain what they need, even if the price is exorbitant. The difference between real and pseudo addiction is that with the latter, people usually stop their drug-seeking behavior once their pain is adequately addressed.

Are You or Someone You Love Addicted?

This is a scary question and one that can be hard to answer especially when you feel you have a deep need for a particular drug. But if you have some question in your mind as to whether this is the case, it's important that you discuss your concerns with your doctor.

Figure 4.2 shows a Web site run by the National Institute on Drug Abuse—available at **http://www.drugabuse.gov/ResearchReports/Prescription/prescription6.html**—which offers four questions to discuss with your doctor about your use of prescription medications to determine if you're developing a dependence on a drug you are taking.

Figure 4.2
Questions to ask
yourself and your
doctor.

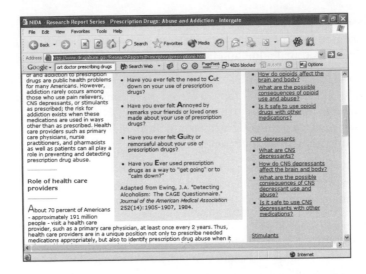

"YOU HAVE TO BE SO CAREFUL"

JC is an online shopping veteran who also describes herself as a recovering prescription drug abuser.

After having back surgery in her early 20s after an injury, JC says she struggled for nearly two years to deal with a mental dependence she formed to Percodan, a painkiller first prescribed right after her surgery. By the time her physical pain began to abate, she was convinced she needed the drug just to get through her day. She lied to her doctor to continue getting the drug until he told her he believed she had a problem. With his help, she was able to wean off the medication.

JC says she was free of all drugs for more than a decade until two years ago, when she re-injured her back. This time, her doctor was very resistant to prescribing pain medication. But JC reports she was in so much pain, it was either effectively manage the discomfort or give up her busy job. So JC went online to one of the online drugstores specializing in chronic pain patients and began to order drugs there.

Unfortunately, JC began to develop the psychological dependence again and noticed she was quickly ordering multiple pain pills from more than one cyber pharmacy. But before she could address this, she says she hit another health crisis. Because her doctor had steadfastly refused to prescribe pain relievers, JC did not tell him about the drugs she was ordering on the side. So her doctor had no idea when he prescribed an antidepressant for her that there would be a dangerous interaction between the chemistry of the antidepressant and the pain drugs.

JC says she was lucky; she got very ill very fast but when she phoned her doctor, she fessed up about the narcotic pain drugs. He knew exactly what was wrong. There was no permanent damage.

"You have to be so careful," she wrote. "Not only did I reawaken the monster of my old drug problem, I nearly killed myself by taking the anti-depressant. My doctor asked me before he prescribed the anti-depressant what else I was taking. I lied and said aspirin. I still order medications online, but now they're all ones my doctor knows about. I don't recommend anybody order drugs without consulting the doctor first."

Drug Company Pressure

If you've visited your doctor's office lately, you may have noticed well-dressed people sitting there with snappy briefcases and boxes of samples. More times than not, these people are drug company representatives or other sales personnel there to provide literature and advertising, to offer free product samples, and to encourage the doctor to use their drugs.

This practice has received much scrutiny in the past couple of years with charges that drug companies push too hard in trying to be sure that doctors prescribe *their* drugs rather than choose the best drug for each patient. Consumer groups and patient advocates voice great concern that some doctors may be lured by financial incentives and heavy-duty advertising against the best interests of their patients. But it's unclear exactly how much pressure (directly or indirectly) gets exerted or how many doctors agree to play ball.

There's also the issue that this is just one of the methods by which drug companies and the pharmaceutical lobby have an effect on medicine in general. They are also involved in support for or defense against legislation that can affect pricing and drug competition and availability, among others things, and provide input to various organizations who design treatment policies or decide what medications get covered under an insurance plan.

However, not all this self-promotion and protecting their own interests is simply that. Drug companies provide a great deal of useful information to doctors—combined with those free samples doctors pass along to us—that can help doctors learn about new treatment methods to help their patients. It's virtually impossible for a doctor to devote the time needed to do large amounts of independent research to keep current about new drugs and treatment regimens and still handle an active patient load.

But there's probably no doubt that the money pharmaceutical companies invest in doctor-related marketing and other materials have some influence on which drugs doctors prescribe. If you see a brand name each and every day, it's going to be implanted in your mind better than one you don't. Doctors are human. As patients, too, we tend to ask for a particular drug by name, and are less apt to know the names of generic versions also available for the same purpose.

Cost Considerations

The best drug in the world isn't going to be of much help to those who can't get it or can't afford to take it as directed. With the rising cost of pharmaceuticals combined with so many people either losing their benefits in full or seeing their coverage become more limited, many doctors are discussing drug costs with their patients.

TIP

If you're a senior citizen or someone on a fixed income who can't afford medication, try to find out if the manufacturer of your drug has a program in place to allow you to obtain it at less cost, as mentioned in Chapter 1. Everyone in this position should take advantage of a visit or call to the reference desk of the local library—or the online Web site for your community—where you may be able to dig up information about other programs to assist with drug costs.

Brand versus Generic

Since the 1970s, generic versions of established brand-name drugs have played an important role in containing costs (since generics are almost always cheaper than the original brand) and giving patients a choice in which drug (of the two, four, or eight versions available) they actually take.

But although generics have been with us in volume for three decades, there's still a fair amount of misinformation about the value of generics against their big name competitors. Some patients insist that they only want brand names, believing them to be of superior quality; others always want the generic to save money.

By FDA mandate, generics must be the full bioequivalent of the original. There should be no significant difference in potency, dosage, or other key factors so that taking the off-brand medication should act just the same for you as taking the brand name. But a brand and generic version of the same medicine aren't necessarily identical. Likewise, people taking generic drugs may respond differently to them than they did to a brand. Active ingredients may be similar, but secondary or filler ingredients may differ. Also, unlike the original branded products, generics aren't treated as new drugs that need safety trials and studies performed before they're released onto the market.

Whether your doctor prescribes brand or generic—and some doctors may ask for your preference—can depend on many of the same issues discussed throughout this chapter. Doctors may be influenced by pharmaceutical reps who keep the brand name in front of a doctor in the form of free message pads, pens, calendars, and other niceties that can make a doctor immediately think only of the brand name when writing a prescription. Other doctors are very price-conscious and usually suggest generics. Still other physicians may use their medical group or HMO's guidelines for which drugs are fully covered, while others may be skeptical about certain generic versions and prefer to write prescriptions for brands only.

You can also ask your pharmacist at the time you fill your prescription if a generic can be substituted.

Insurance Considerations

What kind of health insurance and/or drug plan you use—or don't have—also can play a role in what drugs are prescribed for you. Certain insurance plans including Medicare and state-run Medicaid programs cover very specific drugs for the treatment of various conditions. When you need a drug that is not on this master list, you may have to pay either a higher co-pay (your share of the drug cost) or cover the entire cost yourself.

Some plans exclude whole drug categories altogether, such as psychotropic drugs used for mental illness, highly addictive drugs outside a particular patient profile (so you might be covered for pain medication if you have advanced cancer but may not if you need the same medication for a chronic back problem), or an assortment of other types. In some cases, a doctor or other recognized medical professional may contact the HMO or insurer demanding that the prescribed drug be used. But this doesn't always meet with success.

Sometimes, what a plan excludes or includes doesn't necessarily make sense to the average patient. A good example of this is with some health plans that won't cover the cost of contraceptives, but will foot at least part of the bill for erectile dysfunction drugs like Viagra and Levitra.

Your doctor may factor in the overall price of a drug or how well it's covered by your insurance in making a final decision about which drug to prescribe. Tell your doctor if it's going to be difficult for you to afford a medication that isn't covered or is just partially covered. You can also contact your insurance company to see if there are similar drugs in the same category that your plan will cover.

Issues in Chronic Pain Management

Chronic pain—the type that lasts more than a few days or weeks—is one of the most common and difficult problems facing humans everywhere. In lost work productivity alone, chronic pain costs this country billions each year. We spend billions more every year trying to relieve the worst of that pain.

People who suffer from chronic pain can become desperate for relief while those who love or care for them can feel both totally helpless as well as unhappy about the changes such pain can bring to our lives. Doctors treating those with chronic pain find themselves caught between the medical imperative to reduce suffering and policies and laws that basically treat everyone who uses pain medication as a potential addict.

Because of the breadth of the problems and limitations with pain management combined with the number of people affected (statistics show that many of us at one time or another may face chronic, debilitating discomfort), let's look at this in some detail. Perhaps more than any other category of medication or illness, many different factors play into how your doctor responds to a request for pain relieving drugs. What may seem like a simple and straightforward need to you may present big challenges to a doctor.

NOTE

One of the reasons so much focus is being given to pain medication today is what statistics tell us. While some studies show that illicit drug use among younger Americans is down, others suggest that kids are using prescription drugs, either pilfered from the family medicine cabinet or bought from friends or online, in lieu of marijuana and heroin. The most widely discussed drug related to abuse today is OxyContin, a time-released opioid-based pain reliever. Taken as directed by sufferers of constant moderate to severe pain, it's very effective. When crushed, however, these pills release a powerful amount of drug all at once, making it a popular way to get high. In less than five years, from the late 1990s until today, so-called recreational use of OxyContin quadrupled within the U.S.

THE POLITICS OF PAIN

More and more, you hear the word *politics* used with regard to the concept of pain and pain management. This usually refers to dozens of different aspects of how federal and state agencies, politicians, religious and "temperance"-based organizations and various parts of the medical and patient community have affected the ease with which effective pain relief is available to patients.

Within the past century, pills and potions sold without any prescription were available just about everywhere, from tiny amounts of coca in the original Coca-Cola to "female calming tea" heavily laced with opium. As late as the 1960s, you could easily purchase paregoric, a powerful opiate bottled in a medication used to treat the sore gums of teething babies.

But starting with increased legislation from the time of Prohibition in the 1920s and advancing with major reforms at the federal level in the 1960s and 1970s, and the start of "the war on drugs" in the 1980s, our government began to seriously restrict what drugs are available. The FDA became less just a safety and advisory agency and more a heavy regulatory department involved with every little detail about what you can buy anywhere in the country at any time.

With that decrease in the availability of certain drugs came concern by many medical doctors, communities, and patients that the price for all the regulation was being paid by people with debilitating pain who either found it difficult to find any kind of adequate treatment for their discomfort or who were chronically under-treated by doctors and hospitals who didn't want to draw the attention of agencies that monitor what doctors prescribe.

A survey reported in 1999 by the American Pain Society estimates that more than one in six Americans (or about 50 million) experiences moderate-to-severe long-term pain each year. However, the same study said that only about 25% of those people reported receiving adequate treatment (painkiller and other measures) for their level of pain. Assuming these numbers are accurate, this leaves about 35–39 million suffering at a time in medicine when experts believe that 90–95% of all pain can be effectively controlled.

Doctors and organizations who advocate for better pain control say that a mentality of regulation where we worry more about what might happen (addiction) versus what is happening (suffering) is accounting for unnecessary misery and stigmatization. Pain management advocates charge that good doctors whose main purpose is to alleviate suffering are becoming targets of local, state, and federal "sting" operations and prolonged investigations. During these inquiries, doctors may find themselves unable to prescribe any drugs or may find their practices effectively closed or seriously disrupted.

Some advocates and professionals are also very concerned that the situation is driving desperate people to go online to buy "no prescription needed" narcotic pain relievers at a much higher cost when effective pain management could control their symptoms much more reasonably. Hydrocodone (the generic version of Vicodin, like that shown in an unsolicited ad that arrived in my mailbox; see Figure 4.3), for example, may cost $20–$30 for a 60-count bottle at a bricks-and-mortar traditional pharmacy while the same amount can easily cost $200–$400 through some of the online pharmacies. Figure 4.4 shows one of the sites selling potent painkillers without a prior prescription.

Figure 4.3
A "spam" ad for Vicodin.

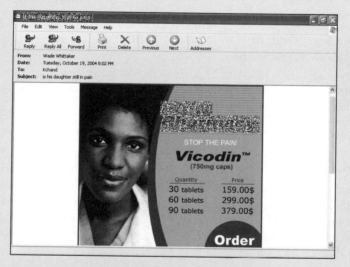

Figure 4.4
Another of the many sites offering strong pain relievers without a current prescription.

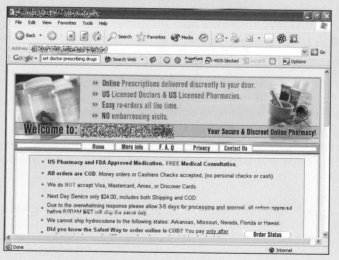

THE HOSPICE MOVEMENT'S ROOTS IN PAIN CONTROL

One of the nasty side effects of the scrutiny under which doctors must operate in prescribing drugs, especially controlled drugs as most heavy-duty pain relievers are, is that the people who suffer from chronic pain or recurring acute pain may find their physicians reluctant to prescribe a narcotic at all or not at the level of dosage needed to successfully manage the pain. Even when a person is diagnosed with an illness that may end their lives within a matter of weeks or months, they can still run up against a mindset of controlling the amount of drugs they receive out of fear of drug abuse or addiction.

With the rise in legislation related to prescription medicine, medical professionals and caregivers became increasingly concerned that patients with terminal illness did not always receive enough medication—or tried in unique combinations sometimes referred to as "cocktails"—to properly control the pain so that such people can enjoy the time they have left. The modern hospice movement, which came to the United States from Great Britain in the late 1970s, was born to address every issue of a terminally ill patient's quality of life, including less restricted access to painkillers.

Interdisciplinary teams made up of doctors, nurses, nutritionists, pharmacists, social workers, and psychologists, and others work together in a hospice to provide support for both the patient and his caregivers.

The Scrutiny Doctors Operate Under

Doctors don't operate in a vacuum. Between the hospitals and clinics, insurance companies (your health insurance and their malpractice carriers), county and state medical boards and agencies at every level of government, and many other organizations and bureaucracies they must involve themselves in, doctors have no shortage of either people to tell them how to practice or those who monitor what they actually do.

When drugs are approved by the FDA, they are usually authorized for specific situations or the treatment of particular conditions. These get written up into policies and approved treatment courses used by medical organizations, hospitals, and clinics. Doctors are strongly encouraged to prescribe those drugs only within the scope for which that drug was intended.

For example, many states—usually through their state medical board—have policies on record that form a blueprint for how doctors practicing medicine within their jurisdictions should proceed when dealing with patients with a particular diagnosis or those needing a specific drug. Those blueprints or protocols can be quite broad or very exacting and different protocols may exist for various categories. One example of this is seen with pain management policies. Here's an example of such a policy from my home state, Vermont, which is similar to those in some of the other states:

Management of chronic non-cancer pain, especially when long-term opioid therapy is involved, presents a time-consuming challenge to the practitioner. Meticulous attention to adequate record keeping is essential. Careful documentation of the rationale for the management plan provides the best defense against any accusation of inappropriate controlled drug prescribing.

When I read this, my first impression was, "They really aren't crazy about doctors prescribing painkillers, are they?" A doctor reading this policy might hesitate before prescribing pain medications for any situation. At the very least, he or she is now on warning that anyone requiring pain management is going to take a lot of their time and they better be prepared to document a good reason for each and every pill dispensed. It's not immediately clear why pain from cancer would be considered significantly different from other types of pain, except that you wonder if it's slightly encoded to mean those with terminal cancer.

But this is just one example. From the FDA and the federal Drug Enforcement Agency right down through local rules and regulations, the doctor's very ability to practice is subject to outside interpretation. At any point along this continuum, an event can trigger an investigation into how that doctor practices. In most cases, this may be a complaint lodged by an insurance investigator, a patient, or almost anyone else. Pharmacists are obligated in most parts of the country to report a doctor who may appear to be violating good prescription practices as are other medical professionals. Patients have the ability to file complaints with county and state medical boards when they think they are not being treated effectively.

Doctors who specialize in chronic pain management or otherwise treat a significant number of patients requiring pain relievers are statistically more likely to feel the heat because drugs used for this are some of the most closely monitored.

THE MYTH OF THE PILL-POPPING DOC

All of us have heard of a case in which some famous or very rich person died or suffered some kind of incident where it was discovered the person was taking huge volumes of different medications including serious narcotics prescribed by one or more physicians. Think Elvis, for example. With these cases, you also usually learn that the doctor(s) in the case become the subject of investigation and possible prosecution.

These stories can lead people to believe that doctors are willing and eager to write lots of prescriptions and "make the drug companies happy." But there is almost no evidence that this is true or that it occurs outside of some very isolated cases.

From the FDA on down, the view tends to be that most doctors prescribe drugs carefully and responsibly. In fact, the results of many investigations show that a very tiny number of physicians account for the large volumes of questionable prescriptions and drug use. While cases are reported and evaluated, there are relatively few prosecutions (let alone successful ones) against doctors for abusing their authority to prescribe.

IS THE WAR ON DRUGS A WAR AGAINST THOSE IN PAIN?

Ron Paul is a doctor who also represents Texas in Congress. He wrote a rather impassioned article about the issue of effective pain management and the increased scrutiny on doctors who prescribe medication for chronic pain in April 2004 on the political blog, LewRockwell.com.

You can read the article yourself at **http://www.lewrockwell.com/paul/paul173.html**, but here is an excerpt:

> The controversy surrounding popular radio host Rush Limbaugh's use of the painkiller OxyContin hopefully will focus public attention on how the federal drug war threatens the effective treatment of chronic pain. In most cases patients are not high profile celebrities like Mr. Limbaugh, so doctors become the target of overzealous federal prosecutors. Faced with the failure of the war on drugs to eliminate drug cartels and kingpins, prosecutors and police have turned their attention to ordinary doctors prescribing perfectly legal drugs. Federal statutes designed for the prosecution of drug dealers are being abused to ensnare innocent doctors…
>
> The real tragedy is that the federal government once again has interfered with the doctor-patient relationship. All decisions concerning appropriate medical treatment should be made between doctors and their patients, without government involvement. But, when threatened with criminal prosecution or loss of their medical licenses, many doctors simply have stopped prescribing powerful pain drugs – no matter how much their patients may need them. Some have even posted signs in their waiting rooms advising patients not to ask for OxyContin and similar drugs. It is shameful that government has created an atmosphere where doctors are afraid of exercising their medical judgment.

NOTE

Some pharmacies no longer stock certain types of pain medication and other drugs for a variety of reasons, including the fact that it can make them a larger target for drug thieves.

Tolerance Levels with Medication

Medication tends to produce the strongest effects—both good and bad—when it's new to us or is one we do not take regularly.

Pain medication along with many other drugs usually require higher and higher doses or more frequent doses over a period of time to achieve the same analgesic effect it did when you first begin to take it. Yet it may not be safe to regularly increase the dosage to get the same results. For example, some pain medication taken in high dosages can affect how our bodies process oxygen. The result can be cyanosis, like the blue-tinged lips often seen with someone who is taking large doses of morphine.

A doctor may decide to discontinue one medication at least temporarily to try a different drug to try to deal with this tolerance. The idea is to give your body a rest from a drug you've taken frequently so that you can return to it again later, when it may be more effective again.

THE STIGMA OF PAIN

When you experience serious pain, you want relief. That's only natural.

But people who suffer from injuries or illnesses that gives them significant discomfort on a daily basis will tell you that the pain itself is only part of the miserable experience. Many report feeling a degree of stigma or isolation over the need to control their pain through medication. They may express a sense of failure that their bodies or minds cannot overcome the discomfort. They also say they sense that society does not approve of people who must rely on drugs outside of life-threatening situations and they also feel that state and local government intrudes upon their care.

That stigma can be intense enough that some people who feel they could benefit from pain medication or higher doses of it refuse to take it. Others apologize to their doctors and loved ones for needing to do so.

THE CONTRACT

Some doctors today require chronic pain patients to execute and live by the terms of a contract specifically designed to address issues related to long-term use of narcotic and other pain management treatments. Some medical boards, like that in Vermont mentioned earlier in this chapter, suggest doctors use a contract to help protect themselves in a situation where a patient is doctor-shopping or a case where a problem develops because a patient has not been forthcoming about all the different types of drugs he or she is taking.

Figure 4.5 shows part of a sample contract made available on a Maine state Web site.

These contracts range from the simple to the complex, usually spelling out what the doctor agrees to do and absolving the doctor of any liability if the patient violates the terms of the agreement. Patient reactions to these contracts vary as well. Many seem to consider them a necessary evil that just adds to the stigmatization, while others are just grateful that it affords them access to some help for pain.

Figure 4.5
A pain contract spells out the exact use for the drug and the responsibilities of doctor and patient.

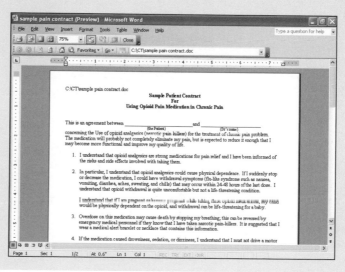

Additional Resources

To learn more about chronic pain, pain management, and advocacy groups as well as about practices and policies for the use of drugs in treatment in your area, start with a good Web search engine such as Google.com or Lycos.com.

To look up pain management policies by state, visit the National Foundation for the Treatment of Pain at **http://www.paincare.org/pain_management/perspectives/government/ government.html**. You can also learn more about the treatment of pain from a medical professional's perspective.

Chapter 5
Patient, Prescribe for Thyself?

The practice of self-medication and treatment has been around almost as long as humans have. We have an ache or a cough and many of us reach into our bathroom medicine cabinets for relief.

Every year, however, we do ourselves an incredible amount of harm through our self-help approach since we're not always good about following drug warnings and dosage details, and tend not to pay a lot of attention to what else we may be taking at the same time. We're also terrible about heeding the warning signals sounded by our own bodies and many of us assume we can "tough" out a situation even when it begins to affect our ability to function properly. Finally and unnecessarily, we also sometimes make worse what's originally wrong by delaying actual treatment long past the point at which we know better.

This is a bigger issue today because so many drug companies reach consumers directly to advertise their products and even offer free-trial doses. Online pharmacies that don't require a prior prescription and may not have many safeguards in place to catch problems effectively allow people to make their own decisions about what drugs they take. They influence us, too, by bombarding us with unsolicited ads that may make us consider a far more potent drug than we normally would.

Also, with medical-related costs so high and more of us facing either no health insurance or policies that don't cover all they once did, we're constantly on the lookout for something that can shave a few dollars off the process. Combine that with the fact that we're working so many hours today, with so many responsibilities, we grasp at shortcuts like self-medication rather than turn to a medical professional.

But if doctors and nurses don't always feel comfortable in going it alone when they themselves are ill, how wise is it for us, without their advanced training, to do this? A pharmacist spends years studying the chemistry of medication and its effects on our bodies, but a pharmacist doesn't usually reach into his or her shelves when sick to self-treat.

This chapter gives you an understanding of what your medical professionals know and the dangers you face in trying to take shortcuts around medical consultation, so that you can appreciate some of the many considerations that have to go into making a choice for which medications should be used. You'll also learn more about online resources that can help you, while emphasizing why your doctor needs to be part of the process.

The Necessary Knowledge

"Good doctors have a keen sense of all they don't know combined with a deep desire to learn more so they can help more people. With science and medicine, we're learning new things every day and a doctor needs to try to keep on top of all of that and more," an experienced doctor of internal medicine once told me.

Consider this: Today's doctors have often spent three or four years in medical school combined with two, three, or even ten years in the additional training involved in internships and residency programs before they go out on their own. Yet these doctors need to keep learning all the time to stay on top of the advances and changes that occur on a constant basis. Many doctors will tell you that their school and training years were just the beginning of their learning curve.

By comparison, most of us mere mortals usually get little or no training in even basic First Aid for emergencies. What we do learn is often quickly forgotten because we don't use the information.

Interestingly enough, consumer studies tell us that a majority of Americans consider themselves at least somewhat health- and medicine-savvy. But in contrast, some of the same studies show that we often fail at basic knowledge about human anatomy and body function, the warning signs for a host of life-threatening conditions, and essential information about common over-the-counter medicines and how we should take them. As I mentioned in an earlier chapter, people aren't usually aware of the risks involved in taking large doses of acetaminophen, aspirin, or ibuprofen, three of the most popular drugs we take. Many of us have no idea what a normal blood pressure range should be (or what our average blood pressure is) either.

This lack of knowledge doesn't spell success when we try to determine by ourselves what medications we need, how we should take them, and what positive and negative effects we should watch for. If you're not convinced, consider this.

Ever have a bad cold and go to the drugstore to buy cough or cold medicine only to be confronted with 5 or 10 different formulas? Do you need an expectorant to help you bring up the fluid from your chest or a suppressant to stop your cough? You might be inclined to stop the cough, but that leaves the nasty stuff in your lungs. Do you want a medicine that takes care of a half dozen symptoms when you only have one or two? Could you end up extending your cold or making it worse even if you take this drug? This is a simple choice we often face and yet it's pretty confusing for most of us. We spend tens of millions of dollars on cough and cold medication every year and few of us are usually satisfied with the results. Your doctor and even your pharmacist has that knowledge. Consulting them before we self-treat so much as a cough is probably wiser than toughing it out on our own.

In Chapter 10, "Identifying What You Really Get," I'll show you how to use online medical and drug information Web sites to check for side effects, drug interactions, and verify the dosage for the drugs you buy (online or off). Yet even if you use these faithfully, you probably won't be able to spot every potential problem or medication conflict. This is true even with the online medical resources presented in this chapter.

Thus, it's unwise for you to try to go it alone, despite the fact that some online drugstores make it pretty easy for you to obtain a range of medicines that were only meant to be used under a physician's supervision.

Danger of Masking Symptoms

Got a cough? Or a pain in your calf only shows up when you walk uphill? Suffer increasingly frequent headaches? These aren't necessarily illnesses or conditions all in themselves; they're more likely symptoms that may point to something else.

It's human nature to want to try to make the symptoms go away. When we choose to self-medicate, however, we often simply mask the effects of those symptoms—through the application of ice to a swelling, through aspirin or Tylenol or ibuprofen to reduce a fever or relieve pain—without addressing the real source of the problem. That's natural, too, because finding the time and money necessary to see a doctor isn't easy. But there really is no adequate substitute here for speaking with a physician.

The symptoms we experience when we're ill or in distress are more than an annoyance or inconvenience. These symptoms—their severity and progress, when they occur or worsen—can be an extremely powerful diagnostic tool in helping determine what exactly is wrong. Masking them too effectively or for too long may place you at risk for allowing the underlying cause to get too far advanced before you seek treatment.

If Doctors Often Don't Prescribe for Themselves, Why Should You?

Not every doctor immediately writes him- or herself a prescription whenever a symptom appears. This is because a doctor is trained to recognize a symptom as potentially more than an isolated event and understand that not all of us make our best choices when we're sick and in pain. Doctors might treat an initial self-health issue, but are probably going to seek out expert advice with the resources available to them.

How much doctors study specific medicines and pharmacological treatment really differs from program to program. Probably their most invaluable experience is in a hospital or clinic setting where they see the results of that medicine on the patients they treat.

Clearly, this is training and experience most of us can't begin to match. If doctors aren't always prescribing for themselves, you have to stop and wonder how well it will work if you try to do it without their advanced knowledge.

TIP

Did you know that the single most powerful way you can fight infection and illness on a daily basis doesn't come in a pill bottle? Washing your hands regularly throughout your day can greatly reduce both your chance of introducing bugs into your body and in spreading those bugs around to others. Experts say that simple measure can help check a flu outbreak or other potential epidemic faster than anything else, including the use of flu vaccines and other drugs.

IS AN ANTIBIOTIC THE BEST CURE-ALL?

One of the types of drugs you'll frequently find available through online pharmacies of all varieties is that miracle of modern medicine known as the antibiotic. You know them by names like Penicillin, Streptomycin, and a host of other "cillins" and "mycins." You'll also see some drug ads and online drugstores suggest you order antibiotic to keep on hand as part of a family medical kit, advice you probably won't hear anywhere else since antibiotics often don't have an especially long shelf life and conditions that require antibiotics really cry out for a doctor's care rather than self-treatment from your medicine cabinet.

When you really need an antibiotic, there is little better to kill bacteria, and bacterial pathogens that are attacking your body or some part of it. Without them, an infection can rage unchecked, driving up your body temperature, fouling up your blood chemistry (because white blood cells are called upon to fight infection), stressing your body's organs, and the result can be extreme illness and even death.

The chief problem with antibiotics comes with how we misuse them. People request antibiotics from their doctors for a truckload of illnesses that antibiotics aren't designed to treat, including common viral infections like a cold or the flu. Antibiotics are essential in the care of something like pneumonia, which can be caused by bacteria, but normally won't do a darned thing for the miseries of a bad cold. Even when people know better they often demand an antibiotic anyway, convinced it will provide a miracle cure. Some doctors, exhausted from trying to explain why these drugs won't help, will prescribe them anyway just for a patient's peace of mind.

But the biggest issue comes because bacteria are smart. As humans, we've had to evolve to survive as a species. So too have bacteria and infections. As we take drugs to fight off that bacteria, the bacteria evolves to resist the antibiotics we use. In the past few years, scientists have identified an incredible number of bacteria strains that have re-engineered themselves to thrive even as we pump ourselves full of antibiotics.

We help bacteria become smarter every time a doctor gives us a prescription for an antibiotic and tells us we really have to take the entire course of the medication, and we don't. We start to feel better, so we stop taking the drug. This "teaches" the bacteria about how to do battle with the antibiotic and then we pass along that smarter bacteria to those around us.

There's also the matter of how our own bodies respond to antibiotics. Studies suggest we're in a much better position to use an antibiotic to successfully fight off an infectious process if our bodies haven't been routinely exposed to these types of drugs.

About Drug Dependence

You know already that one of the factors a doctor must consider in prescribing a drug is addiction potential. Tied to that is a phenomenon known as drug dependence, part of what makes finding the right prescription and then monitoring your use and response so important and why medicine is often best left to the pros to dispense.

We often hear about drug dependence related to taking pain medication where narcotics may be involved, but different types of dependence can occur with various drugs. Even just the term "drug dependence" is a catch-all category for the ways in which both our bodies and minds can be affected by what we consume, both with nutrition and medicine.

Take coffee, for example. If you're a very steady coffee drinker as I am, your body and/or your brain can be profoundly affected when you suddenly stop drinking it (likewise, non-coffee drinkers are apt to feel seriously jolted when they have a cup or two). Your body builds up a tolerance for the effects of caffeine, a drug, and begins to expect to receive a regular refresh of the supply through your coffee. When the caffeine stops, your body wonders what the heck is happening. This is probably the most basic form of drug dependence and can be both physical and psychological in nature.

Physical dependence usually refers to a situation in which the body responds like it's in pain or ill when it's deprived of a drug it's used to receiving. Psychological dependence is tied to a mental desire to feel the way you do when you're taking a drug. A medication can produce:

▶ Little or no dependence whatsoever

▶ Either physical or psychological dependence

▶ Both physical and psychological dependence

Drug dependence doesn't necessarily mean drug abuse, especially when the dependence is primarily physical. Some drugs, in fact, work in part by manipulating our bodies' ability to become tolerant of the drug. However, it's believed that dependence, especially psychological dependence, can make it more likely that a person will come to misuse the drug by taking it longer than necessary, so this needs to be monitored.

But dependence is something very hard for some professionals to assess; it becomes nearly impossible to accurately assess dependence in yourself without expert assistance, particularly once you've developed that dependence. This is another critical reason why a doctor has to be involved in medications you choose to take.

Beyond this, there are risks involved in going off some medications that you've taken for a long period of time and/or in some quantity, particularly if you do it suddenly without tapering down. Withdrawal can result in a host of symptoms and can even precipitate a health emergency. This is another situation in which your doctor really needs to be involved to provide expert advice and to be available if you experience serious problems.

A Look at Pharmacological Study

Think your pharmacist just counts and dispenses pills and potions all day? Think again.

Today's pharmacist has had nearly as many years of school as an entry-level physician and may specialize in various disciplines, such as the following:

▶ Geriatrics—working with older adults

▶ IV nutrition support—to find the right alternate diet for those who cannot eat normally

▶ Nuclear study—focusing on chemotherapy regimens

▶ Oncology—treatment of cancer and tumors

▶ Psychopharmacology—the study and practice of medical effects on the brain and mental illness

In 2002, there were about 230,000 pharmacists working in the U.S. with their employment divided between consumer pharmacies, hospitals, special treatment programs, both private- and public-sector research and development, and pharmaceutical manufacturing companies, with a median salary of about $77,000.

A pharmacist must obtain and hold a valid license, graduate from a fully accredited four-year college of pharmacy and pass a state exam. Most pharmacists today hold a Pharm.D, or Doctor of Pharmacy degree, although there are many still practicing with a B.Pharm, or 5-year Bachelor of Pharmacy degree. Although the four-year program is required, many practicing pharmacists actually complete a 5-, 6-, or 7-year education. In some programs, the pharmacy student actually goes out on rounds much as physicians do.

Once they pass the exam and get their license, pharmacists are required to stay current in their education and training in the newest health- and medication-specific areas. Every two years, by federal mandate, a pharmacist must complete 30 credits of continuing education programs on drug therapy.

Here are these specifics from the Bureau of Labor Statistics (**www.bls.org**):

> A license to practice pharmacy is required in all States, the District of Columbia, and U.S. territories. To obtain a license, one must graduate from a college of pharmacy accredited by the American Council on Pharmaceutical Education (ACPE) and pass an examination. All States except California require the North American Pharmacist Licensure Exam (NAPLEX) and the Multistate Pharmacy Jurisprudence Exam (MPJE), both administered by the National Association of Boards of Pharmacy. California has its own pharmacist licensure exam. In addition to the NAPLEX and MPJE, some States require additional exams unique to their State. All States except California currently grant a license without extensive re-examination to qualified pharmacists already licensed by another State. In Florida, reexamination is not required if a pharmacist passed the NAPLEX and MPJE within 12 years of his or her application for license transfer. Many pharmacists are licensed to practice in more than one State. States may require continuing education for license renewal. Persons interested in a career as a pharmacist should check with State boards of pharmacy for details on examination requirements and license transfer procedures.

Questions to Consider Before You Order

If you've gotten this far in the book and you're still interested in using a "no prescription needed" site to get a drug that you don't feel comfortable in asking your doctor to prescribe, you should be asking yourself certain questions because you are assuming a degree of risk in doing so. This section looks at some of the very basic questions.

If you're going online to purchase a medication that you and your doctor agree you should take, then you still probably want to be completely certain you know about the dosage and possible side effects of the drug.

Are you certain this is the medication you need?

This is a huge concern, especially if you're ordering a drug outside of your primary doctor's knowledge.

Are you sure there is not going to be a conflict with some other medication you take or that the drug you order won't exacerbate another problem you have?

Again, this is a major issue when you're working with a "no prescription needed" site. A doctor evaluating your order can only base his or her decision on the details you present during the consultation, so you need to spell out every relevant bit of information. Even then, there's a risk to getting any medication without a thorough medical evaluation by a doctor.

What happens if you have a bad reaction to this drug?

If you end up in a medical crisis after you begin to take this drug, it's extremely important you seek help immediately and that you tell your doctor or emergency personnel what you've taken. But you also need to be prepared in the event you won't be able to tell them, which means family members or your significant other must know you're taking the drug so they can report it.

Do you know exactly how you're supposed to take the drug?

Most drugs aren't a one-shot deal where you take it once and get instant relief or a cure. In fact, many types of medicines work on a time table of sorts. For example:

▶ Some drugs should not be taken longer than several days or a full week before they lose their full effectiveness or can result in increased side effects as our bodies build up a concentration of the drug (part of what is referred to as the drug half life).

▶ Other drugs may not produce any noticeable benefit or needed changes until they have been taken as directed for 2–6 weeks.

▶ Specific drugs may require they be taken at set times around meals.

▶ Antibiotics and other anti-infection drugs must be taken for their full and complete course, often 7–10 days.

▶ Certain types of drugs should not be stopped suddenly; for best results, you need to wean yourself off the drug by slowly reducing the amount of medication you take until you work down to zero.

▶ Some drugs require blood tests and other monitors to be sure you're getting an adequate dose and that your blood chemistry remains normal or improves as a result of taking the medication.

▶ Many drugs should be taken at the same time each day, both to help you remember to take them and to give your body adequate time between each dose.

▶ Several types of drugs should never be taken when you need to drive or otherwise operate heavy machinery (most of these will bear a label warning you about that).

CHAPTER 5

Empowering Yourself Through Research

Knowledge empowers you. It also provides you with much more information with which to become a real partner in your overall health and health care and to make better decisions when your doctor offers you a choice.

From diabetes to various types of cancer to heart and respiratory disease, immune system disorders, to combating high cholesterol, high blood pressure, and thinning bones, people are turning out in force on the Internet to learn more about the health-related issues that affect them and the ones they care for. In fact, health-related research accounts for one of the 10 ways we use the Web most frequently.

Some of the things you can find online include:

▶ Health professionals presenting their own unique information and experience on a host of different subjects

▶ Communities of other patients and caregivers offering suggestions and moral support along with stories of how people have overcome debilitating illnesses and even terminal diagnoses (like that shown in Figure 5.1 for WebMD.com)

▶ Databases of details about various illnesses and conditions, medicines and side effects, and alternative therapies including holistic and all-natural treatments

▶ Articles offering preventive measures to keep you healthy or reduce your risks once you fall ill

▶ Notices of studies where researchers are seeking people to help them test the effectiveness of drugs and other therapies

▶ Programs to help you bear the financial cost of treatment

▶ Community sites that inform you about health care choices in your area

▶ Hospital and medical center sites that detail special programs or services they may offer to people suffering from a particular illness or condition

▶ Electronic forms to report problems with ordering or using medication or to blow the whistle on sites offering "miracle" cures and bogus medical help

▶ Resources to check drug pricing

▶ Your health insurance company may provide a number of online resources to help explain your coverage, find a doctor or hospital, and get additional assistance (Figure 5.2 shows the Blue Cross-Blue Shield of Vermont site, for example, with its options)

Online Resources

In this section, I'm going to help you jumpstart your online medical education by pointing out several Web-based resources. Most of them are either free or give you features you can access without joining. Where special registration is required, I'll note that.

Figure 5.1
Busy health support
communities on
WebMD.com.

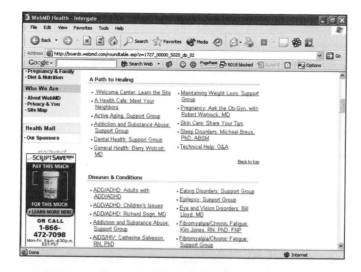

Figure 5.2
Your health insurance
carrier may offer a wide
variety of online tools
and help.

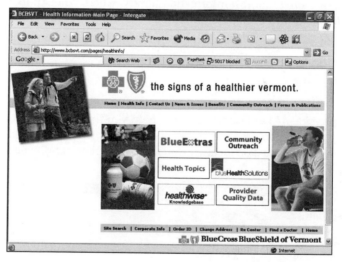

CHAPTER 5

But consider this a starter list, since new and better help references go online all the time. Also, besides major health organizations offering information, you can find a number of other types of resources, including pages started by patients or caregivers with a particular health issue. If you take my suggestion in Chapter 7, "Finding Good Stores Online," to journal your work, you might want to jot down health sites you visit that you think are particularly useful so you locate them again later.

Note, too, that none of these resources is ever going to take the place of the help you can obtain through your doctor or local health care facility. Instead, use them to augment your knowledge in between office visits and to aid you in coming up with a good list of questions to ask your doctor.

American Medical Association

(www.ama-assn.org)

This is the official Web site for the largest doctors' group in the country. You'll see that most of the information available on the site is geared toward physicians, medical students, and other association members.

However, you can click Go next to the Patients listing from the home page to locate consumer tools to help you find an AMA member doctor in your area and links to additional resources, such as the following:

- ▶ Patients Action Network—for legislative measures related to health care
- ▶ State medical society Web sites
- ▶ Patient education resources (shown in Figure 5.3)
- ▶ Smart Parents Health Source

Click the Patient Education Resources link shown in the previous figure and you jump to the Medem award-winning medical information library, where you can look through a wealth of articles organized around popular and important topics including pain management, infectious disease, asthma, organ transplants, and heart disease and stroke.

Doctor Directory

(www.doctordirectory.com)

Don't have a physician? Let Doctor Directory help you find one in your area. Click Consumer Services and you can then search by specialty (allergies, ophthalmology, endocrinology, and more) or by state. You can also locate hospitals, health plans, and even medical schools.

Figure 5.3
The AMA official site lets you access other resources such as the Medem medical library for patients shown here.

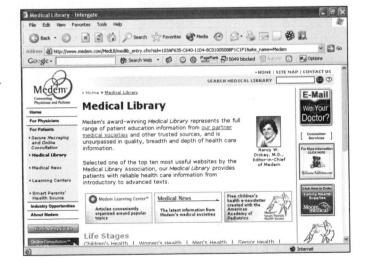

DrKoop

(www.drkoop.com)

Named for a former U.S. Surgeon General (C. Everett Koop, M.D.), this is another consumer health site not unlike WebMD. Choose to browse through the Drug Library or Natural Medicine sections or use the home page's convenient alphabetical guide to diseases and conditions (see Figure 5.4) or the Symptom Finder to research a problem you have.

The Drug Center provides information on medicinal uses, interactions, and provides a handy pill identifier so you can be sure that what you get from the pharmacy is the correct drug. Other helpful resources include individual sections on a wide range of topics including men's and women's health, rheumatoid arthritis, lung disease, and eczema.

HealthCentral

(www.healthcentral.com)

Health Central (shown in Figure 5.5) is a simple, plain English consumer health site. If you aren't familiar with medical issues in general, this one makes a great introductory resource that's both easy to navigate and understand. You won't confuse this site with a serious medical reference, but it helps you get up to speed so you can tackle the more in-depth sites.

It covers a wide range of topics from asthma and diabetes on to mental health, nutrition, the skinny on vitamins and supplements, as well as parenting and sex and relationships. Under Choose a topic from the home page, select a topic like Drugs and Medication or Diet Drugs and you can learn some of the basics. Click Cool Tools and you find a mixed bag of quizzes and calculators for body weight and height.

Figure 5.4
DrKoop.com organizes consumer-oriented medical information into digestible chunks you can read at your leisure.

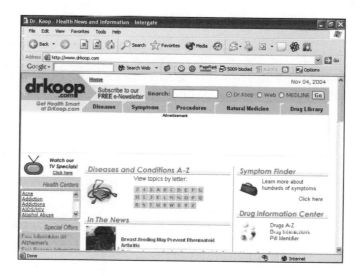

Figure 5.5
HealthCentral provides easy-to-read articles on a number of general and specialty topics.

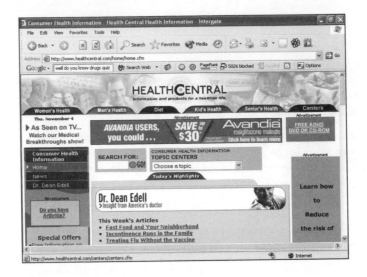

HealthGrades

(www.healthgrades.com)

The focus here is on health care quality, with the main site divided between information helpful to professionals and hospitals and consumer quick links. Here, you can look up "grades" for quality of care assessments for a specific physician or group, a hospital, or a nursing home. It boasts reports on more than 5,000 health care facilities nationwide.

HealthWeb

(www.healthweb.org)

HealthWeb is a simple portal, or a place of entry on the Web, where you can seek out information on a variety of subjects, with this portal devoted to various aspects of medicine. Click one of the links provided here such as Obstetrics & Gynecology or Telemedicine to find links to material found on other sites on the Internet.

HealthWorld Online

(www.healthy.net)

Calling itself "the home of self-managed care," HealthWorld Online (shown in Figure 5.6) presents you with a mix of categories you won't find everywhere else. These include herbal medicine and mind-body health, which are paired with more traditional topics such as information on healthy aging, children's health, and how to find a health care practitioner.

Figure 5.6
HealthWorld Online also offers expert columns, a bookstore, and special areas devoted to men's and women's health.

InteliHealth

(www.intelihealth.com)

Visit Harvard Medical School's consumer health information annex here. Search for drugs or illnesses by name. Look up health topics by gender or age (men's vs. women's, children vs. seniors). You can also access a complete medical dictionary to help you understand some of the terminology you see in use as well as a drug resource center and "ask the experts" option.

Mayo Health

(www.mayohealth.org)

Just as the Mayo Clinic is renowned as a medical facility around the world, its Web site is highly respected for putting so much expert information online and accessible to all. Here you can look up diseases and conditions, drugs and supplements (as shown in Figure 5.7), and articles on healthy living. You can also take advantage of specialty areas that zero in on diabetes, alternative medicine, fitness and sports, heart disease, mental illness, women's health, and pain management.

Several online medical community enthusiasts pointed to Mayo's Health Decision Guides (see Figure 5.8), which look at some of the different treatments available for topics such as early-stage breast cancer, children's ear infections, and prostate cancer. You can also use helpful tools like a depression self-assessment survey or measure your heart disease risk or daily calorie intake.

Information here tends to be presented intelligently, giving you important facts and options without talking down to you. The content is geared toward all types of people, from caregivers of the young and the old to others at all stages of life and health.

Figure 5.7
Look up information on
drugs and supplements
on all kinds while also
researching a variety of
health issues and
treatments.

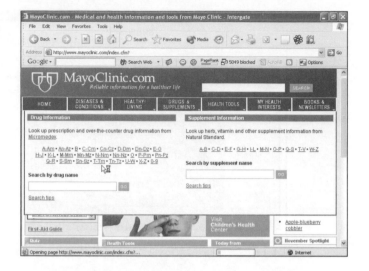

Figure 5.8
Use guides and tools on
the Mayo Health site to
measure your risk and
examine different
treatment options for a
host of health issues.

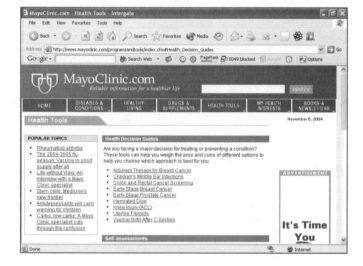

National Institutes of Health

(www.nih.gov)

Paid for at least in part by your tax dollars comes the official site for the National Institutes of
Health. Click on Health Information to see an A–Z index of NIH resources, clinical trials, health
hotlines, and drug information. You can also use the MedLinePLUS online medical library to
research medical topics, available either from this site or directly at **www.medlineplus.gov**.

It even has a rather special tool that lets you track the journey medicine takes once it enters your
body. Click this option, and you get your ABCs of pharmacology. Additional links tell you about
the life of a drug in your body and how small things we might consider—such as a simple glass
of grapefruit juice—can affect how our bodies process the medications we take.

You can also visit the National Library of Medicine (see Figure 5.9), part of NIH, if your focus is on serious research of medical conditions and diseases. Find them at **www.nlm.nih.gov**.

NIH Senior Health

(nihseniorhealth.gov)

Looking for a resource that specializes in health issues for older people? Try NIH Senior Health, again part of the National Institutes of Health. One big benefit here for all ages are controls right at the top of the page (see Figure 5.10) to enlarge the type size used so you don't have to squint. You can turn speech on and off, too.

Figure 5.9
Use the NIH's National Library of Medicine to look up articles, studies, and other health- and medicine-related information.

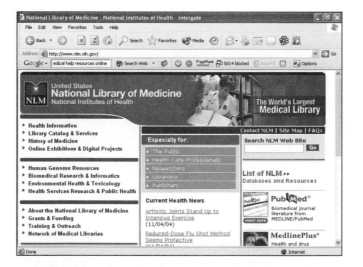

Figure 5.10
The National Institutes of Health's senior citizen–oriented site lets you research and even allows you to adjust the size of the type shown.

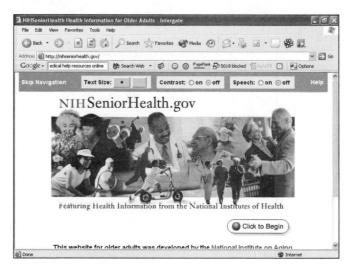

Senior World

(www.seniorworld.com)

Whether you're an older adult yourself or care for one, this is one of the places online you should become familiar with because it offers good basic material organized into commonsense categories. One key topic covered is health (see Figure 5.11) and tackles serious subjects like Alzheimer's, osteoporosis (thinning bones), the changing face of senior nutrition and fitness, longevity, and care giving.

When I last visited it, the site was undergoing some changes to add forums and other areas that may make the site far more interactive. Check them out.

WebMD

(www.webmd.com)

WebMD is one of the oldest and best-known of the consumer health-oriented Web sites. It boasts a regular community of people who visit to grab information or participate in its offerings, both asking questions and seeking support.

Some of the information on this Web site is available to everyone, but areas like the message boards where you can post questions and read through discussions on various medical topics require membership, as do special live events and other services. Click the Ready to Join link from the message boards or other areas online, and fill in the registration form shown in Figure 5.12. Review your information and then click Submit. Once you're registered, just click the Sign In link on the site to type in your username and password to access the message boards.

Figure 5.11
The Health section at Senior World provides needed information on nutrition, health care options, and other wellness issues.

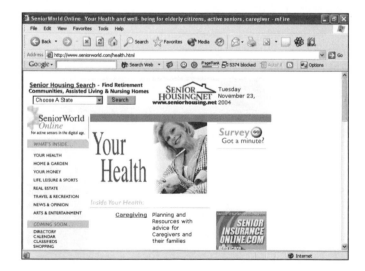

Figure 5.12
Register as a member on WebMD to use message boards and access other key features like newsletters and live events.

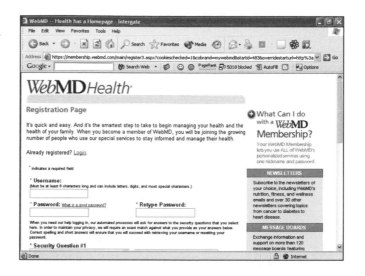

Why a Consultation with Your Doctor Is Important

You may feel like I'm beating you over the head with this brick, but if you care about some aspect of your health enough to seek medication, consider seeing your doctor rather than purchasing prescriptions without your doctor's knowledge.

Although you can get prescriptions over the Internet authorized by a physician you never meet, and you can get dosage and side effect information from online resources, that physician usually isn't going to be available to answer questions or address problems that arise from taking the drug. Combine that with the fact that not every drug can be taken the same way by different people and you really do have a recipe for possible disaster unless you involve your doctor in the process.

Doctors have to make highly individual decisions every day about how to treat us. They'll tell you it isn't always easy to get something like the right dose—or even the exact right type—of medicine for a person on the first try. Follow-up and adjustment are often necessary, and you have to be prepared to deal with a medical emergency that may arise as a result of taking a new medication.

Even when you have prior successful experience with a particular drug, that doesn't mean your system will always respond the same way when you begin to take it again. Besides interactions with other prescription and non-prescription medication and food that can affect the mix, body changes that come with age or health problems can produce stronger or weaker results. A drug that was safe and effective for you in the past may be toxic for you on a later try or simply not resolve the problem or symptom as it did before.

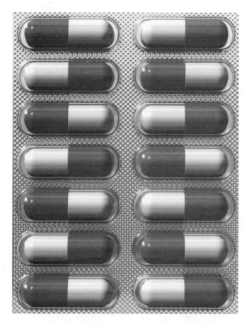

Part III

Shopping the Virtual Shelves

Now we move from all the background information into the actual choices you have online for seeking prescription medications. You learn about the most frequently prescribed drugs and how they differ from those most popularly sold online, and some of the many ways you can distinguish a legitimate, trustworthy online drugstore from one just trying to sell you a product regardless of whether it's the right one for you.

Chapter 6
The Drugs You Want and Need

"I'm never surprised by anything I find for sale on the Web," a friend and Internet marketer likes to say, eager to point out some of the silliest and most bogus items he's ever encountered online. He points to bogus sprays to increase your cell phone reception and a prayer bracelet targeted at children with AIDS that promises a cure.

This is definitely true with some online drugstores that hawk miracle weight-loss pills, age-reversing creams, and bust-uplift gels right next to life-saving medication and donut pillows for those with hemorrhoids. Even in "no prescription needed" pharmacies, you can shop for quite a range of medications. There are the dangerous ones we'd quickly identify like sleeping pills and heavy-duty painkillers, but with them are several drugs you might not view as dangerous—like some forms of heart medicine—that can be quite deadly when used improperly or consumed by someone without that illness. Even aspirin and Tylenol, those staples of the American medicine cabinet, can be fatal when taken in volume, as you've already learned.

This chapter looks at the range of pharmaceutical products available, and explores some additional variations between more traditional drugstores offering their full range of standard products and medicines, and less mainstream ones that offer morphine and heart stimulants without a doctor's exam. Along the way, I'll share with you some of the top-selling prescriptions.

The Range of Pharmaceuticals Available

One of the greatest differences you see with various types of online pharmacies is obvious the minute you look at their "product catalog"—as some call it—or their medication list. Go to Drugstore.com or CVS.com, for example, and you'll find pretty much the full range of drugs available that you would find at your local pharmacy. By comparison, many cyber-pharmacies like the one shown in Figure 6.1 carry just three, six, or a dozen drugs of the tens of thousands on the market.

One of the oddities of less traditional pharmacies is that they tend to limit their inventory to drugs that people are known to use for less than strictly medicinal purposes, including:

▶ Pain relievers used for their "euphoric" effect or to dull psychological discomfort
▶ Sleeping pills used by people who don't have traditional insomnia

Figure 6.1
Some pharmacies have
a very limited offering.

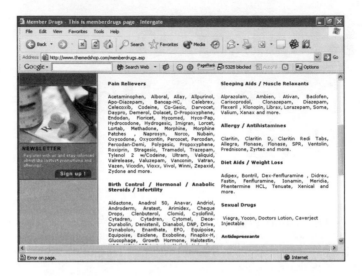

▶ Anti-anxiety pills for those who are not diagnosed with an anxiety or panic disorder, like those shown in Figure 6.2

▶ So-called vanity uses of diet pills, or hair re-growth products like Propecia

▶ Muscle relaxants used more for their sedative properties than to overcome muscle pain, stiffness, or spasms

The vast majority of online pharmacies (like that pictured in Figure 6.3) that I researched for this book carry fewer than 30 medications, stock just one or two dosage strengths of each medication offered, and stock just one brand or one generic version of a drug.

Figure 6.2
Anti-anxiety pills for
sale online.

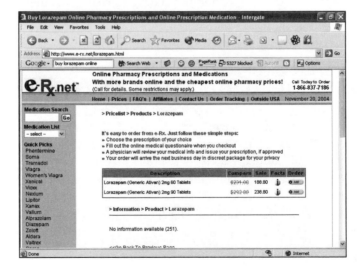

Figure 6.3
Another cyber-
pharmacy selection.

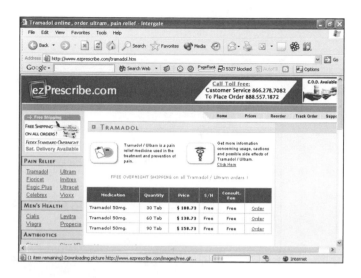

The Most Sought-After Drugs

Remember when I mentioned before that many cyber-pharmacies often sell just the most popular drugs? Well, that's not always true. There are plenty of popular drugs you won't find on the virtual shelves; instead, you'll often find the drugs most often sought by those who aren't working through a traditional doctor-patient relationship.

This section looks at the most widely prescribed drugs, then moves on to the drugs most often sought by shoppers not going through traditional means. You'll see some overlap, as in the case of some contraceptives, cholesterol-lowering medications, and antibiotics.

Table 6.1 (and Figure 6.4) lists the top-selling drugs for 2003 as reported by NDC Health (**www.ndchealth.com**) and available on a number of Web sites, including Drugs.com and Rxlist.com. Of interest is the fact that while so much attention is given to painkillers and pain management policies, only one serious addictive pain reliever, OxyContin, is on a list mostly populated by cholesterol- and stomach acid blockers, anti-inflammatory medications, and both antidepressants and anti-psychotic drugs. Narcotic pain relievers disappear from the list altogether when you look at top pharmaceutical sales by overall prescription and patient count, too, where anti-cholesterol, beta blockers used for heart patients, arthritis medications, and synthetic thyroid drugs top the list.

Notably, sales of other "embarrassment" related drugs such as Viagra, Cialis, Levitra, contraceptives, and anti-anxiety drugs are also mostly absent, yet these represent the most popular drugs sold on the Internet. This is true even when you look at drug sales by top therapeutic classes (meaning what the drug is used to treat), where cholesterol fighters, antidepressants and anti-psychotics, and red blood cell stimulants dominate. In fact, a pain drug only shows up on top 2003 sales by patient—this for Hydrocodone, the generic form of Vicodin—detailed in Table 6.2 (also from information available at NDCHealth.com).

However, one thing that isn't clear is whether the illegal Web-consultation-only-based sales of painkillers, antidepressants and anti-anxiety medications, erectile dysfunction treatments, and diet pills factor into reported pharmaceutical sales.

Figure 6.4
Top drug sales as
reported by NDC
Health.

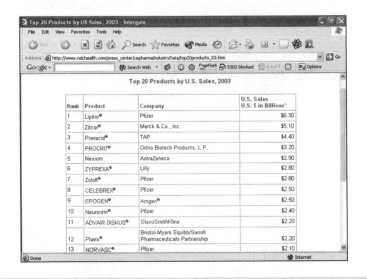

TABLE 6.1 TOP DRUG SALES FOR 2003

Rank	Sales in Billions	Drug Name	Manufacturer	Purpose
1	$6.30	Lipitor	Pfizer	Reduces cholesterol
2	$5.10	Zocor	Merck	Lowers cholesterol production
3	$4.40	Prevacid	TAP	Decreases stomach acid
4	$3.20	Procrit	Ortho	Stimulates red blood cell production
5	$2.90	Nexium	AstraZeneca	Reduces stomach acid
6	$2.80	Zyprexa	Lilly	Anti-psychotic
7	$2.80	Zoloft	Pfizer	Anti-depressant
8	$2.50	Celebrex	Pfizer	Anti-inflammatory
9	$2.50	Epogen	Amgen	Stimulates red blood cell production
10	$2.40	Neurontin	Pfizer	Treats seizures and neuralgia
11	$2.20	Advair	GlaxoSmithKline	Prevents asthma attacks
12	$2.20	Plavix	Bristol-Myers Squibb	Reduces blood clots
13	$2.10	Norvosc	Pfizer	Calcium channel blocker
14	$2.10	EffexorXR	Eisai	Anti-depressant
15	$2.00	Aciphex	Eisai	Decreases stomach acid
16	$2.00	Protonix	Wyeth	Decreases stomach acid
17	$1.90	Risperdol	Jannsen	Anti-psychotic
18	$1.90	Pravachol	Bristol-Myers Squibb	Blocks cholesterol production
19	$1.80	Vioxx	Merck	Anti-inflammatory
20	$1.70	OxyContin	Purdue Pharma	Pain reliever

TABLE 6.2 2003 TOP DRUG SALES BY PATIENTS FILLING PRESCRIPTIONS

Rank	Drug	No. of Patients Filling Prescriptions	No. of Prescriptions Filled
1	Hydrocodone	38.7 million	85.7 million
2	Zithromax	32.3 million	39.5 million
3	Amoxicillin	31 million	37.5 million
4	Cephalexin	19.5 million	23.8 million
5	Ibuprofen	16.6 million	24.9 million
6	Albuterol	14.4 million	30.6 million
7	Amox TX/Potassium CL	12.5 million	14.6 million
8	Trimox	12 million	15.1 million
9	Prednisone	11.6 million	22 million
10	Lipitor	11.5 million	65.5 million

THE WATCH LIST

Look up the details for most of the medications listed both on the top-20 list shown in Table 6.1 and the top 200 drug sales as reported by NDCHealth and you see many drugs that offer complications that takers of this medicine need to be aware of before starting on the pill or daily injections (most of the red blood cell boosters like Procrit, for example, require injections).

Many of these drugs should not be taken if you're regularly consuming alcohol. Several of them have not been thoroughly tested for use in women who may be pregnant or breast-feeding (and others aren't meant to be used by one gender at all), while cholesterol-blocking drugs themselves should normally be avoided in women of child-bearing years.

Virtually all of these drugs bear a warning about their use in patients with liver disease. The liver is an integral part of our bodies' ability to both process and store medicine along with anything else we consume. Likewise, known kidney disease is a no-no with many of the drugs. A diagnosis of hypertension (high blood pressure) is also worrisome with some of these medications that may act, at least short term, to raise blood pressure.

Not Every Drug on the Virtual Shelves Should Be There

Unfortunately, some of the drugs sold online include those either never approved by the FDA or since pulled off the market because of health concerns. You'll see that in Chapter 13 when we discuss Vioxx, the non-steroidal anti-inflammatory placed under voluntary recall by the FDA after reports of thousands of cardiac deaths were brought to light. There are plenty of places to still buy Vioxx, months after the recall.

Remember Fen-Phen? That was the diet drug combo linked to dangerous cardiac symptomology and subsequently removed from pharmacy shelves. However, you can still buy Phentermine (the Phen in Fen-Phen) separately, and I found several overseas pharmacies where Americans can still shop for Fen-Phen. One person who ordered the drug from a site based in Russia did indeed receive Fen-Phen, but the pills were minted in 1996 and had long since expired.

You'll also find foreign prescriptions for diet and weight-loss drugs online. But unless you're a chemist or specialist with a background in human physiology, it's going to be very difficult to tell if any prescription will work for you without causing side effects that can range from inconvenient to life-threatening. This is the case whether you're buying Meridia here in the U.S. or some Russian formula available mostly from foreign sites.

Diet pills are yet another category of drug that really cries out for medical supervision and an approach to life changes that depends on more than just a pill. Most diet drugs, after all, still require you to watch your food intake and to exercise. A foreign formula isn't apt to change that recipe for success.

Life-Saving Drugs

Often enough with online pharmacies, you can tell the legitimate from the less-than-traditional by whether the cyber drugstore sells anything besides pain relievers, sexual function medications, diet formulations, antidepressants, and anti-anxiety prescriptions. But that isn't always true.

There are plenty of online pharmacies—both here and abroad—where you can buy a broad range of drugs normally prescribed only to seriously ill cardiac or cancer patients, including cancer-fighting chemotherapy drugs such as Tamoxifen, nitroglycerine (usually table sub lingua or under the tongue to fight angina and heart attacks), anti-blood clotting drugs like Coumadin and Warfarin, and liquid morphine.

Buy them from a non-traditional pharmacy, however, and you could be looking at a price that may exceed normal by two or three times at least. That doesn't make a lot of sense if you have a legitimate medical need for the drug. It's better to go through your doctor and a more standard pharmacy (online or not).

Most Popular Drugs Sold Online

Now that you know some of the best-selling and more popularly prescribed drugs, this section lists the drugs you're most likely to find while shopping online. In fact, you'll find many pharmacies that only sell these drugs—or sub-categories of these drugs—to the exclusion of everything else you may need or want.

Understand that this list and its information isn't intended to replace the kinds of details you should get from your doctor and pharmacist. Consider it warning that many of these drugs are not just unintended for self-medication, they can be quite dangerous to you if you try to manage them on your own.

Alprazolam

This is the generic name for Xanax, a benzodiazepine developed to fight the addictive qualities of Valium only to produce many more people who became strongly dependent on the "fix." Like all benzodiazepines, alprazolam serves as an anti-anxiety agent, used to calm nerves or terminate panic attacks. This drug acts to block chemicals in the brain that produce a sense of tension or anxiety.

THE SYMPTOMS OF AN ALLERGIC DRUG REACTION

Allergic reactions to drugs can vary widely since there are tens of thousands of different medications on the market at any given time. Symptoms include the following and should be immediately reported to your doctor:

▶ Nausea, vomiting, or sudden abdominal pain or tenderness

▶ Shortness of breath or overall difficulty breathing

▶ Rapid or slowed pulse

▶ Swelling of lips, tongue, throat, or face

▶ Hives or other areas of swollen, tender skin

▶ Yellow eyes or skin

▶ Unusual fatigue or weakness

Some of these, like a ballooning throat or difficulty in breathing, mean you should seek help quickly, whether or not you can reach your physician. If you head to an ER, take along any medications you're taking or the emergency medication list I recommend you create in Chapter 13.

Remember: Don't assume that you can't have an allergic reaction to a medication you've taken before without incident. Our overall health at the time we take a drug can combine with certain types of food we may eat or other preparations (herbal and over-the-counter) we take to produce an allergic reaction even in those who have developed a tolerance to a prescription drug they've taken for some time. Most allergic reactions do, however, appear shortly after you first begin to take a medication.

In some patients, alprazolam can worsen some types of glaucoma. It can also make breathing more difficult for those with lung disease, including emphysema and chronic bronchitis.

Use of this drug without good medical supervision can more readily lead to drug dependence, and withdrawal usually needs to be done by slow reduction of dosage over a period of days; in some cases, withdrawal is best handled as an in-patient in a medical facility because the symptoms can be severe.

Ambien

Also sold under the generic name of Zolpidem, this is a sedative/hypnotic type of drug that induces sleep and causes a person to relax. Like most sleeping pills, it's intended only for short-term use; longer use can result in psychological and/or physical dependence and actually worsen insomnia. Ambien should not be stopped abruptly, especially if you've taken it every night for a week or two; withdrawal symptoms may appear.

This drug passes into the breast milk of nursing mothers. It's not approved for use in those under 10 years old, and those over 60 may experience increased side effects.

Ativan

Ativan, also sold as Lorazepam, is also a benzodiazepine similar to Alprazolam/Xanax. It was engineered to react against chemicals in the brain that may produce insomnia, anxiety, and even seizures.

Although this drug may be habit-forming and can result in either or both physical and psychological dependence, it's frequently offered online at "no prescription needed" sites like that shown in Figure 6.5, where I ordered it from a so-called foreign pharmacy that actually shipped from a warehouse in Flushing, Queens, New York. There were no instructions on dosage included, just the blister packs shown here.

This drug can worsen narrow-angle glaucoma as well as breathing problems in those with respiratory disease. It's also known to be harmful to unborn babies and passes into breast milk. Those taking it who are 65 and older may see more side effects.

Buspar

This is another anti-anxiety drug, although it's considered to have less of an addiction potential than drugs such as Ativan and Xanax. Unlike those, Buspar (also sold as the generic Buspirone) usually works over a period of time to reduce tension; many people see results only after taking it for several weeks. However, it's about as widely available through online channels as the other anti-anxiety medications, including those not requiring a prescription.

It's also one of the drugs that responds poorly when you eat grapefruit or drink grapefruit juice; consult your doctor. You should also inform your doctor if you've ever had an allergic reaction to Buspirone or similar drugs since there's an allergy potential here. Nursing mothers should also talk to their doctors before taking it since this drug can pass into breast milk.

Carisoprodol

See **Soma**.

Cialis

Often referred to as "weekend Viagra," Cialis (also called Tadalafil) is one of the "male potency" drugs. It acts to relax the muscles in and around the penis and to increase blood flow, allowing a man to achieve and maintain an erection.

Figure 6.5
An order of Ativan purchased online with few questions asked.

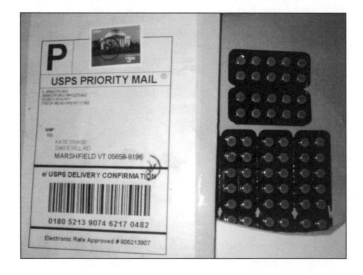

Although they are sold widely on the Internet without a prescription (see Figure 6.6), most drugs of this nature have some risk. This is especially true in men with a history of uncontrolled heart attacks, stroke, or cardiac disease, but may exacerbate problems for those who haven't been diagnosed yet. When used in combination with various heart or blood pressure medications or recreational use of amyl nitrate or nitrates (called "poppers"), you can create a situation where you experience dangerously low blood pressure.

Just like the commercials say, you need to contact your doctor immediately if you experience either of the following:

▶ Erections that last longer than four hours
▶ Tingling sensations, jaw or chest pain, shortness of breath, or other unusual symptoms during sexual activity

Unfortunately, because of its wide ability online, at swap meets and flea markets, and other non-authorized venues, this drug has become popular among young men 25 and under—a population this drug really wasn't designed to help. Without trying to sound too flippant, many sex experts agree that use of these drugs is less likely to help if you don't know what to do with an erection once you get one, a fact that experts feel applies to younger men using the drug without any history of impotence.

Codeine

Codeine is an opium derivative related to heroin, long and frequently used as a way to combat mild to moderate pain. You used to be able to purchase it over the counter in many medications in the U.S., but this is no longer the case, although other countries, including Canada, still include it in "on the shelf" pain relievers such as the one shown in Figure 6.7. When sold over the counter, codeine is usually combined with caffeine (the ingredient in coffee that can have some not-completely-understood positive effects on pain) and another, anti-inflammatory pain reliever such as aspirin, ibuprofen, or acetaminophen (the active ingredient in Tylenol).

Figure 6.6
Buying candy online can involve more questions than some sites offering "male potency" drugs.

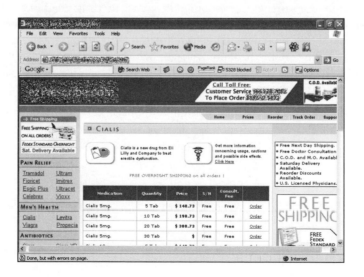

Figure 6.7
An over-the-counter pain reliever sold in Canadian drugstores without prescription.

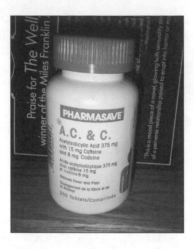

Considered a narcotic analgesic, codeine can produce drowsiness and fatigue in some and a sense of euphoria in others. It also has strong properties to those allergic to the drug, something you're not apt to know unless you've used it before. Since codeine is also used as a cough suppressant, those with breathing difficulties aren't normally good candidates to take the drug.

Another nasty side effect is that people who use it regularly or in routinely high doses may develop constipation (true with opium and any opiate derivative like OxyContin, Percodan, morphine, or Vicodin/Hydrocodone). This can often be avoided by adding extra water and fiber to your daily diet.

Of the pain relievers, it's probably the most frequently available online even though it's also capable of producing dependence and addiction. It's sold under a number of names, including Tylenol #3, Codecol, and "European Vicodin."

Codeine isn't quite the same as the codeine-like synthetic drug used in medications such as oxycodone, OxyContin, and Vicodin/Hydrocodone. It takes about six times the amount of codeine to produce the same narcotic pain relief as a 5- or 10-mg dose of oxycodone, for example. But because codeine is often packaged with moderate to high-level doses of a less powerful pain reliever like aspirin, it can be very rough on your stomach as well as the rest of your body if you try to take enough codeine to get the effect of these stronger synthetics.

Never take codeine while pregnant or nursing without talking with your physician. Older adults (those age 65 and older) should watch for stronger side effects and take special care driving or operating machinery.

NOTE
While I mentioned before that the use of caffeine isn't fully understood, enough is known about it to appreciate the fact that it tends to relax constricted blood vessels, which can play a factor in pain and pain relief.

Darvon

Darvon is also a narcotic analgesic or pain reliever made up of a compound called propoxyphene (and sometimes sold by that name) that's related chemically to codeine. This is often packaged together like codeine with another less powerful pain reliever like aspirin, acetaminophen, or ibuprofen (many formulas use caffeine, as well), and it's habit-forming. It also makes a bad medicine if you aren't careful about dosages, since taking too much can result in anything from vomiting to a life-threatening situation.

An old standard used for moderate to severe pain, Darvon in its many different forms is available through many online pharmacies, especially those operating overseas. However, experienced online shoppers report that foreign versions of the drug, often with far less of the active ingredient, are often what you get when you order it. Figure 6.8 shows receipt of an order from an Indian pharmacy, no prescription or consult required.

Fioricet

Fioricet has been used for decades to relieve the misery of migraines and other types of severe headaches. This pill is actually a combination of drugs: butalbitol, which is a barbiturate that acts like a sleeping pill to slow down your central nervous system for relaxation, acetaminophen, and caffeine. Fioricet is often sold online both with and without codeine.

However, even without codeine, Fioricet can be habit-forming because of the presence of the barbiturate. You should exercise great care with dosing to make certain you don't exceed your directed dose levels because any of these ingredients can cause problems in large quantities. It's also possible to increase the number of "rebound" headaches you experience, which are headaches that come roaring back stronger than before after taking a headache relief medication. This is not a great drug to take if you have to drive or operate a construction crane, but both of those are hard to do with a migraine as well.

Figure 6.8
Darvin, an Indian version of Darvon, sold through an overseas Web pharmacy.

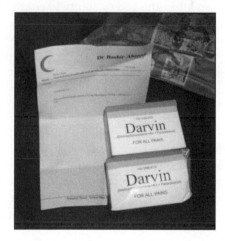

NOTE
Most people should never exceed 4,000 mg of acetaminophen a day from all sources. If you take Tylenol separately or take different drugs that include acetaminophen, you need to factor in the total amount you take. Taking too much in either a large single dose or over a period of time can result in liver damage and other health issues.

Flexeril

Sometimes also sold by its generic name (Cyclobenzeprine), Flexeril is a muscle relaxant that acts to block nerve signals that can produce pain with muscle injuries and other muscular problems like chronic back or leg cramps. As such, it's used to relieve pain, reduce tenderness, and stop the limited motion normally found with these kinds of health problems.

Use of this drug is normally limited to just two or three weeks and most doctors prefer to taper patients off the drug slowly for best results. Those with congestive heart failure or other cardiopulmonary illnesses should be monitored carefully by their doctors and promptly report any unusual symptoms. This is also the case with people suffering from kidney disease or urinary retention, irregular heartbeat, or narrow-angle glaucoma.

Glucophage

Glucophage (Metformin) is used to control blood glucose levels in those with non-insulin-dependent diabetes, also known as diabetes mellitus.

While taking this medicine, you need to avoid excessive alcohol use, and consultation with a doctor is necessary if you have a history of heart attack, stroke, require major surgery, or have a tendency to be dehydrated. Contact your doctor immediately if you develop an infection or suffer a serious injury because these can affect the body's ability to control blood sugar. You should also call your physician should you experience sudden weakness, general discomfort or malaise, sore muscles, difficulty breathing, unusual nausea, drowsiness or dizziness, or change in heart beat while taking the drug.

Hydrocodone

See **Vicodin**.

Ibuprofen

Ibuprofen is a non-steroidal anti-inflammatory drug (collectively called NSAIDs) commonly sold over the counter in 200 mg tablets and caplets. However, ibuprofen started out as a prescription-only medication typically used with sports injuries. As people began to discover its pain and swelling-relieving properties for menses, arthritis, and other painful maladies, ibuprofen was made available over the counter, with stronger, therapeutic doses (800 mg or more) available by prescription only.

Levitra

Similar in nature to Viagra and Cialis, Levitra (Vardenafil) is another of the popular male "potency" medications available at hundreds of cyber-pharmacies, with or without a prescription. Just like the other types, Levitra acts by relaxing the muscles involved with the penis which improves blood flow, allowing erections to occur and last.

Check the warnings for use.

Lipitor

Another drug frequently available online through a number of types of drug vendors is Lipitor, the best-selling cholesterol fighting medication. It's also known as Atorvastatin. Technically, it's known as an HMG CoA reductase inhibitor, an elaborate way of saying that it tries to boost levels of HDL, or good cholesterol, while working to reduce the body's production of

- ▶ Bad (LDL) cholesterol
- ▶ Total serum cholesterol levels
- ▶ Triglycerides
- ▶ Apolipoprotein B (a special protein that helps in the manufacture of cholesterol)

Lipitor's job is to drop the body's cholesterol level when diet and exercise don't do it well enough. High bad cholesterol and triglyceride levels can hasten hardening of the arteries, a major factor in the development of heart disease, heart attacks, and strokes.

The use of Lipitor is usually done in conjunction with blood monitoring to check cholesterol levels to be sure they're decreasing. For those with liver problems, additional tests may be necessary to be sure there are no adverse side effects. Use of alcohol while taking Lipitor and similar drugs may affect the liver. Those with muscular disease should also be watched carefully under a physician's care.

Since Lipitor is known to produce birth defects, women who are pregnant or plan to become pregnant should not use this medication. Those nursing babies should be sure their doctor knows this fact. Should you develop symptoms such as unusual muscle soreness, yellowing of the eyes or skin, tenderness in the region of the liver, or other serious issues after starting the drug, contact your doctor immediately.

Lorazepam

See **Ativan**.

Meridia

Meridia, also known as Sibutamine, is a drug that acts on chemicals in the body that affect weight and weight maintenance and is used in the treatment of obesity, usually in association with diet and exercise. However, it's usually used as a short-term supplement rather than a long-term solution.

Tell your doctor before you take Meridia if any of the following are true:

- ▶ You suffer from high or low blood pressure
- ▶ You have anorexia nervosa
- ▶ You use an appetite suppressant or amphetamine
- ▶ You have been diagnosed with heart disease, diabetes, gallstones, or glaucoma

CHAPTER 6

▶ You're apt to use any other prescription or non-prescription drugs during the time you would use Meridia

This drug may cause dizziness, restlessness, and/or difficulty in mental concentration.

Ortho Evra

Also frequently referred to as "the birth control patch," this contraceptive drug combines estrogen and progesterone to reduce the risk of pregnancy as well as to treat severe symptoms of dysmenorrhea (abnormal menstrual cycles).

Like many contraceptives, its use is not advised in those who smoke because the combination can increase your chance of blood clots, heart attacks, and strokes. Your use should be monitored closely if you have already diagnosed elevated blood pressure or notice heightened blood pressure after you begin taking it.

Don't take while pregnant or nursing.

Paxil

Paxil (Paroxetine) is one of the new generation of antidepressants called Selective Serotonic Reuptake Inhibitors, or SSRIs, that act on brain chemistry to try to adjust imbalances that may cause depression, anxiety, panic attacks, obsession-compulsive behavior, social anxiety, premenstrual difficulty, and post-traumatic stress disorder (PTSD). Such drugs can often take several weeks (as many as four to six) to begin to show noticeable results.

SSRIs in general should never be stopped abruptly; talk with your doctor if you want to stop taking this medication. They should also not be taken with alcohol, heavy-duty pain medication, and antidepressants referred to as MAOI inhibitors.

You should also contact your doctor immediately if you notice that your depression, anxiety, or similar symptoms worsen, especially during the first several weeks you take this drug.

Unborn and nursing babies that come into contact with SSRIs like Paxil may suffer medical complications; talk with your physician before taking it during pregnancy or while nursing.

Phentermine

Phentermine is related to amphetamines or the "speed" we typically associate with some types of diet drugs like Dexedrine. It acts to stimulate the central nervous system, and increase heart and blood pressure while also decreasing your sense of appetite. Most experts agree that such drugs should only be used for short periods of time because of the "wear and tear" effect they can have on the body and should be used in concert with a low-calorie diet and exercise to achieve best results.

Like amphetamines, Phentermine (shown for sale in Figure 6.9) can be habit-forming and should be used with care. It should only be taken under a doctor's care, especially true if you suffer from elevated blood pressure, heart disease (including arteriosclerosis or all the makings for it like high cholesterol), respiratory illnesses, diabetes, epilepsy, or other seizure disorders. Those who take MAOI inhibitors (a form of antidepressant), who abuse alcohol, or have a history of alcohol or drug abuse may have serious problems.

These kinds of drugs should never be taken in the evening or late at night since they can often produce insomnia or troubled sleep.

Figure 6.9
Phentermine can be both habit-forming and dangerous when taken without medical supervision.

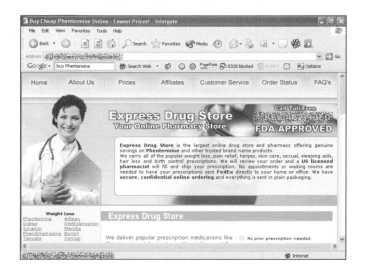

Retin-A

This drug (also called Tretinoin), usually sold in gel form, is a topical form of Vitamin A, important for skin care. It's used to treat acne and is often employed as an anti-aging cream to reduce fine wrinkles, lessen skin discoloration, and to reduce the development of pimples and other blemishes.

Many weeks or months of use may be required to produce visible results and you're cautioned to avoid any activity (like exposure to the sun) that can damage your skin further. While taking it, your skin is apt to feel more sensitive. You should never use Retin A—sold under a number of names including Retin A micro gel, Renova, Altinac, and Avita—near open wounds or patches of very dry skin or eczema.

Soma

This is probably the most widely available muscle relaxant sold online, where it goes by both the brand name Soma as well as the generic Carisoprodol. It's used to relax muscles and relieve muscle pain and spasms and it's usually combined with careful exercise and rest. But many doctors also prescribe it as a combination sleeping pill and muscle relaxant for people who find their sleep affected by back and leg cramps.

Yet the very properties that make it an effective sleeping pill can also depress your breathing, so people with respiratory difficulty need to be careful. You also need to avoid taking anything more than the doctor-approved dose and no more times each day than prescribed; you also need to consult your doctor before you combine the use of such a drug with antidepressants, other sleeping medication, anti-anxiety drugs, narcotic pain relievers, antihistamines, and alcohol.

Those who have kidney or liver disease usually require special monitoring while using this drug, although this is true with most prescription medication.

Sonata

Sonata is a sedative/hypnotic used in the short-term treatment of insomnia as well as anxiety that may keep you from sleeping. Most medical sources advise that this drug, also known as

CHAPTER 6

Zalephon, should not be used for any longer than a few days to two weeks. It's also one of those medications where you should not stop taking it abruptly without a doctor's recommendation since withdrawal symptoms and increased insomnia may result.

You're usually not a good candidate for this and similar drugs if you have respiratory problems (including asthma, emphysema, or sleep apnea), heart problems (including congestive heart failure), kidney or liver disease, or you have a history or drug or alcohol abuse. In fact, you should never mix alcohol and Sonata and like drugs, and you should avoid taking anything else (prescription or not) that may cause dizziness or drowsiness, since the combination can be severe.

This medication is known to pass into breast milk, so advise your doctor if you are nursing or plan to nurse. It is not known whether Sonata affects unborn babies.

Tramadol

See **Ultram**.

Ultram

Ultram, also sold as Ultracet and the generic Tramadol (shown from an online order in Figure 6.10), is a pain reliever that is usually not as habit-forming as some of the narcotic pain control medications. It acts by working on the chemicals and receptors in the brain associated with pain and can treat moderate to moderately severe discomfort.

Talk with your doctor before using or continuing to use this drug if you take any of the following other medications or experience any of the following illnesses or injuries:

> ▶ Tricyclic antidepressants such as Elavil (amitryptilene) or Sinequan
>
> ▶ SSRI antidepressants such as Paxil, Lexapro, or Zoloft
>
> ▶ Psychotic medications such as Haldol or Thorazine
>
> ▶ Narcotic pain relievers
>
> ▶ Muscle relaxants
>
> ▶ Certain diet drugs such as Meridia

Figure 6.10
Tramadol ordered from online without a prescription.

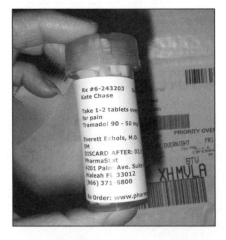

▶ A central nervous system infection

▶ Traumatic head injury

▶ Epilepsy or seizure disorder

This may be the most widely available non-narcotic pain reliever in the majority of online pharmacies.

Valium

You've no doubt heard of Valium, a benzodiazepine (its other name is Diazepam) that acts on brain chemistry to treat imbalances that may lead to anxiety or even seizures, migraines, and muscle spasms. Valium has been used to treat all of these and more in its many decades on the market. It's also sold online through a number of venues both with and without a prescription.

Because it's habit-forming, Valium is usually a bad match for those with a history of alcohol and/or drug abuse. You should consult your doctor before taking this medication if you have a history of breathing problems or respiratory illness, regularly consume alcohol, suffer from kidney or liver disease, or are depressed or having suicidal thoughts.

Valium has the potential to harm unborn babies if taken during pregnancy. It's also known to pass into the breast milk of nursing mothers.

Viagra

Also known as Sildenafil, Viagra was the first of the well-known male "potency" medications. Similar to the others, it works by relaxing muscles in or near the penis and to increase blood flow which allows erections to occur and be sustained.

Those with unmonitored coronary heart disease and those with a history of non-medically-controlled strokes or heart attacks should have a full medical exam before using any erectile dysfunction drug. It's not advised for use in those who take other types of male potency drugs, those with blood disorders including leukemia and sickle cell anemia, those with liver or kidney disease, or those with retinitis pigmentosa, a degenerative eye disease. Avoid taking alcohol with it and don't use heart medications containing nitrates or recreational "poppers" because this can create a dangerously irregular heartbeat.

Contact your physician immediately if you notice strange tingling, breathing difficulty, unusual nausea, or other serious symptoms while engaging in sexual activity. Sex can be strenuous—mentally and physically—and regardless of whether you take erectile dysfunction drugs, you've got to watch that you're not overtaxing yourself.

Vicodin

Vicodin is the best known of a class of narcotic analgesics—and sometimes cough suppressants—that go by a variety of names including the generic Hydrocodone, Lorcet and Lortab, Norco, and Zydone. Used to treat moderate to severe pain, this drug is usually combined with another pain reliever/anti-inflammatory compound such as acetaminophen or ibuprofen (example: Vicoprofen). Because its an opioid, it can cause constipation (extra water and more fiber can help), and it's occasionally used as an anti-diarrheal medication as well.

This is a drug that is both widely used and abused, with about 85 million prescriptions filled or refilled for it in the U.S. last year alone. Like other narcotics, it should be used with extreme care in conjunction with other pain relievers as well as drugs that may cause drowsiness such as antihistamines, sleeping pills, muscle relaxants, and alcohol.

Wellbutrin

Wellbutrin and its look-alike Zyban are both types of bupropion, an antidepressant often used to treat both anxiety and to reduce the symptoms of withdrawal associated with stopping smoking. However, experts are not quite sure exactly how buproprion works.

Regardless of this lack of understanding, both Wellbutrin and Zyban are available through the majority of online pharmacies, even without a prior prescription. Notify your physician immediately if you notice an increased level of depression or suicidal thoughts once you begin taking the drug.

Bupropion drugs should not be used if you suffer from an eating disorder such as anorexia or bulimia or you have diagnosed heart, lung, or kidney disease. Avoid alcohol and the use of any "street" drugs while taking them and don't use them if you're taking an MAO inhibitor antidepressant.

Xanax

See **Alprazolam**.

Xenical

Xenical is one of a range of different diet drugs sold online (see Figure 6.11, a pharmacy offering it without prior doctor's prescription). Like the others, it's usually used as one part of a total weight-loss program that includes diet and exercise. Xenical has been used to treat obesity in both adults and adolescents.

It works slightly differently than some in that it actually tries to stop your body's ability to absorb certain fats derived from the food you eat. Because of this, you usually need to watch for

Figure 6.11
A cyber pharmacy offering Xenical.

changes in bowel movement and other problems you may associate with changes in how your body processes food. Continuing a diet high in fat while taking a drug like this probably won't work too well.

Zoloft

Zoloft (shown for sale online in Figure 6.12) is an antidepressant prescribed in the treatment of a number of conditions, including premenstrual syndrome (PMS), depression (including post-partum), obsessive-compulsive and panic disorders, and post-traumatic stress disorder.

Figure 6.12
Zoloft is yet another drug you can purchase without a full doctor's evaluation even though that's strongly recommended.

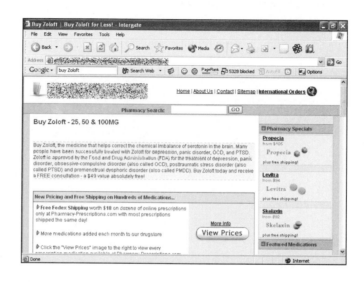

Chapter 7
Finding Good Stores Online

With online pharmacies, the devil is in the details. Fly-by-night drug dispensaries aren't going to advertise themselves as such and all those cyber drugstores calling themselves U.S. FDA approved pharmacies may be anything but. Your very best bet is always to get a prescription from your doctor and then go online to shop through very credible sites.

Unless you're dealing with a large regional or national pharmacy chain with an online sales site or your local drugstore's Web site, you're going to have to take a long look at the site to determine whether it's a place where you feel you can safely do business. Details found within the site—often kept very separate from the products you order—can help you decide whether you're visiting a legitimate and consumer-oriented pharmacy or a site where they are simply trying to move a great deal of merchandise very quickly before the authorities discover them and they must close up shop.

This chapter is all about helping you make the determination between the good and the bad, the right choice and the risky one. Take the information here combined with the additional detail covered in Chapter 8, "Placing Your Order Online," and you have a powerful checklist from which to work. As you go, don't be afraid to exercise your common sense. If something seems too good or easy to be legitimate, you very well may be correct.

Yet one piece of information you won't find in this chapter or Chapter 8 is a list of online drugstores where you should shop. There's a good reason, too. Existing virtual pharmacies close and new ones pop up all the time.

As you look around for best prices and good service among stores that offer the types of medication you need, you're going to have to evaluate and re-evaluate these for yourself as you discover a new one. So like that old wisdom about how when you teach someone to fish, you give them a way to feed themselves, it's really more important that you know how to separate the wheat from the chaff than it is to reference a list here that could be out of date by the time you read it.

TIP
Chapter 8 shows you how to check an online pharmacy's customer contact, order process, and privacy information and where the site is registered to do business before you hand them your credit card information or medical history.

How You Find Cyber Drugstores

The first online drugstores you may want to explore are the virtual flagship pharmacies already mentioned in this book, such as:

- ▶ CVS.com
- ▶ Duanereade.com
- ▶ Drugstore.com
- ▶ RiteAid.com
- ▶ Walgreens.com

CVS.com, for example, has a pharmacy processing and distribution center equipped to easily handle 50,000 or more prescriptions each day; because of this, CVS is called upon by some other pharmacy chains like Eckerds to process their orders as well.

Also ask your friends and family, co-workers, and good shoppers you know if they're using online pharmacies. If they are, ask if there's one they can recommend to you. Talk to your doctor and any other health professionals you know, too: they may know of great sites that are less well known by the public at large. In my research, several people told me their own doctors had passed along the names of good Canadian online pharmacies and others.

If you're already using online medical community sites like WebMD, post a message asking others for recommendations. A great deal of these tips get shared through sites like this, and it can help you narrow down your Internet choices to a small group of likely drugstores you can check for yourself.

Web search engines like Yahoo.com and Altavista.com can also offer you a jump-start. However, the search results you get tend to be a huge mixed bag of listings that includes legitimate and questionable drug vendors, plus the drug membership clubs disguised as pharmacies discussed in the next section along with a host of related listings, such as drug treatment centers and articles for pharmacy and other medical professionals. Figure 7.1 shows the mixed bag I got from Yahoo.com after doing a search on the single word "Lipitor" where I got over one million (1,262,000 to be exact) matches.

I don't know about your schedule, but I really don't have time to go through more than a million sites. I need to be able to weed the results down into a much more select listing. For that, I'll need to search smarter. So let's tackle that next.

TIP
Also, beware of prescription drug clubs that offer you great extras and guaranteed drug approval. See "About Drug Membership Clubs" at the end of this chapter.

CHAPTER 7

Figure 7.1
Searching on a single drug can return thousands of results.

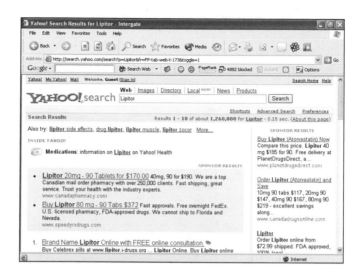

Searching Smarter

If you're accustomed to performing just simple searches using Web search engines where you simply type in a single word, click Search, and see what comes up, you may want to refine your skills a bit when looking for cyber pharmacies. If you don't, you may get thousands of hits (or matches for your search)—or even that million-plus we saw with Lipitor earlier—making the task seem pretty overwhelming.

Most search engines offer a help link to let you learn more about doing smarter searches to refine your results to try to obtain better matches for what you're specifically seeking. Because this can be so helpful to you regardless of what you're looking for on the Internet, I recommend you take the time to learn some of these tips.

Let me show you by using the popular Google.com as an example where we'll look for pharmacies that sell the widely used medication prednisone. Let's assume that we want to locate a pharmacy that addresses the issue of insurance coverage. We also want to limit the matches to English sites and ones that have been updated recently, plus we want to see 50 matches per page rather than the default number of 10.

Follow these steps:

1. Open your Web browser and go to **www.google.com**.
2. When Google opens, click Advanced Search, which opens the Advanced search window shown in Figure 7.2.
3. In the Find Results section, in the box to the right of "with all of the words," type Prednisone pharmacy medication.
4. Just to the right of what you typed, click in the drop-down list box and select your desired number of result listings per page (here, choose 50).
5. Click in the drop-down list box to the right of Language and select English.
6. Click in the drop-down list box to the right of Date and choose "past 3 months."
7. Click the Google Search button.

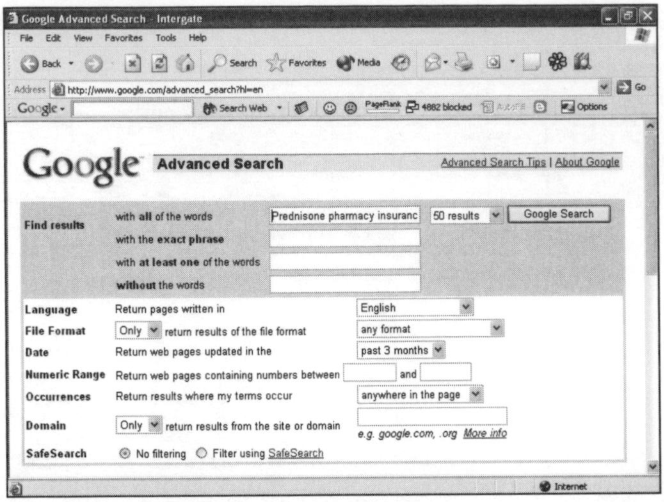

Figure 7.2
Set your Advanced
Search options such as
language and looking
for specific words.

Now look at your search results when they appear, like those shown in Figure 7.3 (yours may differ since new listings are being added and old, dead ones removed all the time). To view a listing in detail, click on its link from the search results list. In fact, one of the listings is for a tool called Pharmacy Checker (available directly at **www.pharmacychecker.com**) that lets you evaluate prices and view a "service" rating for a listed pharmacy. See Figure 7.4.

You can begin to do your research by clicking on these sites, or go back and refine your search further if you don't like the matches you get. So let's turn our attention to the kind of qualities you should look for in a cyber pharmacy and what the warning signs are that should send you looking elsewhere.

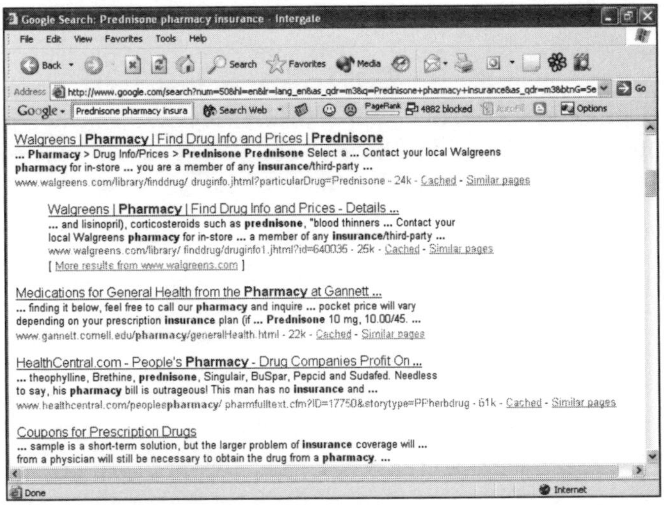

Figure 7.3
Your Advanced Search
results.

Figure 7.4
Pharmacy Checker, a site for evaluating drug prices, is one of the results from an advanced search.

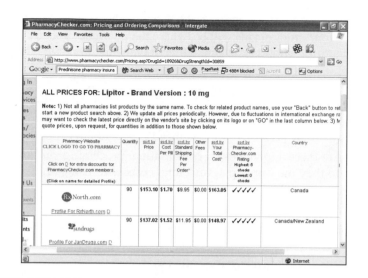

CHAPTER 7

TIP

Chapter 9, "The Price You Pay," shows you how to check pricing on your medications to determine whether a specific site is offering you good competitive prices or inflated ones.

DON'T MAKE A PHARMACY CHOICE SOLELY ON ADVERTISING

Because ads are often designed to jump out at us and because Web search engines like Yahoo and Google allow merchants to buy ads that will appear whenever you search on a related word, it's easy to just click on an ad to check it out.

However, don't use advertising as your primary means of selecting a pharmacy, because advertising alone simply means the vendor has a budget to buy ad space. Today, Web-based ads can be very cost-efficient compared to print avenues like magazines and newspaper or broadcast options like TV or radio, so almost any company can afford to advertise.

Your Questions Checklist for Finding Good Online Pharmacies

Once you begin to look at online pharmacies, you can either simply browse through them and note which ones you want to evaluate further, or immediately go through each with a virtual fine-tooth comb as you look for specific features along with the medications you need. The more checking you can do, the better your results should be.

At this point, questions should be popping into your brain. Begin to jot them down (and check the sidebar about recording your efforts later in this chapter). Then look back at your first pharmacy site and start browsing through it for answers to those questions. Look at what's available under different links such as FAQ (or Frequently Asked Questions), Privacy, About Us, Customer Support, and How We Work, as well as the actual product pages for the medications you need. These pages should give you an idea of how the ordering process will go, how secure and confidential your order details will be, where the pharmacy gets its stock, and who you're dealing with. Figure 7.5 shows an example from a Canadian drugstore that spells out the order process for you.

Some of your common questions are likely to include the following:

▶ Does this pharmacy offer all of the medications I need?

▶ Are their prices within the range I expect to pay?

▶ Are there added fees for consultation, processing, and/or shipping? If so, how do they measure up against total costs with using another drugstore without these fees?

▶ Are these drugs the exact same ones I usually get?

▶ Is this a recognized professional pharmacy? Who are they and where are they based?

▶ What will I need to place my order?

▶ Does this pharmacy accept my health insurance or drug coverage benefits?

▶ How private and secure will my order be?

▶ How long will it take for my order to arrive?

▶ What do I need to do if there's a problem with my order? How can I contact them?

▶ What shipping method is used and do I need to be there at my mailing address to sign for my order?

▶ Is this pharmacy part of a bricks-and-mortar drugstore or drug chain, which might indicate it follows local and federal guidelines?

▶ Does this pharmacy have the VIPPS seal first discussed in Chapter 2?

Figure 7.5
A Canadian pharmacy's "How To Order" page spelling out the process for you.

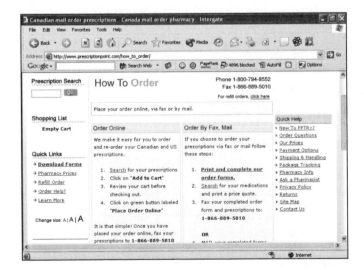

Unanswered questions account for a big reason why people feel less comfortable about ordering online, yet medication represents enough of an important matter in our lives that we simply don't need the doubt. When you don't see information on the pharmacy site to address your common questions, you want to delay ordering until you know everything you need.

Have your questions ready, then take advantage of links such as Ask a Pharmacist (with an example shown in Figure 7.6) or Live Help since these may give you immediate access to someone to answer your questions right then without having to wait. You should also locate the pharmacy's toll-free customer service number and call them directly if you can't locate a "live" question feature and don't want to send email.

Only use email to ask a question when you've got time before you need to place your order. It typically takes a business (at least one receiving a volume of email) 24–48 hours to respond to email requests, and longer if you happen to contact them at the start of a holiday weekend. However, despite the delayed response, email has one big bonus: you've got a copy of their answers, which can prove your case if you get into a dispute with the cyber store over some detail covered in that email.

If the online pharmacy doesn't answer your specific questions or responds with only a form or boilerplate response, find a different pharmacy. You have enough choices online today that you don't need to waste your time or effort on a less than professional drugstore.

Figure 7.6
Use the Ask a Pharmacist or Live Help feature to contact customer service immediately.

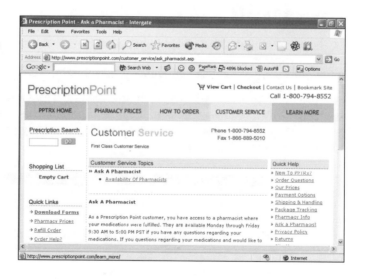

"THERE OUGHT TO BE A LAW..."

Believe it or not, there is not a single law on the books in the United States that specifically requires drug-selling Web sites to disclose anything to you except the basics of your actual order transaction. They don't have to tell you who they are, where they actually operate from, who the doctors are that write prescriptions on those sites where they take orders without prior prescription, or anything about the pharmacy that dispenses your order. That's extra frightening if you try to avoid seeing your doctor and depend instead on "no prescription needed" sites because you're placing your trust in an entity you don't know.

As you'll see in Chapter 8, many sites that promote themselves as U.S.-based actually operate in a foreign country. There are also those that are registered in a different nation to place them outside U.S. law enforcement jurisdiction, but are actually run from a warehouse in New York or somebody else's garage in Florida or Cuba.

However, there are laws covering lies and misstatements on medical sales Web sites like online pharmacies. The FDA and/or the Federal Trade Commission (FTC) can take action against an online pharmacy purporting to offer an unproven "miracle" cure, or that says its selling a diet drug when it is actually selling you a salt tablet. Considering the abundance of sites you can visit daily that violate these laws and the overall low number of prosecutions the federal government undertakes, some online drugstores may not be too worried about getting shut down by making fraudulent statements.

Journal Your Work

If you plan to use the Internet to do your drug buying on at least a semi-regular basis, it's easy to quickly go through a few dozen online pharmacies and then begin to have difficulty remembering which ones were of interest and which you wanted to avoid.

What you may want to do is invest $2–$3 in a small notebook or create a file using your word processor or spreadsheet software to keep track of the online pharmacies you evaluate in your research. Figure 7.7 shows a sample research page kept in Excel 2003 by one of the long-time online drug shoppers interviewed for this book.

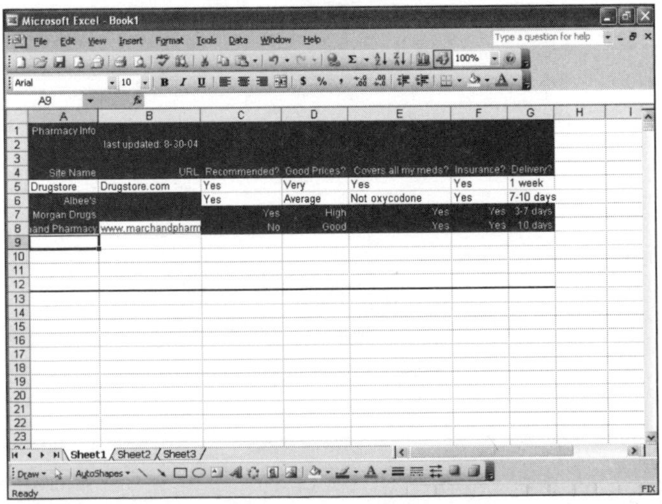

Figure 7.7
Log the results of your research efforts so you can consult them again later to compare a number of different pharmacies.

How you document your work is entirely up to you. To keep it simple, you could just keep lists divided between the good, the bad, and those you've learned about but haven't checked yet. Or you may want to do an elaborate checklist that roughly follows some of the information presented earlier in this book as well as here and in Chapter 8.

Table 7.1 shows a checklist much like the one I used in my early research (although I've changed the names of the Web sites to protect both the innocent and the guilty). You can make a copy of this to start your pharmacy journal or use it as the basis for one you create for yourself.

TABLE 7.1 PHARMACY RESEARCH CHECKLIST

	Drugs4less.net	GoNowDrugs.com	Val-U-Drugs.org	Mintnerdrugs.biz
U.S. site?	Yes	No	No	Yes
Good prices?	Average	Cheap	High	Average
Extra fees?	Yes ($35.00)	No	No	Yes ($39.99)
Carries all drugs I need?	Yes	Yes	Yes	No
Customer Service contact info supplied?	Yes	No	Yes	No
Rx needed?	Yes	Yes	No	No
Medical consultation type	None (supply Rx)	None (supply Rx)	MD phone consult	Online form only
VIPPS approved?	No	Yes	No	No
Guarantee?	No	No	No	Yes
Free Shipping?	No	Yes	Yes	No ($15)
Takes insurance?	No	Yes	No	Yes

About Drug Membership Clubs

Once you begin looking online for medication, you're going to discover the phenomenon of drug membership clubs. These frequently pop up when you're doing a Web search for medication (as shown in Figure 7.8) in a way that makes you think you're actually visiting a cyber pharmacy; it can be confusing enough that you believe you're placing an order when all you're doing is joining what are usually at best service clubs.

Figure 7.8
Drug clubs ads/sites easily mix in with actual pharmacy ads/sites.

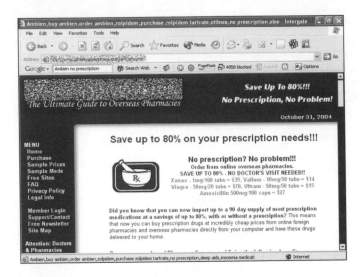

The help offered by such clubs is often just what you might be looking for: discount prices, easy access, no embarrassing questions, and a roster of thoroughly screened pharmacies you won't find anywhere else, guaranteed to deliver just what you're looking for better than any competitor. Figure 7.9 shows just some of the benefits offered on one site and common to many similarly advertised drug clubs.

But what do you actually get? In some cases, the most noticeable difference over what you can do all on your own is just a bigger credit card bill.

Visit a drug club site like the one shown in Figure 7.9, and you'll see that it guarantees almost certain approval for any drug you want to buy. This is a common offer by drug clubs of this type. But no pharmacy should be able to make that offer because it implies you can order a drug even if a doctor says no, even if it's not a good choice for you, and whether or not you happen to take other medications that might interact with the drug you want to order. Other claims include

Figure 7.9
A sample of the benefits drug club membership can offer.

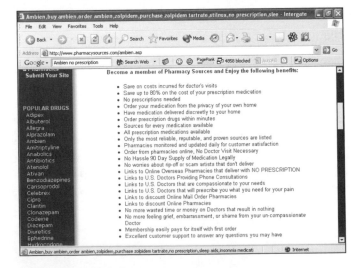

the ability to legally obtain any medication on the market and "no hassle 90 day supply" of any medication. Again, these are not issues you can guarantee. If these are shipped from a foreign country, they may violate U.S. law, and many controlled substances cannot be supplied in 90-day quantities.

In talking with online drug shoppers, none of them could recommend a drug membership club that had been helpful to them, which may be telling in itself or may just mean they didn't happen to find a good club. When I looked at these clubs, I found many that sounded like a great idea for the confused beginner shopper who doesn't understand the process. Yet what I actually found in joining three clubs at random—along with two additional ones that allowed a trial one-week or one-month free membership—was not usually worth the cost (anywhere from about $5 to nearly $30 per month).

On the plus side, at least one of each of the test sample clubs offered these helpful tools:

- ▶ Message boards or some kind of posting area where members can share their experiences and offer suggestions (two of these had fairly active communities even if these help areas didn't seem to get much attention or comments from the club's management team)

- ▶ Comparative prices for different drugs for multiple pharmacies

- ▶ User satisfaction scores where members rate how good a particular pharmacy is at fulfilling your order quickly and accurately and at providing customer service

- ▶ A way to get help from the drug club if a member pharmacy fails to treat you properly

- ▶ Access to a newsletter or help article with medical information presented in plain English

Yet except for the ability to use your drug club's customer service line to help resolve order problems, almost all of these features can be found at various spots on the Internet without the need to pay a recurring fee. Also, a couple of the drug club sites I fully evaluated gave me absolutely nothing I couldn't obtain without them.

Here are some other disappointing findings:

- ▶ Almost all clubs supplied out-of-date pharmacy lists or links with one or more member pharmacies no longer available.

- ▶ There was rarely a wide selection of member pharmacies to choose from and some of those listed either offered a very limited choice (only brand names with no generics), small order caps (you can only order 10, 20, or 30 pills at a time), or only foreign versions of drugs (not always the same drug or containing similar ingredients) although they advertise American brands.

- ▶ One drug club appeared to be nothing more than a representative for the one online pharmacy the club gave access to, although the benefits promised members access to a number of different drugstores with highly competitive pricing.

- ▶ In all cases except one, there was no significant (10% or more) price savings; in fact, a few of the drug clubs' member pharmacies charged higher prices for drugs you could buy directly (without a membership) from the same sites.

▶ In the worst example, the list of member pharmacies—advertised as American drugstores—were entirely foreign, all pharmacies listed were available to use without membership in the club, and the price for ordering two drugs directly versus through the drug club was actually 10–15% less expensive.

▶ Some clubs only do two things: provide you with a list of pharmacies and collect a monthly fee.

Now all of this isn't to say that there are not very useful drug membership clubs; some traditional organizations are experimenting with this concept so they can offer drug discounts to their members. However, the ones you tend to encounter as you're looking for online drugstores may not be worth your time or money. If you happen on one that makes almost ridiculous claims or promises you something no one else does, ask tough questions before you join or simply go elsewhere.

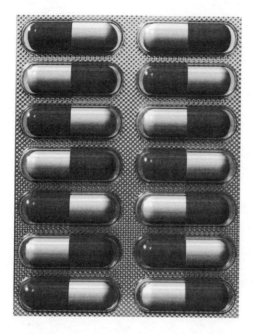

Part IV

The Process, the Practice, and the Prices

This section gives you a look at the actual process for placing an online prescription order. You learn what to expect in terms of information you must provide and how you provide your paper prescription to an online pharmacy. Just as important, I'll show you how to check prices so you can be sure you're not paying through the nose for a prescription from a pharmacy that boasts low prices.

Chapter 8
Placing Your Order Online

Have you decided you want to go ahead and try an online pharmacy?

This chapter is designed to let you take what you've learned so far, including the qualities of a good online drugstore just covered in Chapter 7, and use it to place a medication order. Here, the focus is on what you actually see as you shop and the kinds of information you'll be asked to provide.

However, if you're concerned about making sure the price you pay is fair or the great bargain many online drugstores promise, you may want to wait until you've read Chapter 9 to learn how to check prices before you buy. Even if you're willing to spend just a little more for the convenience, you certainly don't want to get ripped off.

What to Watch For

Caveat emptor means let the buyer beware. This concept is built into American law as it relates to shopping for just about anything, and it's a smart rule to follow when you're buying something as important as medication needed to maintain your health.

The best favor you can do yourself in shopping for your medications online is not to suspend your usual good common sense. If you were out looking at new cars and the dealer sales rep started the aggressive sales pitch on you, up to and including offering you something that doesn't smell right, you'd walk away. Right?

Well, with buying online, up until the moment you submit your order and confirm the purchase, you can step away at any time. Also, if you notice that something doesn't feel right, you may not want to get past the points at which you need to provide personal information or your credit card details. Most companies probably just discard the records for incomplete transactions, but why take the chance?

When I placed test orders, I was always careful about what details I provided before I had to confirm my order. Often, I would step through a test order three or four times before I actually placed it. This wasn't just to make sure both prices and process stayed the same (although I did that for some electronic stores, too), but also to get a feel for what they would want before I went all the way through with the order.

Guidelines to Help Determine Legitimacy

Unfortunately, non-standard online drugstores won't have a scarlet letter or some other sign indicating that you're in a shop that's either operating illegally, distributing drugs and counterfeits illegally, or both.

Understand that a fancy Web site isn't necessarily indicative of much. Smaller pharmacies, for example, may not have a budget or the expertise to have all the nice extras and great-looking graphics that a large chain of stores may offer. In my travels, I saw a few for individual local-pharmacies-gone-global that were very simple sites, usually just allowing existing customers to order their refills online or to reach out to U.S. customers from Canada. However, with the expertise or one of the software packages that allow you to create a very polished Web site with little effort, a big budget isn't always required. You'll see some non-standard "no prescription needed" online drug shops with rich looking sites that don't necessarily operate with all the safeguards of normal, licensed pharmacies. Your concern is more with the product they deliver to you than with how elaborate the pharmacy's Web site is. After all, the most important issue is the legitimacy (in all senses of the word) of the drugs they offer and the safety checks they have in place to protect you.

Issues to watch for include:

> ▶ If the site uses a strange address, such as all numbers (for example, 999.125.198.43) or the name of the site doesn't sound much like a pharmacy.

> ▶ If you receive a fair amount of unsolicited email that seems to be the same ad but the name of the online drugstore, its address, or the prices change with each new copy you get.

> ▶ If you visit an online drugstore that displays ads for certain drugs suggesting recreational purposes ("chase away Monday blues with Xanax" or "have a great Saturday night with Cialis").

> ▶ If a site assures you that you can obtain a prescription drug with absolutely no prescription or doctor's visit or consultation needed.

> ▶ If the prices listed are well above market price (see Chapter 9 to learn how to determine prices for a drug) and where generics are always the same price or higher than name brand medications.

Finally, assume nothing. In talking with electronic drug shoppers, I found many believed the "FDA approved" pharmacy statement on some of the "no prescription needed" sites (see Figure 8.1). Others felt that a site must be legitimate if it links back to the FDA's site providing tips on buying drugs online.

But when you go to the FDA pages some of these sites link to you sometimes discover either very dated material from before the recent concerns about shopping in Canada spurred some crackdown in over-the-border shipments, or information that is so filled with legalese you're not sure what it's telling you about the legality. Unfortunately, such online drug warehouses don't have to look hard to find a lot of differing information available on the FDA and other government Web sites.

Figure 8.1
Just because a pharmacy says its drugs are FDA approved may not mean much toward legitimacy of the pharmacy.

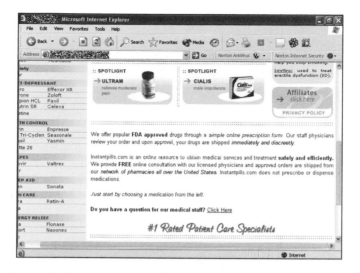

A SUBTLE DIFFERENCE

There is one subtle difference in overall site design between more standard online pharmacies and those that seem to largely operate as prescription mills: the emphasis on the prescription drugs themselves. You see this in two different ways.

Most standard online pharmacies—like their brick-and-mortar colleagues—offer a range of prescription and over-the-counter products along with general merchandise. By contrast, less standard online pharmacies often carry only prescription drugs, and their inventory is more apt to be limited to one or both of the following categories:

▶ Most popular drugs sold (you may see only one drug of a particular type)

▶ Commonly abused drugs (sedatives, painkillers, and sleeping aids)

A few sites sell just one brand or category of medication. Ever been to a regular pharmacy that just sold one drug?

Beyond just the emphasis on prescription pills comes something more subtle. You may see graphics with a shower of brightly colored pills and capsules (some look very much like mouth-watering candy) or text suggesting you stock up on a number of drugs at once, much as you might stock up on canned soup or toothpaste. That's also unusual for a regular pharmacy.

The VIPPS Seal

One indication that you're looking at a legitimate pharmacy Web site is the presence of the VIPPS seal (see Figure 8.2) that you learned about in Chapter 2. However, not every legitimate pharmacy may choose to participate in the VIPPS program.

Remember, too, that the VIPPS seal on a Web site isn't just a symbol or graphic. You click on the seal and it takes you to the VIPPS site, where you can check to be sure that the site using the seal is a member in good standing that is judged to meet the National Association of Boards of Pharmacy criteria for running a virtual pharmacy. Figure 8.3 shows the member information available if you click the VIPPS seal on CVS.com and then click the link on the VIPPS site to verify that CVS is a member in good standing.

Figure 8.2
The VIPPS seal
displayed.

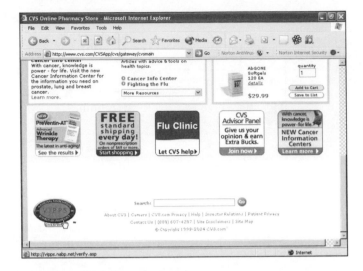

Figure 8.3
VIPPS verification
information for the CVS
online pharmacy.

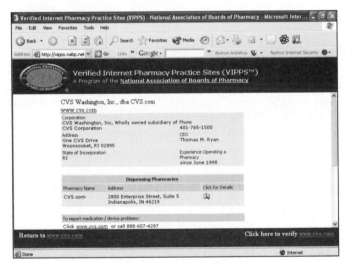

You may see that some sites use different organization seals—other than VIPPS—whereas some won't display one at all. Right now, VIPPS is the only one that is recognized pretty much throughout the U.S. and beyond. Most of the pharmacy organization seals I've seen in my Web surfing either don't seem to stand for anything or don't indicate that membership has anything to do with meeting standards for customer service or pharmacy professionalism.

If you run into ones other than VIPPS, click the seal to see if you can determine whether the organization provides any consumer protections for you or a way to report problems. But don't stop there. Use a Web search engine such as Google.com or Lycos.com to look up the name of the organization so you can locate other references to it besides the organization's own site. A few minutes of checking may give you some idea as to whether the seal or membership means anything for you or not.

The Too-Easy Alarm Bell

Some of what you read in this chapter and others about sites that make it very easy to obtain medications, especially controlled or highly dangerous medications, should make you worry rather than appreciate the lack of fuss.

A pharmacy isn't a candy store where you pick some of the red ones and some of the blue ones. Even too much candy or a volume eaten in the wrong combinations (lots of watermelon sours and double fudge bars, anyone?) has bad side effects.

If you don't see your doctor for a few years, then call up one day and announce you want a prescription for a drug you've never taken typically used to treat an illness or condition you have never been diagnosed as having, a good doctor is at least going to ask questions. He or she is likely to suggest you make an appointment to come in for an exam—in other words, you need to be evaluated in a way that allows them to eyeball you, check your vitals, and talk with you about the request.

Sure, the doctor could save you both time (and some cash or insurance form filing) if he or she just calls the pharmacy to give you want you want. But a doctor's job and responsibilities go well beyond pill approval, as you learned in Chapter 4, "When and If Your Doctor Says No." In good faith, doctors aren't supposed to prescribe anything they don't feel is justified. Saying you want it usually isn't enough.

Read Those FAQs

Almost every site has a special page that addresses Frequently Asked Questions (aka FAQs). You can find this listed under FAQ or different names like How to Order or Instructions for Ordering or Have Questions? Figure 8.4 shows a button link on a pharmacy site to open such a page.

Figure 8.4
Look for the FAQ or How to Order page and then read it.

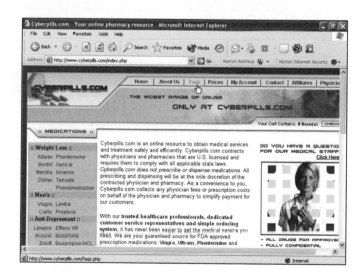

Think about what types of questions you have and you should have a pretty good idea of the information that should be addressed on such a help page. The whole focus with a FAQ is giving you answers to the most common questions to remove the mystery from the process and aid you in feeling more comfortable in placing your first order.

Sites that offer a decent FAQ usually give you a basic run-down of the following:

▶ How the shopping and ordering process should go

▶ What the site does once it receives your order

▶ What additional steps you may need to take to finalize the order once you submit it

▶ How long it should take to receive your order

▶ What you can do if the site fails to provide your order

But each site's FAQs may be quite a bit different—one you'll bless for its completeness of information and another you'll know was written by a lawyer because all the language is deep in qualifiers and statements such as, "We take no responsibility…"

Do you want to shop at a store whose first comment to you is to absolve itself of any responsibility for a problem? Probably not. Likewise, if the FAQ gives you practically no answers—making you wonder why it's supposed to help—you also should go elsewhere.

Yet the FAQs often do more than just give you a question-answer format. Many provide you with a sense of how these sites view their relationship to you as a potential customer combined with sometimes broad hints about the overall legitimacy of their sales process. Figure 8.5 shows you a FAQ from an online pharmacy with a statement that should have your alarm bell ringing.

Figure 8.5
A legitimate pharmacy usually doesn't offer drugs without a prescription.

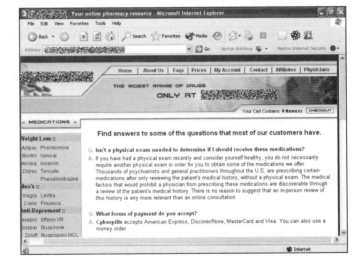

If the FAQ tells you an order will step along one way but, once you start the order, you see that the procedure is quite a bit different, don't continue without considering whether you want to shop there. Although most of the FAQs I read (hundreds) provide an accurate representation of the process, some clearly used the FAQ to put on a public face for visitors that is quite different from how they actually handle matters.

TIP

One thing to note in the FAQs is what steps you need to take to cancel your order or obtain a refund if you realize for any reason that you don't want to go through with the order. Some allow you to cancel the order and obtain a full refund (or your credit card will not be charged at all) if you cancel the order before it's sent to be filled, but you may have to act fast (within a matter of hours) to do that. Other sites consider the transaction done and over once you click Submit and insist they have no way to cancel the order after that point.

WHEN THEY TELL YOU ONE THING AND DO ANOTHER

Here's an example drawn from one site (no longer in operation) which purported to be a compassionate resource for chronic pain sufferers who have trouble obtaining enough medication to control their pain. That sounds noble enough, right?

Its FAQ spelled out a rather thorough procedure before the site would dispense orders for any of its drug offerings, which ranged from muscle relaxants and sedatives to mild-to-major narcotic pain relievers including Vicodin, Darvon, and OxyContin. It indicated that the site submits each order to a panel of doctors for careful review. It said that a doctor from the panel would likely call you to perform a more thorough evaluation. Then it noted that you would be asked to supply a copy of your most recent medical records that document your need for pain relief along with your doctor's contact information. Expect the process to take a minimum of five business days before your order is shipped by overnight delivery, it said.

Yet when I placed a test order for Fiorinal (a medicine used for migraine headaches that also contains a small amount of barbiturate) all I did besides provide my payment and shipping details was to fill out a medical form. Because I wanted to test the review process, I added a few pieces of information that should have drawn attention. Specifically, I noted the following:

▶ That I have a history of a breathing problem that can become more severe if I use the kind of drugs that contain barbiturates (which Fiorinal does)

▶ That I am currently taking an over-the-counter allergy medication—one with a label stating it shouldn't be taken with painkillers or sleeping aids

▶ When asked if I had ever been treated for "drug problems," I clicked Yes

The first statement is true. Since I was a teen, I've had to avoid most drugs that have a sedative effect because my breathing can become labored. Thus, I'm not a very good candidate for anything containing barbiturates that act to make me sleepy. Likewise, the note about my allergy medicine is accurate; I included this knowing that my allergy medicine and Fiorinal aren't a good match for concurrent use, something a medical professional should realize.

Continued

CHAPTER 8

The final piece of information isn't true, but I chose it because it definitely should have raised concern by any doctor reading that medical form. Granted, the site did not ask me to specify what those "drug problems" were so it's possible to assume the problem was something other than drug abuse. But the potential for abuse among stronger pain relievers is pretty high.

What happened? Interestingly enough, my order was approved less than 30 minutes after I submitted it. No physician called me. I didn't provide my doctor's name and I was not asked for it. Nor was I asked for the copy of my medical record. Also, no one asked me to explain my breathing difficulty, the exact nature of my headaches, advised me not to take the allergy medicine with the Fiorinal, or sought more details about the "drug problems" requiring treatment.

However, the order itself never showed up. Although I received approval by both email and through the Web site's order tracking tool, the order never progressed past "pending shipment." My credit card was never charged. A few weeks later, I noticed the site was no longer available. There's nothing to suggest that concern for the safety of the drug for me played any role in the failure to receive my order; otherwise, I should not have been approved for it in the first place.

Find Out How to Ask Questions

One of the great points of a bricks-and-mortar pharmacy is that you can usually walk up to the counter, ask to speak to a pharmacist, and then get the chance to drill this professional about questions you may have about a particular drug or its interaction with other medications you may be taking.

An American pharmacist undergoes years of rigorous training to obtain an R.Ph. degree and then regular in-service or extra training to keep current on all the newly released drugs. This can make a pharmacist an invaluable resource who is often more accessible than your overworked M.D.

Avoid online drugstores where you can't find any way to submit questions before or during the ordering process. You should be able to consult with an actual pharmacist at an online drugstore rather than just a customer service rep, but this can get tricky depending on the electronic storefront you use.

Not all virtual pharmacies are what they appear. Some aren't pharmacies in the usual sense of the word. Instead, they are management companies that offer a service by which they wed a medical staff who can prescribe your drugs with a pharmacy that can fulfill your order, but really have no way for you to communicate directly with either the medical staff or the pharmacist. Their emphasis is on order fulfillment; they aren't designed to handle special situations or act as a medical resource for you either before or after you get your order.

Also, steer clear of online pharmacies where your every question to them is answered through a form letter sent by email. This usually indicates the site has warm bodies there to respond to emails but not to provide any real information beyond standard answers.

You'll discover that many online drugstores offer a live customer help feature. Click on it—a note on the tool will tell you when such help is available—and a special chat window usually opens in which you and the service rep can type your questions and responses. You may want to avail yourself of this tool to ask questions such as "Is there a U.S.-based toll-free number I can call to speak to the pharmacist?"

Also check the FAQ again as well as any links labeled "Contact Us" or "About Us" that should spell out your contact options. If there's a toll-free number, don't be afraid to dial it just to be sure humans answer the phone. Some pharmacies—and this appears to be especially true with foreign-based outlets—simply contract with another company to provide a mailing address and phone number they can supply to customers, but customers trying to use those numbers or addresses can be met with voice mail or long delays in reaching anyone actually working for the online shop.

Why Companies Touting U.S. Services May Be Continents Away

Like people in many countries, we take a fair amount of pride when we take the time to shop for products made and sold in our own country. While some people hear *foreign* and think higher-end products like Swiss watches and German cars, studies tell us consumers place importance on "buying American"—even if the American flag they buy was actually produced in China (for several years until the terror events of 9/11/01, it was actually tough to buy a U.S. flag made here). We think of U.S. products as superior and created using the best standards and we disapprove of American companies that move their "on paper" addresses out of the country to take advantage of tax loopholes.

This phenomenon hasn't been lost on Web-based pharmacy operations where American flags are often displayed on Web site banners (see Figure 8.6) and the label "U.S. pharmacy" is touted. The majority of online drug consumers I talked with in researching this book usually stated that they looked for the American label on a site when they weren't specifically trying to get cheaper drugs from Canada or Mexico.

Studies bear this out. A Pew Research study just released at the time this book is being written says that U.S. consumers tend to avoid buying online from overseas sources, providing they can identify the difference, because they've heard the warnings about foreign drugs being prepared using different formulas and varying manufacturing standards.

But you can't rely on a Web site's content alone—such as advertisements that they're a U.S. pharmacy selling only American-made products—to tell you whether the site is based in the United States. There aren't many authorities around to police statements made on Web sites. Anyone who wants to include a U.S. flag on their site just adds one.

The same holds true for sites with USA or American in the name or that use a domain name like www.GreatDiscountPharmacy.us. The "us" at the end of the Web site address—called the extension (common extensions are .com, .org, and .net)—certainly makes it seem like an American-based site. But again, this is no guarantee that it is.

When I checked the registrations of 50 different online drugstores not affiliated with a leading pharmacy or pharmacy chain that used something like "USA" in the name, an American flag, or otherwise indicated they were U.S.-based pharmacies, I found that nearly 80% (or 39 of the 50) of these were run by companies registered outside the U.S.

Figure 8.6
Just because a site says it's a U.S. pharmacy doesn't necessarily mean it is.

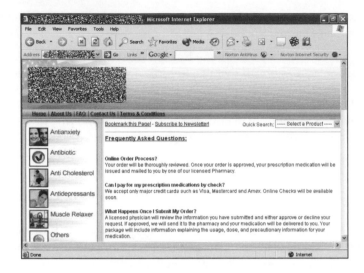

By registered, I'm referring to the manner in which Web site domains (the names used to help you get to a site in your browser, like CVS.com) must be registered to use the name. As part of the registration process, you must supply the name of the company or people who get listed in a domain registration database as the designated virtual tenants of the name (I say tenants because Web site domain names are leased rather than owned).

But here again, as long as you give a domain registration company its payment, you usually aren't required to prove you are who say you are or that you live or do business where you state. Add to that the fact that some companies and individuals lease domain names that they then sell or lease again to others, and it becomes even more difficult to figure out if an online drugstore that touts it's U.S.-based is the real deal.

HOW TO CHECK SITE REGISTRATION

You know now that before an organization or a person can use a specific Web site name, called a domain or domain name, they have to register their contact information—as well as pay a fee—with a domain registration firm. Once registered, you can then look up the domain name for a site and see what details are listed there, free of charge.

Here's how. First, you get an address that you want to check. If you click on an ad, for example, your Web browser moves to a new Web address (also called the URL or uniform resource locator), which is displayed in your browser's address bar, like that shown in Figure 8.7. You usually only need to worry about the main part of the address, like drugstore.com or fda.gov and not all the forward slashes and extra text that comes after it.

Once you have the address, you can use any of the domain lookup sites to pull up the domain's details. You can find two of the best known of these at register.com and Whois.net (see Figure 8.8). But if you happen to have your own Web site, it's likely your Web host has a domain lookup tool on its main site.

Figure 8.7
The browser address window in Microsoft Internet Explorer.

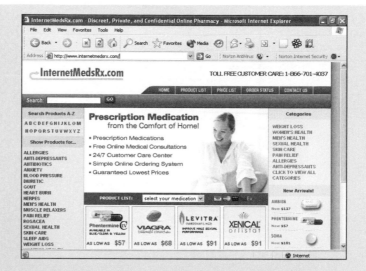

Figure 8.8
Use sites like Whois.net to check registration information.

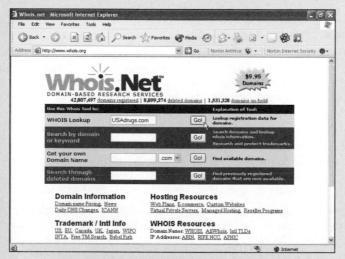

Let's assume you hear of a site called USADrugs.com and you want to see who they are. Here's how to perform your lookup:

    1. Open your Web browser (be sure you're already connected to the Internet).

    2. Go to Whois.net.

    3. Click under Domain Lookup, type in usadrugs.com, and click Go.

Registration information opens in a new window (see Figure 8.9), along with a disclaimer telling you that you aren't supposed to use the details found there for any bad purpose. Here we discover that USADrugs is registered in Hong Kong.

Continued

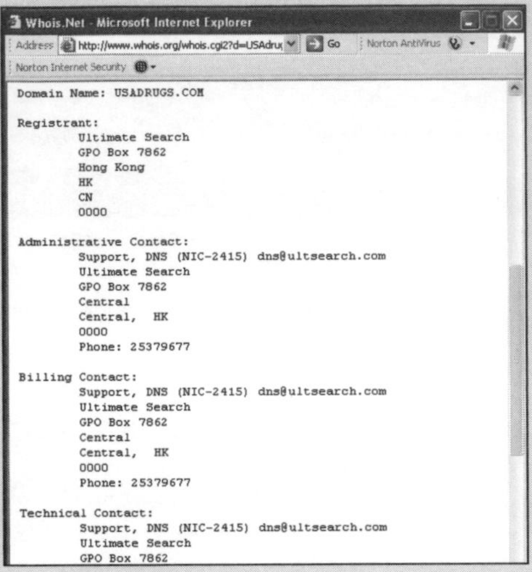

Figure 8.9
An example of the details found for each site lookup.

WATCH FOR SPYWARE AND ADWARE

One of the fastest growing ways for people to get information about other people is through the use of special software designed to monitor what you do on your PC and what types of sites you visit on the Internet. Such software is all over the Internet. Just visiting some Web sites—and some very nice ones with big names, let me add—can turn your PC into a tool for others to watch what you buy.

Spyware usually refers specifically to special programs designed to record your activities—and even your keystrokes as you type in passwords and user names—and then report them back to whoever wants to know them. Adware, by comparison, is designed to eavesdrop on your Web browsing habits to see what you may be interested in and shopping for, then report this back to something like a marketing or ad company to help target you for competing ads.

Let me give you an example that may sound pretty familiar. Ever go online looking for information on a particular illness or condition or shopping for a specific product only to find that you suddenly begin to get email about that condition or product from some company you've never heard of? Or perhaps you start to see pop-up windows advertising other sites that either offer drugs to treat the condition or other products competing with the one you're shopping for? If so, you may have adware and/or spyware on your PC that is feeding details about what you're doing back to some central database.

Before you say, "they can't do that; it's illegal," understand that at the time I'm writing this, this practice—called data mining—is not strictly forbidden by law. We may not like it and find it pretty intrusive, but there has been nothing but a sense of ethics in place to prevent companies from doing this. Yet this may change soon.

Two bills have just passed the U.S. House of Representatives in a step toward outlawing the transfer of this software to your PC without your permission. Still, when other Internet-based laws like the CAN Spam Act of 2003 have been enacted to address a problem, companies have found loopholes to continue targeting potential customers. So we'll have to wait to see if the

Continued

anti-adware bills become law, how well they're enforced, and how well we're served by them as consumers.

Do you use any kind of Internet protection such as Norton Internet Security Suite or firewall software like Windows Internet Connection Sharing firewall, Zone Alarm, or Black Ice? If so, you may be equipped with what you need to try to protect your PC from spyware and/or adware being downloaded through your Web browser to your system without your knowledge. Check the online help for any of these products to find details on configuring your system for good security.

If you don't happen to use any of these, you might want to consider getting free or free-trial adware and spyware checkers. Some of these products include Lavasoft's Ad-aware (see Figure 8.10) available at **www.lavasoftusa.com**, WinPatrol at **www.winpatrol.com**, and SpyBot at **www.security.krolla.de**.

Figure 8.10
Ad-aware is one of the adware/spyware checkers that can scan and remove these snoops from your PC.

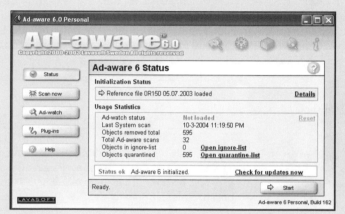

What to Expect When Ordering

Before you actually place your order, it helps to know what to expect to see as well as what information you'll be asked to provide or which option to choose during the process. This can remove a lot of undesirable mystery from the process. By knowing some of the common practices and choices ahead of time, you also may be better equipped to spot situations in which an online pharmacy's practices seem out of the ordinary.

LOOK FOR SECURE TRANSACTION SITES

It's wise to have a certain amount of concern about submitting confidential information through a Web browser as you do with almost any online store. The amount of confidential details required often jumps considerably when you're using an online drugstore. But there's a way you can reduce the chance that anyone with snooping tools can intercept your private information when you submit it to a site.

Most online ordering sites today use security tools that try to ensure that any data entered into a form, like you'll see with medical consultation forms and credit card forms, is only seen by the sender (you) and the store itself or the agent the store may use to process your order. At some point in the ordering process, you may see a note appear on your screen that you're being redirected to a secure transaction site, sometimes referred to as a secure server.

But you should also check your Web browser. At the very bottom of the window, below the actual page being displayed, you will normally see a globe icon that is labeled "Internet." When you're using a secure transaction form, the icon either changes into or is joined by a lock or padlock with the word "Secure" or "SSI" listed once you run your cursor over it, as shown in Figure 8.11 for Microsoft Internet Explorer.

Figure 8.11
Look for the lock icon at the bottom of your browser window.

Understand, however, that secured sites help but don't necessarily mean your data is kept safe under lock and key once you submit it. Not every site practices really good security, meaning that hackers—and sometimes a site's own employees—can get access to credit card and other information, which can be abused. This happens with sites of all types.

Shopping

If you've shopped online before, you're accustomed to dealing with virtual shopping carts where you select items, and store them in the cart while you continue shopping. Once you have all you want in your cart, you click Checkout or Order and go through the checkout procedure to actually place your order. Nearly all online pharmacies use a shopping cart (also sometimes called a shopping basket).

In a few situations, however, an online pharmacy may require you to order each drug in a multiple medication order separately, meaning that if you need to fill three prescriptions, you'll have to go through the entire process three different times. What fun! However, this is usually not done for any great reason other than that the online store hasn't been designed well. It's probably wiser for them to process your multiple-drug order together so they will be more likely to spot possible drug interactions. If you like a particular online pharmacy but notice it uses this extra-steps method, consider dropping a suggestion to the email address listed on the Contact Us page to suggest they fix it.

Registration

Some online pharmacies as well as other Web sites like online publications require you to create an account with them that you sign into each time you re-visit the site. Usually, this registration is free of charge and often allows you to fill out just your email address and a password to become a registered member.

Others may ask you to fill out additional information to be stored as part of a profile such as your real name and phone number, actual versus shipping address, and a credit card you want to store as part of your account. This information can then be used to automatically fill out forms for you when you return to a site so you don't have to type these same details again and again.

Filling Out the Medical Consultation Form

Medical consultation forms—which ask you to list details about your current condition or illness as well as your medical history—are used on just about every online drugstore site that does not require an existing prescription from your regular doctor. Often, this serves as the only medical information about you that a site has before it issues or rejects your drug order; this happens even though the FDA has stated that an online-only consultation isn't enough to be considered an adequate medical review.

You may see the same form used on a number of different sites, but you'll also see some big changes between forms used. Some can be completed thoroughly in just a moment or two, whereas others can request information like dates of past surgeries and last chest X-ray that require more time and perhaps a bit of digging into your records. Figure 8.12 shows you one of the sample online forms used.

It's probably smart if you take the time to read through the entire form before you begin to answer. This way you can spot details you need to look up yourself (for example, date of your last physical exam) as well as identify forms that request unusual information you normally aren't asked to provide to your doctor. If you question some of the requested information, it's better to bail out of the order before you complete and submit it than afterwards. You can always check the site's Contact Us or Ask a Question link to ask the online drugstore's customer service representative about the form or voice your concern.

Also, remember to look for the "secure" icon at the bottom of your browser. If no lock icon is present (and check your Web browser's Help menu if you're using a browser other than Internet Explorer or Netscape Navigator to see how that browser notifies you of secure access pages), then your medical information is not being sent through secure means.

If you have genuine concern about filling out a medical form that is not on a secured server, look again at the site's FAQ page or find the Contact Us or home page to see if you can locate a toll-free number where you can supply this information and place your order over the phone. Most sites that allow online ordering also have a toll-free order number.

At the end of most of these forms, you're asked to agree that you've read certain Web documents such as a "customer responsibility" form and an "informed consent" form like that shown in Figure 8.13. If you don't agree or click Yes that you've read them, your order will usually be

Figure 8.12
One of many varied medical consultation forms used by online drugstores.

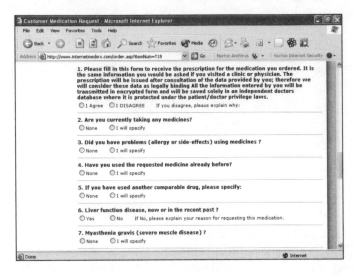

rejected at least until you do so. Unfortunately, most pharmacy sites don't actually require you to open these consumer Web pages before you agree to them and some don't even offer links to these pages so you can read them.

Always read these consumer Web pages, like that shown in Figure 8.14, before you submit your order. Failure to read a contract almost never absolves you of responsibility, so you need to be aware of what you're agreeing to by clicking Agree or Yes. Often these pages basically state that the site isn't responsible if you don't provide accurate answers to your medical history form or choose to use this site without discussing the matter with your doctor.

Figure 8.13
You must agree that you've read the customer/consumer/ patient forms.

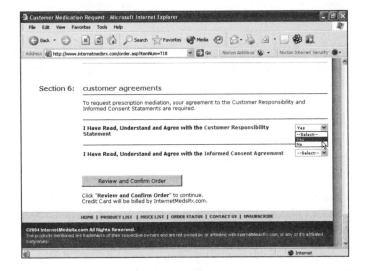

Figure 8.14
An example "informed consent" consumer page on an online pharmacy site.

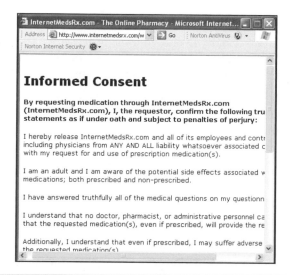

TIP

Remember that tip I suggested in Chapter 3 of taking screenshots of your order process? I usually capture shots to specify what I've filled out in the form as well as shots of the customer agreement pages. Then I store them in a separate folder on my PC's hard drive named for the online store I've used.

NOTE

Not all online stores are designed to work well with the browser that comes with America Online software. However, most sites that recognize the problem usually provide special instructions for AOL customers who experience problems filling out forms or submitting orders. Look for such instructions, often found right on the home page when you first open a Web site.

BE TRUTHFUL. BE THOROUGH.

We hate forms. We approach them with the same relish we normally reserve for root canals and tax preparation season. The result is that we often try to provide only what information is absolutely required and not one bit more.

But ordering medication isn't a game you score points for completing quickly. You want the right drug to treat your condition or illness and you want to be sure the medication won't interact badly with something else you already take.

Resist the urge to rush through your form or only to list the details you think will help in fast approval of your order, especially when using "no prescription needed" sites. You want to offer every bit of relevant information you can and try not to make assumptions about what isn't necessary.

If you have strong doubts about your desire to provide this level of personal information about yourself to a complete stranger, then a) you may not want to use a particular site or b) you may be better off going through your doctor and a more traditional pharmacy.

Questions Asked

Expect to see certain questions about you and your medical history asked on virtually all online medical consultation forms you fill out. These usually include standard questions that you might be asked when seeing a new doctor or entering a hospital.

Among the questions will be some that you are required to answer in order to process the order. Usually, these will be noted with the word "required" or special instructions outlined in red. If you try to submit the form without responding, even if just with a "not applicable" or "no," you'll be returned to the medical form page with the required but missing entries noted. A few badly designed forms may erase all the information you previously filled out, which means you have to type and/or click your responses all over again.

Questions you'll be asked include:

▶ Your age.

▶ Your height and weight—often, you'll see this listed as your BMI, or body mass index, which is a calculation of our overall size when height and weight are factored together; most sites allow you to simply type in your height and weight while a tool on the site automatically calculates your BMI for you. Since this calculation is often used to compute the right dosage for you, don't fib.

▶ The current medical condition for which you're requesting the medicine.

▶ Your specific symptoms.

▶ Date of your last complete physical exam.

▶ Pertinent medical history (major illnesses, previous drugs prescribed, and the like).

▶ Whether you suffer from common or high-risk illnesses such as diabetes, high blood pressure, cancer, immune deficiencies, or obesity.

▶ Your primary physician's name and contact information.

▶ Medications you currently take (some will ask for all formerly prescribed drugs, including over-the-counter drugs such as allergy formulas and herbal remedies).

▶ If you've ever been prescribed a drug identical or similar to the one you're ordering and your experience with it (used to try to determine how safe a match the drug you're ordering is for you).

▶ If you've filled a prescription like this recently (used to try to determine whether you're drug shopping for other than legitimate need) through another online store.

▶ If you've ever been treated for drug problems in the past.

You also may be asked for other specifics, such as whether you've alerted your doctor to your need for this medication and whether you've ever been issued a valid prescription for the drug in the past. Again, be as honest as possible. If the site does indeed have a doctor review your application, you want the information he or she has to be as complete as possible so that a professional can spot problems before the drug reaches you.

Types of Medical Consultation

The range of medical consultations that are offered through online drugstores can run the gamut from a very simple form to a process by which a health care practitioner in your area contacts you to make an appointment to come in for a physical examination. The price differs considerably as well. Some charge no extra fee for a form-only or form-with-follow-up-call but hit you with a $200 fee (or higher) if an exam is required to determine your drug eligibility.

You now know that the U.S. government's federal agencies don't acknowledge an online form-only consultation as providing enough basis for a doctor to write a prescription. The American Medical Association (AMA), probably the most powerful and influential of all U.S.-based medical organizations, also feels that a medical form alone does not provide enough information on which a doctor can properly make a decision about prescribing a drug.

Yet you'll see that the form-only practice is probably the most commonly used consultation type on "no prescription required" online drugstores. You saw one of these sites back in Figure 8.5 where the FAQ stated that the store makes a policy of using just the information provided in the form to make its judgment on whether to approve or reject an order.

But let's go through all the types you may find as you check various online pharmacies and what each can mean for you in terms of time, cost, and convenience.

Form-Only

If the online drugstore you choose specifies that it prescribes medication solely on the basis of your form, you need to take special care in filling out the form to be sure it reflects everything you believe a doctor needs to know in making a decision to give it to you. However, you may not be aware of your complete medical history, presenting another situation where going through your doctor is a smarter choice.

Your goal, regardless of how you shop online, should always be to obtain the right prescription-based treatment for your illness or condition rather than "I need to get this particular drug; what do I have to do to accomplish that?"

But bear in mind that a form-only consultation may not be a wise choice for you if you tend to have lots of special circumstances. For example, let's say that you have experienced several non-typical reactions to drugs you've taken in the past. This might be compounded by one or more allergies to drugs or chemicals often used as the foundation in a compound formula (for example, you can take codeine if it's mixed with ibuprofen but you can't if it's mixed with acetaminophen or aspirin). Or perhaps your health just isn't great in general. If this describes your situation, you're probably much better off having a regular physician who can help coordinate your care and treatment. Then, with prescription(s) in hand, you can try to shop competitively online or offline for the drugs you need at the best prices.

Form-with-Phone Follow-Up

Some online drugstores use a procedure in which, once the consultation form is submitted and reviewed, a call is then made to the person placing an order to ask specific questions. These questions may be related to something troubling or unclear found in your form answers or simply to review what you've already told them.

The simple addition of a follow-up phone call to the process can help, although it's not clear how many drugstores go this distance. From your viewpoint as the customer, it gives you a chance to ask questions or provide additional facts that the form didn't allow. It also allows the pharmacy to confirm your details (typos or accidental omissions can matter) and try to be sure you're not just shopping for a drug you want regardless of whether it's the right one for you. Finally, the follow-up call can reduce the chance that someone else using your credit card may be obtaining drugs under your name. A follow-up call has alerted some parents, for instance, that their teens were drug shopping.

However, even with the follow-up call, this system is far from perfect. A phone follow-up won't verify your blood pressure or blood chemistry. It can be far more prone to error than having a doctor see and evaluate you.

Yet how often the follow-up call is made by a doctor or other medical professional versus a normal customer service sales representative isn't clear. Sometimes, whether the follow-up call is made at all is in question.

When NBC's *Dateline* program did a story on the ease of getting prescription drugs on the Internet, it was discovered that many of the authorizing physicians appeared to be based outside the U.S. even when customers thought they were ordering from U.S.-based drugstores. In one case, a doctor interviewed insisted he had called a patient and performed a phone consultation before he prescribed a powerful drug, only to later admit that he had not done so.

This order had been placed to test the system and the designated patient was actually a small dog. To see how thorough the review process was, the person placing the order specified the dog's age (two years) and weight (under 40 pounds) on the form but did not mention the order was for a dog. Despite the fact that no two-year-old human (let alone a dog) would be prescribed this drug and certainly not one weighing just 40 pounds, no warning sign aroused the attention of the site's staff, no follow-up call was made, and the order was processed and delivered to the dog's owner.

Form with Primary Physician Follow-Up

Sites offering this feature will insist that you provide the name and contact information for your primary care physician as part of your order. The site should then follow up by contacting your doctor to be sure the drug isn't contraindicated or the wrong choice for you. If your doctor agrees, the site's medical staff then authorizes the new prescription, which is then filled by the pharmacy.

At first blush, this may sound like the "safest" way to obtain a drug online without a prior prescription outside of actually going to a doctor for an examination because this process implies your doctor will be involved in the decision making. But once you go through this process, you have to wonder if it wouldn't be easier to just go through your doctor without the intermediary. Remember that "no prescription needed" sites often charge more for medications than a pharmacy filling a standard prescription. You might actually pay less to see your doctor and get a traditional prescription than it costs for the "convenience" of not doing so—and so much safer, too.

You also have to wonder what your doctor may think about this. Although you're not obligated to go to him or her for every medical service you need, it's usually good for all parties if the doctor who knows you best is consulted. If the doctor's first call comes from a third party, such as another doctor working for a pharmacy site, your doctor may wonder what's up. I suggest you touch base with your own doctor before the pharmacy makes contact

---

ABOUT DRUGSTORES CALLING YOUR DOCTOR

Here's something interesting about how some sites conduct primary care physician follow-ups. Pointing to a desire to maintain your privacy, some online drugstores state that they need to contact your doctor but will only do so to verify that you are a patient; some say they also ask your doctor to verify that you've had an exam within the last six months to one year.

Yet your doctor's office generally isn't going to provide this information to callers. Physicians are obligated to federal law to keep patient information confidential except in a case where someone else has a power of attorney or the patient has provided written permission for the doctor to share details.

When I asked a couple of doctors how they would respond to a call like that, they said that the only verification calls they usually get are from Canadian pharmacies filling lower-cost prescriptions for their patients. One said it was not his policy to divulge information about a patient—even whether the person is under his care—without a specific okay from the patient.

This means it's probably important that you at least make contact with your doctor when ordering a prescription online that your primary doctor hasn't written. Beyond letting the physician know to expect a call from an online pharmacy, your doctor should know what you're taking, especially if it's being used at the same time with other medications he or she has prescribed.

Physical Required

To address the concerns voiced about whether form or phone follow-up is enough to properly order a drug, some sites go the extra step of insisting that you undergo a physical exam by a doctor of their choosing before any prescription order is drawn.

You usually start this process by filling out a form that may be either far more or far less exhaustive than the questions you're asked when you won't have any type of follow-up. Once you submit the form through the online drugstore, the pharmacy arranges for you to see a health care practitioner of its choosing.

This additional step is usually the most expensive option. Although you might pay less for the prescription drugs ultimately ordered than you may through some "no prescription needed" drugstores, you often face a fee of anywhere between $125 and $300 for the consultation on top of the price of the ordered medication.

The quality of the medical evaluation you receive with this can differ widely, just as noted by some of the online drugstores that offer this service. You could see just a simple exam very much like a routine doctor's office visit where your height and weight is verified, your blood pressure taken, and questions asked, except that it costs more than most of us pay for a routine office visit. The possibility also exists that you're basically being sent to the office of someone contracted by the online drug service to perform very speedy evaluations where little in the way of a real examination takes place.

But as with some of the other consultation methods already discussed, how much some sites actually require the actual physical follow-up is open to question. Check your next credit card statement to be sure you aren't billed for an exam or consultation fee when no follow-up is provided.

In test orders, I used two services where the ordering process stated exams were required to fulfill orders (or to fill an order for a specific controlled drug) if:

▶ You don't have a current valid prescription for the same drug being ordered, and/or

▶ You fail to provide the name of your primary care doctor whom the site can contact to confirm your need for the drug

In one case, the medication was sent even though I didn't list a primary care physician and offered no history of taking the same drug in the past. No doctor called me let alone scheduled an appointment to examine me. The only mention of examination was listed in the rules for ordering on the site, which apparently the site did not follow.

With the other order, a hold was placed temporarily on my credit card for the amount of the drug but without the $125 consultation fee that site said it would charge for the physical examination. A confirmation message on the Web site informed me that the company would be in touch about scheduling my visit with the doctor. But a few days later, without any explanation, the credit card hold was released (meaning they didn't charge me for the order), and I noticed the site was also no longer available on the Internet. I heard nothing more from them. For the next few months, I checked my credit card bill each month to be sure they did not bill me.

At the end of the test orders, in fact, no one ever asked, much less insisted, that I talk to a doctor or be examined by one before an order was filled. Only one site refused an order because I didn't provide them with my doctor's name. Among those consumers who talked with me regarding their online order experiences, none said they were ever required to submit to a full doctor's exam even when a site listed this as a possible requirement.

Only one respondent said she saw a doctor as part of the process of getting a regular prescription to treat chronic pain. Once she placed her order, a representative from the site contacted her and explained that the only way this woman could receive refills of the drug beyond her initial order was to undergo a physical at a cost of $150. Knowing that she would need refills, the woman agreed.

She noted that she was sent to a local hotel where a "traveling physician" was registered as a guest. Once there, she joined a group of between 15 and 20 other people also there to see the doctor. When she was called into the room, the man identified as the doctor simply asked her questions, many of which she had already answered on the form. In less than three minutes, he approved her prescription, which was then delivered a few days later. This doesn't sound like a remarkably safer improvement over getting the same drug based on the information provided by a medical consultation form.

WHY NO REVIEW IS NOT A GOOD REVIEW

Don't fool yourself into thinking you're getting off easy if an online pharmacy doesn't seem to offer a careful review process in approving your order before it's shipped. If you think I'm belaboring this point, there's a good reason: You need someone knowledgeable watching over the process

This review can be very important, especially if you're doing this outside the bounds of your doctor, to identify key points in your medical history, the drugs you're currently taking, and what reactions (if any) you may have had in the past to similar drugs you're ordering now. A good pharmacy that protects your interest isn't going to ship a drug simply because you want it, and certainly not without a thorough review of the details that you provide about yourself.

Earlier in the chapter, I told you about a test order for Fiorinal that should have raised alarm bells among those reviewing my medical consultation form. But it did not. Potentially, the results could have been disastrous if I received the order and used it because there was a conflict with an over-the-counter drug I use as well as my history of breathing problems when taking drugs similar to Fiorinal. If this had been a normal order rather than a test, it would have been bad news for me if I assumed I could take the drug as prescribed.

If you encounter an online drugstore that doesn't seem to read your form information, this isn't a good place to shop. But how do you tell if they read it or not? If your order is approved very quickly (usually in less than two hours), or you never have to fill out a medical consultation form at all before approval, that's a sign.

Some of the experienced online drug shoppers I talked with suggested people add notes to their forms specifically requesting follow-up. For example, one woman said she had shopped via some European and other foreign Web sites to obtain an anti-migraine drug not approved by the FDA. She had questions that the sites did not answer. As she filled out her form, she noted some special circumstances and stated she would be more comfortable if a medical professional contacted her before the order was finalized. The first foreign pharmacy that did follow up with a phone call to get more details and provide her with more information was the one who got her business; she canceled the other orders.

Payment Options

Using a credit card to make your purchases usually offers you the best protection if there is a problem with your order. Although some sites give you many more payment options beyond credit cards, all involve putting your money upfront before you see what you actually get. You might feel comfortable doing that once you come to trust an online drugstore where you've placed several orders but in the beginning, you don't know.

With a credit card, you're putting the finance company's money upfront. If there's a problem with your order, you can dispute the charge with a chance to explain why. The finance company may be willing and able to retract its payment to the offending pharmacy.

STORES THAT DON'T TAKE CREDIT CARDS

What if you encounter an online drugstore that does not let you use any credit cards? If all it accepts is cash on delivery (COD) or pre-paid orders, it doesn't hurt to wonder why. This is true even when you want to pay by cash or check because you either don't have a credit card or choose not to use one.

It's not that difficult to obtain what is called a merchant's account that allows online vendors to accept and process credit card transactions. Although vendors typically pay a small fee (usually a percentage of the total order) for each sale paid for by credit card, most are willing to accept this because the convenience of credit card purchases tends to increase their overall sales.

Sure, it's always possible that the company simply prefers cash only. You will also find foreign pharmacies that don't have the ability to process U.S.-only credit cards.

Yet you should consider the possibility that the vendor may have had his or her merchant's account suspended because previous problems (fraud, failure to deliver, improper charges) have been reported. There is also the chance that this is a fly-by-night drugstore that might not be open long enough to process those credit card charges before it disappears.

NOTE

Triple-check prices to make certain the price of the drug itself does not change from the beginning of your order process; also be sure that additional unexplained charges are not added.

Shipping Options

You definitely need to look at the shipping methods offered by each site (and some just offer one type) before you place an order. If you need a drug in the next few days but the pharmacy you're looking at can't deliver it that quickly, you may want to go elsewhere.

How your order gets shipped can mean the difference between getting it within a day or two and waiting one, two, or more weeks to receive it. You also need to factor in the time it takes for a pharmacy to process your order, which can typically add 1–4 business days before your order is actually sent.

Free shipping is more difficult to find online than it used to be, probably owing to higher transportation costs due to high oil prices. At the other end of the spectrum is expedited shipping, which can cost anywhere from $10 to $40 depending on the site and the parcel service used.

If you live in a very rural area with limited delivery service, check ahead to determine which service provides the most thorough coverage in your area. I happen to live in rural north central Vermont, for example, and not every parcel service makes deliveries out here on a daily basis. Some come out just a couple of times a week, so paying for overnight service often amounts to a waste of money because the delivery isn't going to arrive sooner than it would if a package is shipped by 2- or 3-day service. Try to pick the most reliable service for you as well. If you've had problems initiating a complaint about a lost order through one shipper, you might want to use another service for delivery of a very-much-needed drug. You don't want to have to wait days for the delivery service to check on a missing shipment before you can get the pharmacy to re-issue the order.

Finally, there's another factor to consider when having your drugs shipped. If small parcels are delivered to an open mailbox or to your porch, they could be stolen. Also, if you have children at home, you may not want them to have access to a box of medications—and we all know how irresistible kids find a package delivery. Think about whether you would prefer to have your package shipped to your office address (if acceptable with the folks at work).

TIP

If you want to shop for your drugs online but don't want to have to wait for delivery to begin taking a new medication, ask your physician to provide you with two prescriptions: one he or she can call in to a local pharmacy for enough medication to cover you for 7–10 days and another for your online pharmacy.

Reviewing Your Order

At some point in the ordering process, you'll be presented with a screen that details the contents of your shopping cart. Depending on where in the ordering process this appears, this review screen may also state your shipping costs and any additional fees that may be charged as part of the order.

Look over the information carefully to be sure you have ordered the correct medication (including the right strength and number, that the price stated for each drug is the same as when you first placed it in your shopping cart, and that no unexplained charges are added in). Once you click Submit Order or Confirm Checkout, you may not have another chance to change incorrect information before the order is processed.

Once the order has been submitted, you should see a final screen listing details about your transaction: what you ordered, which payment method you used, and how much your credit card was charged. You should also receive an order or tracking number, a detail you should note and keep right through to the point you receive your order and verify that it contains what you purchased. This order or tracking number often provides the key to checking the status of your order once you submit it.

You may also receive an email with the same basic information; this usually arrives within minutes of placing your order. If you fail to receive any kind of confirmation or order number, don't just assume the order did not go through and try to resubmit it. The result could be that you get a duplicate order. Instead, use the email address or phone number provided under the Contact Us link to ask customer service if your order has been received.

TIP

If you're following my advice about taking screenshots of your online orders (and I use this for more than simply prescription orders), you may want to take a shot of both the order preview as well as the order confirmation page. In one of my test orders, I was able to get a pharmacy to reverse $35 in unexplained charges made to my credit card between the time I clicked Submit and the moment I saw my order confirmation. Should the pharmacy fail to respond to problems with unexplained fees, your screenshots could help you prove your case to the credit card company when disputing the charge.

Checking Your Order Status/Tracking

Most but not all online drugstores provide you with a tool to track your order from the moment you submit it until the package arrives at your delivery address. This allows you to check to be sure everything was authorized through your credit card, that any needed approval has been obtained on the pharmacy end, and when and how your order ships out to you.

If you received an email confirming your order, check that email for a link to the store's order status page. If you didn't get an email, you can return to the site where you placed your order to locate and click a link labeled Order Status or Check Your Order. You'll usually need to provide your order or confirmation number and usually one other piece of identifying information, such as your email address, your zip code, or your phone number.

A Walk-Through of a Safe Online Purchase

Let's walk through the process for placing an order via an established Canadian pharmacy offering sales to U.S. residents. Then I'll show you the differences you may see in ordering from U.S. pharmacies instead. Much of it will be the same, with Canadian pharmacies able to accept most of the same payment types, such as credit cards that U.S. pharmacies accept. By comparison, several of the Mexican pharmacies I checked don't take credit cards at all and may require you to pre-pay by check, bank debit card, or money order.

With legitimate Canadian pharmacies, be prepared with your written prescription form or be prepared to call your doctor to either have him or her call the number provided by the pharmacy or to receive a call from the pharmacy to confirm and obtain a copy of the written order. All pharmacies that met the standard I use here for legitimacy require your prescription, and some specify that the prescription order itself must be submitted directly by your doctor (to reduce the chance that a forged prescription could be passed). Once the pharmacy receives the order, it then verifies the prescription and gets it authorized on their end (U.S. doctors usually don't have drug ordering authorization north of the border).

NOTE

Notice that I'm not using the names of specific pharmacies here. The intent is to provide you with information, not offer you referrals.

Here, let's assume you need to fill three prescriptions:

▶ One to treat high blood pressure (Diovan HCT)

▶ One to regulate blood sugar for diabetes (Glucophage)

▶ And one muscle relaxant (usually sold as Soma or Carisoprodol) to help you sleep when you have back spasms

The first job before you is to choose a Canadian pharmacy that ships to the United States (many do). Once you find the online pharmacy, follow these basic steps (your results may vary slightly):

1. Most sites allow you to search for a particular drug alphabetically. Since in this example, you're trying to locate three drugs, let's start with Glucophage. Once you find it, locate the dosage strength and number that you want. Click Order or Add to Cart (see Figure 8.15).

2. Your shopping cart page will open showing the drug you just added. Click Continue Shopping (or its closest equivalent).

3. Now locate Diovan HCT on the site and add this to your cart, then click Continue Shopping again.

4. Using the same search tool, look for Carisoprodol. If nothing comes up, check for Soma. One of two things should happen here: either you won't be able to find it or you see it but it's listed as N/A (not available) so you can't add it to your shopping cart. There's a reason for this: Carisoprodol is a controlled drug used also as a pain reliever, so most Canadian pharmacies will not ship it outside the country. Make a note that you're going to need to get your Carisoprodol or Soma elsewhere, either from a U.S.-based online pharmacy or at your corner drugstore.

5. Once you have all the drugs you need to order, click your shopping cart icon again, but this time, click Checkout or Proceed to Checkout or Order (see Figure 8.16).

6. You may see a subtotal for your order now along with the newly added shipping charge. Click the appropriate button to proceed with the checkout.

7. Provide your name, address, and email as requested.

8. At this point, you also reach a point where one of two things may be needed. Either click on a link to complete an online form (see Figure 8.17) or follow a link to download or print a form that you must fill out and send to the pharmacy—at the fax number and/or address it provides—along with either the original (in some cases) or photocopy (in other cases) of your doctor's prescription form.

9. You will then be asked to choose a payment option. Some pharmacies may allow you to send a check or international money order (or traveler's cheque) along with your mailed form and prescription, but you usually are given the chance to use a credit card as well through an online form.

10. Once this phase of your order is complete, follow the site's instructions to supply your prescription sheet(s) and any forms it requires you to complete and send.

CHAPTER 8

Figure 8.15
Add your first
medication to the
shopping cart.

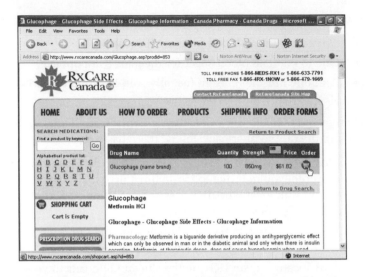

Figure 8.16
Proceed to checkout.

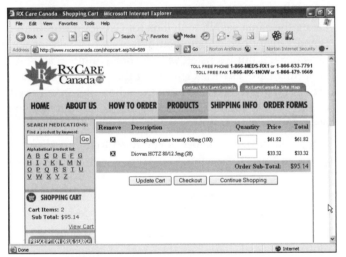

Now, provided your order doesn't happen to be one of those stopped by Customs or the mail system (and you've learned they have the right to seize your order and notify you by letter), your paperwork should get processed soon after you send it to the Canadian pharmacy, with your order arriving within the scope of time (often 1–2 weeks by standard delivery).

Figure 8.17
Fill out your online medical form or download/print the form they provide you to send back (by mail or fax) with your prescription sheets.

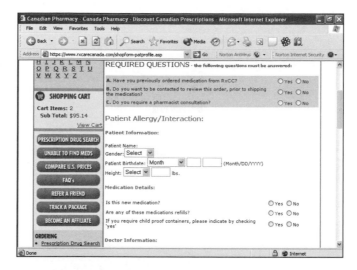

HEED THOSE WARNINGS

With all the warnings I've offered in the last several chapters, you might be hesitating before you place that first online order, wondering if it this move is truly right for you. Yet it's by heeding the warnings that you reduce your risk and increase the chance that your first online medication purchase is a good one. The best advice of all, of course, is to go through your doctor to get a prescription and then have it filled online; any other method is too fraught with danger.

As this book was going to press, the Pew Internet and American Life Project released the results of a study that said that of those who had purchased drugs online already (still a small part of the American population), 9 out of 10 considered their experience a good one and that they expected to buy drugs online again in the future. Shop carefully with the precautions offered here and you're apt to join that large majority of happy customers.

Although I've tried an assortment of different types of online pharmacies to place test orders for the book, I've very much appreciated the convenience along with the wealth of information I can find online when I shop for my own personal medications. It lets me feel a bit more in control of the drugs I need to take because I now have a good idea of the price I need to pay, the precautions I need to take, and where I can go to get good service without paying extra.

Yet again, the very best fact to take from all the information shared here is to see your doctor, go through the traditional process, and then do your shopping online. This gives you far more safety than going it alone in a world filled with pills and potions and possible interactions.

CHAPTER 8

Chapter 9
The Price You Pay

One of the biggest misconceptions about shopping for medications online is that—in part because the volume of online shops would seem to promise stiff competition—you can save big money. Yet you might not find this very accurate if a) you don't know the going price for the drug and b) you don't look around.

Yes, it's possible to reduce costs but this really depends on a number of different factors, including:

- ▶ What you shop for
- ▶ Whether you already have a prescription for the medication
- ▶ Where you shop (the U.S. vs. Canada or other countries)
- ▶ Which service you use
- ▶ How prepared you are to make your mouse do a fair amount of virtual legwork in research

Probably the fastest thing you will discover is that if you're searching for drugs without a valid prescription, you are typically going to pay for the privilege in money, if not in larger problems. You will find plenty of sites stating that they have the best prices on a particular drug, but you're still likely to pay two or three and sometimes even twenty or more times what you would pay for the same pill obtained through a more traditional method. This is true even if the online pharmaceuticals site does not require and charge for a medical consultation (some sites may charge anywhere from $25 to $200 and up for this beyond the price of the medication).

Figure 9.1 shows a site advertising warehouse-stocked medications at great discounts. Note that it promises no doctor appointments and no prescription needed. The "no medical history" part is actually the scariest, since medical history can sometimes provide information that might signal whether you're a bad candidate for taking such a drug. However, if you look at the prices and do some research, you quickly see that this site overcharges above and beyond what you would pay for some of these drugs at other "no prescription" sites.

CHAPTER 9

Figure 9.1
This site promises 80% off drugs, but their prices are sometimes several times the normal drugstore price.

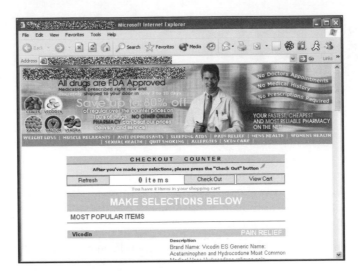

Research and Consideration

If your primary motivation for shopping for medication online is to save money or at least keep the price you pay within the realm of being reasonable (minus a bit of added expense for overall convenience), it's crucial that you educate yourself about the current price for the exact prescription you want to fill.

Whether you're shopping online or in a bricks-and-mortar store, even small variations in a prescription can substantially impact the price. For example, if you choose a generic over a specific manufacturer's product you may see savings of anywhere from 5% to 25% or more but there is always the possibility of at least a slightly different response to the generic over the brand.

Yet there's more to consider. Depending on how the manufacturer prices the drug and supplies it to pharmacies, you can pay substantially less if you can purchase in volume (for example, a 90-day supply vs. 30-day supply). Volume purchase is sometimes available in HMO mail order companies.

In some situations, you can find even more variation. Say you need to take 15 mg of a particular medication for each dose and that this drug is packaged and sold in three different strengths: 7.5, 15, and 30 mg. You may want to analyze the prices of the drug at each strength to see whether it's cheaper to obtain a prescription for twice as many 7.5-mg pills (but take two pills at a time) than the 15-mg level. Similarly, perhaps the 30 mg is the best deal, although this means dividing the pill in half, something obviously not possible if the medication comes in capsule form.

Many, however, advise against any practice that involves pill-splitting. What sounds like a simple enough task isn't always easy, even with special cutting devices you can buy to do this. Some pills are scored in such a way to make it a breeze to break them in half. But with lots of others, it can be nearly impossible to slice a pill exactly in half. When the pill crumbles in the process, you either have to wash down often bitter powder or face the waste of some product along with a slightly lesser quantity than was prescribed for your dosage. There's also the issue of the jagged edges from split pills that can irritate your esophagus as they go down.

Understand, too, that not every pharmacy—either online or off—may carry every different strength. Sometimes, there can be a dozen or more generics for a single drug. Also, while there may be a number of different generic types of a brand-name medication you take, such generics may vary widely in price and again, every pharmacy may not carry every generic version. You'll want to check to see which generic or brand is the least expensive and then be sure that the site you want to buy from carries that specific label at or very close to the price you expect to pay. If you fail to do this, you may cost yourself money, which could amount to just pennies or an amount far more appreciable. Legitimate pharmacies can almost always get a drug within 24 hours if it's not currently in stock.

However, here's an issue with generics that not everyone considers. If you or someone you care for, such as a very elderly patient, takes their medications by sight (example: the blue ones every four hours and the red ones every six), changes from brand to generic or even one generic to another may be confusing.

TOP WAYS TO RESEARCH DRUG PRICES

1. Use sites like drugstore.com to check pricing, looking carefully at dosage strength and generic versus name brand to compare.

2. Call local bricks-and-mortar pharmacies, including the large bulk stores like CostCo that offer pharmacy services. Most will gladly quote you the current price. Some may allow you to fax them a list, which they'll fill in and send back.

3. Check local organizations. Some senior groups and others have organized bus trips or discount drug buying services to get access to lower-priced drugs in another community, state, by mail in volume, or even across the U.S. border. Some have sample price lists for common drugs.

4. Likewise, if possible, take advantage of the American Association of Retired Persons (AARP), which negotiates better pricing for its members.

5. Find out if your work or employee health program provides any type of discount drug eligibility. Some unions, for example, have negotiated contracts that include the mail order or Internet ordering of drugs through specific outlets to cut price.

6. Ask friends and associates. They may have located a pharmacy—online or otherwise—offering lower prices than you're already paying.

DO YOU HAVE A SPECIAL HARDSHIP?

Many drug companies have special options available to help people with limited incomes and/or other strong financial hardships obtain needed medications at a reduced cost or by a special subscription (for example, pay $25 or $30 per month to get a card that you can use to purchase the drugs through your pharmacy at little or no cost). Some of these programs, however, are limited to just senior citizens based on stringent income requirements.

You may be able to locate information about such programs via the drug company's Web site. If not available there, use a major Web search engine to locate the company's toll-free number, call them, and ask for more information, especially the guidelines and any required application form. Use the Web search engine, too, to look up drug company Web site addresses, although you'll find many are quite obvious (for example, **www.watson.com** takes you to Watson Pharmaceuticals, and **www.pfizer.com** is the location for Pfizer Pharmaceuticals' site).

If you aren't sure of your drug's manufacturer or you want to investigate what other companies make a version of your needed medication, you can use a site like **www.rxlist.com** to search by the drug's name and obtain a list, as shown in Figure 9.2.

Figure 9.2
RxList.com is just one of several highly useful sites for researching medication and even obtaining a quick price quote.

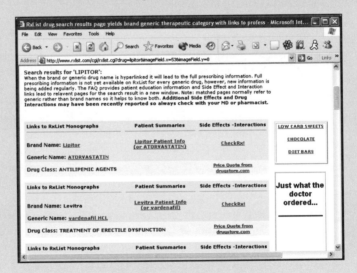

How to Determine Prices

A smart consumer always does his or her research and this certainly applies to the issue of medication prices, as we've already discussed. Thankfully, you can determine an average price or price range for a particular drug in a number of ways, along with obtaining information about generic varieties and different strengths available.

Several online sites, including drugstore.com, allow you to search for prices of a number of medications. Using drugstore.com as the example here, you would follow these steps:

1. Determine the basic information about your needed prescription (name and dosage).

2. Using your computer and available Internet connection, go to drugstore.com.

3. Click on Pharmacy.

4. Under Prescription Price Checker, type in the name of the drug you want to locate (or browse through the list by alphabetic links), as shown in Figure 9.3.

5. Click Go, then examine your results (see Figure 9.4).

Figure 9.3
Use drugstore.com's prescription price checker.

Figure 9.4
Examine the prices for the various drug strengths and from different manufacturers, depending on the type of drug.

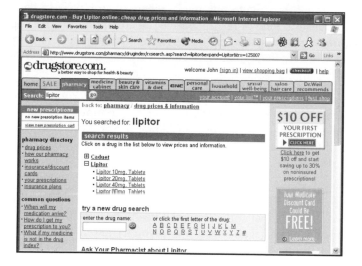

Shop Around

Don't assume that if you get the best price on one drug from a particular pharmacy you will automatically save similarly if you need to order other prescriptions. In fact, you may find that one site offers a particularly good deal on one of your drugs, but a higher price for a second or third prescription you obtain.

For this reason, you probably want to research each medication separately. Unlike shopping in bricks-and-mortar stores, you don't have to exhaust yourself running all over town to take advantage of one good price here and a better price on a second drug elsewhere. After all, it's pretty easy to move between different Web sites and once you've set up an account with each and started ordering prescriptions, you usually don't need to re-supply your information again and again. Just keep a record of where you shop each time and a reminder when you need to refill each.

Shopping with an eye toward assertive competition represents a bit more work, but your savings may be worth the trouble.

A Practical Shopping Example

Now let's look at an example using a commonly used drug, this one focusing on Lipitor, a popularly prescribed anti-cholesterol medication. Through a traditional prescription, about five minutes of research showed me that it would cost about $45–$55 (before insurance co-pay) to fill a 30-count bottle of 20-mg tablets at one of three area pharmacies. In some other parts of the country, I could order the same drug for both about 25% less as well as 20%–30% more. Although not every doctor or pharmacy will agree to do this, you can sometimes arrange to have your prescription in one state filled by a reputable online pharmacy in another. For this, you'll need to check to be sure that the destination pharmacy is willing to ship.

Likewise, I could order the drug from Canada, where the savings can be substantial. In this instance, I would need to mail or fax the online Canadian pharmacy a copy of my prescription (some may require supporting medical documentation in addition to the paper prescription) where a doctor there may re-originate a Canadian-based prescription, which a Canadian pharmacy can then fill and ship.

What if I decided I wanted Lipitor without a doctor's 'script? You might question why anyone would do that. No medical professional would ever recommend it. Yet it happens, as you saw in the profiles of online pharmacy users in Chapter 3. For those who want to go that route, dozens if not hundreds of online pharmacies exist where a doctor you will never meet or talk with writes a prescription for which you would pay usually anywhere from $74 to $140 via credit card.

But there is more than just cost at issue with Lipitor, true with similar drugs as well as certain other types of medications that support overall health or a specific, potentially life-threatening illness. These present a special challenge when you try to omit your doctor. Medications that affect blood chemistry usually warrant follow-up testing to monitor both the success of the treatment as well as to ensure there aren't any nasty side effects that may appear in blood work before they produce demonstrable symptoms.

Some people can take advantage of community health fairs and screenings, usually available at a much reduced rate, to check for high blood pressure, elevated cholesterol, and other standard health issues. But unless you have access to a regular system—doctor, clinic, senior center program, or other wellness program—where blood workups can be performed, it's going to be pretty difficult for you to assess your immediate situation and whether a drug you've chosen to take is effective.

Other Issues to Investigate or Beware

Now that you've looked at some of the most basic issues in online pricing and price research, let's explore some of the finer details. Legitimate questions you should have, especially when dealing with the less-than-standard drug ordering sites, include the issue of whether your health insurance or prescription drug plan will help offset costs, and what extra fees, if any, may be added to your order before or *after* it has been placed.

Insurance and Tax Deductions

A key difference between traditional online pharmacies where you fill standard prescriptions ordered by your doctor and the new wave of pharmacies that do not always require a previous prescription is that the latter is far less apt to accept health insurance in order processing.

Think about this and it makes sense. Many health care policies limit benefits to recognized care and service providers, and hardly need to look for an excuse not to cover a questionable purchase.

This issue may not matter for certain prescriptions that aren't always covered through the pharmacy portion of health insurance in any event. For example, some policies specifically exclude contraceptives, homeopathic and/or herbal-based remedies, as well as non-FDA approved drugs (such as the kind you might order from another country to treat a particular ailment). Thus, you would not be able to get insurance coverage for them regardless of whether you shopped at your local drugstore or bought from a site in India or Thailand.

However, look at the pharmacy section of your health insurance manual. In some cases, even when a pharmacy site does not take billing for insurance directly, you may still be able to submit proof of purchase to your insurer for reimbursement of all but your usual co-pay amount.

There is also the issue of tax deductions. For U.S. income tax purposes, medications can be included under the medical expenses listed in the Schedule A deduction form. Whether or not the medication is covered by insurance, the tax man usually accepts any needed drug properly prescribed as a legitimate expense worthy of deduction on the form. For this, you will want to keep records of the order and proof of payment (such as your credit card statement) along with a copy of the prescription (if available). In this way, if you are questioned about such a deduction later, you have the evidence for the Internal Revenue Service's consideration.

With that said, understand that if you have serious questions about the methods by which you obtained a drug—for instance, it's specifically banned in this country or you procured recurring refills of pain medication from an out-of-country pharmacy for which you have no printed prescription—you may want to weigh carefully whether or not you want to list this on your tax form. An IRS review might lead to some unpleasant questions.

What Consequences?

Since the preceding section covered what you may wish to include and exclude on your taxes based on prescriptions ordered online, it seems an ideal time to raise the issue of another price you may pay. This is one that is not strictly financial, although fines and potential legal fees could place quite a dent in your wallet as well. It's also one discussed before but it bears further consideration.

Besides the risks you run with your overall health by ordering from a site that does not require a prescription drafted by a physician who has actually examined you, there are legal consequences, which were covered briefly in Chapter 2 when we talked about federal agencies related to medication sales and distribution.

As you learned in the chapter about the products you actually receive, it's very possible that your medication ordered through one of the online drug mills that don't require a prior prescription may actually supply you with the drugs but minus any real documentation.

U.S. federal law requires that you have a valid prescription issued in your name for any prescription drug in your possession. If an overseas-originated drug shipment is stopped at Customs on its way to you, the only way you may be able to receive your shipment is if you produce documentation proving your prescription, something you're unlikely to get from one of the drug mills. In fact, even if the shipment arrives at your home or office unburdened by Customs questions, you may open the package to find that there is nothing specifying your prescription.

As an example, Figure 9.5 shows a picture of one of the results of the test orders I did for this book. Note that the prescription bottle states nothing but the drug name, quantity, and strength, and the briefest of directions for use ("Take 2 tablets a day"). The name of the pharmacy that supplied it and the name of the doctor who supposedly prescribed it are missing, as is the patient name, expiration date, and whether or not the prescription can be refilled.

Figure 9.5
One prescription I ordered online arrived without any documentation and with a label that does not list the patient's name, prescribing doctor, or the pharmacy.

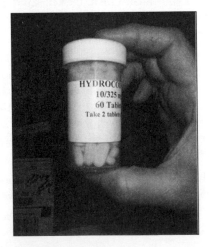

If you get a medication like this and happen to carry it with you into a situation where you may be searched by police or some other security officer, you risk immediate arrest for possession of medication without a prescription. In this case, the ordered drug is the powerful, highly addictive and often abused synthetic opiate-based medication hydrocodone (also known as Vicodin, Norco, or Lortab), one that is apt to get the attention of law enforcement considering that the label offers no identifying information.

Possession of a Schedule II or III (see Chapter 2 for a list of "scheduled" drugs) narcotic without a valid prescription is a serious charge that can bring with it the potential for incarceration, one every bit as complicating as being caught with an illegal drug such as marijuana.

Also, you may find that not all of the prescriptions you order from some of these more dubious vendors will arrive in a standard pill vial. In two ordering tests, for example, I received flat blister packs of pills stapled within plain white cardboard without so much as a small printed sheet stating what the medication was or how to take it. Two other test purchases brought pills in their original packaging, with boxes that contained no English translation of the drug name or instructions for use. Yet another was accompanied by a printed prescription sheet, photocopied from one of the popular drug information books, but for a medication other than the one supplied in the shipment. All of these would be considered illegal by federal standards, even when such shipments originate in the United States.

If it sounds like buying the so-called "pig in a poke," it is. Many of these sites really involve a roll of the virtual dice, one where your ultimate safety may largely depend on your research and resourcefulness.

One final thing to consider before you use such sites is that although sites will often feature the American flag and talk about being a U.S. pharmacy utilizing U.S.-licensed doctors and pharmacies, this may not always be the case. One of my test orders at such a site ended up with a shipment from the Netherlands. Another arrived from India. Conversely, on one foreign order, the package was shipped instead from Flushing, Queens (New York).

The foreign-based nature of certain drugs is an issue because some medications are illegal to bring into the U.S. even for proper personal use, such as some narcotic pain relievers. You will also find that you can purchase codeine products over the counter in both Canada and Mexico that would require a prescription here to obtain. Technically speaking, you are not supposed to bring these into the U.S., although actual enforcement of such rules tends to be few and far between.

Many Canadian pharmacy sites, for example, simply will not ship orders of such drugs into the U.S. To handle that, some services have cropped up that do allow you to place orders for these drugs—often at greatly inflated prices (for example, $45 for a bottle of aspirin with codeine that costs $5–$10 in Canada). These services skirt the laws by employing private shoppers within Canada who will go to a pharmacy, purchase the over-the-counter drug, and then ship it to you directly, much as you might send a gift to a relative in a neighboring country. Such actions tend to fly below the radar of Customs and the shipping services.

Watch the Shipping Charges

Good organization and pre-planning will usually save you money when shopping online for prescriptions. This is because many sites may not offer free FedEx overnight delivery, or at least not without charging a premium for the medication itself.

Both for cost and to be sure that you don't run out of needed prescriptions, always research the shipping prices and policies for the online pharmacy sites you want to use. Some, like drugstore.com, offer free 3-day shipping for prescriptions, but may add several dollars onto the price of the order if you forget to refill in time and have to bump the shipping method up to overnight delivery.

In fact, with a particularly inexpensive prescription, one less than $20, the potential exists that you could pay more for shipping and handling than for the drug itself. In such a case, advance research will tell you, so you may prefer to opt to buy the medication locally based on the cost you attach to your time and convenience.

Check also to be sure that there is no separate shipping fee for each medication you order if you purchase more than one. A few sites—either the less legal ones or those poorly designed—will actually make you order each drug separately. This appears to be particularly true when ordering pain medications, sleep aids, and sedatives. Usually, however, you should be able to obtain more than one prescription for the same shipping cost as one unless you have a particular situation in which one drug is provided in large liquid format (a heavy bottle can mean a higher shipping fee).

You'll find that some online stores won't ship liquid-format medicine at all out of concern that the bottle may break and produce a scare among the shippers handling it. The anthrax scare of 2001 has resulted in some general nervousness in package handling. While some rules exist about shipping liquid forms, especially those where any chemical compounds are concerned, many online drugstores do indeed ship syrups and other liquids—including ampules for injection-form drugs such as insulin and even morphine sulfate—as readily as pill form.

When you're dealing with an overseas or out-of-country drugstore, however, you may sometimes have to wait anywhere from 4–5 days to 4–5 weeks to receive your order. Not only do such drugs have to travel some distance, but they usually have to go through at least a customary stop at Customs (and this book tackles the issue of Customs elsewhere). This must be taken into account when ordering because you probably don't want an interruption in taking your prescription, especially since some sites require you to wait 30 days from shipment to consider an undelivered package as lost.

Beware of Fake Low, Low Prices to Get You in the Virtual Door

Many people learn about online pharmacies through unsolicited email. Such ads may promise extremely low prices and even offer some specific examples. If you go to the site you may see even more savings listed.

But look carefully: the price you pay may end up being substantially more. Some of this may be because special charges have been added for shipping, for an online (or by telephone) medical consultation, and even sometimes for a pharmacy processing fee. These charges can usually be found before you order by viewing the Frequently Asked Questions (FAQs) page on a drugstore site or looking at instructions for placing your order; so they aren't hidden per se but reduced to what amounts to small, fine print you may not bother to read until it's too late.

Once you review the supporting documentation for the site, you need to add up the costs and see if it still makes sense to order your medication from a given online store. In reality, most legitimate pharmacies build order processing charges directly into their bottom-line pricing and don't tack on extra charges. Your research may show that you can ultimately pay less for a medication if you order it from another site where the per-pill price is higher but which doesn't tack on these different, extra fees.

Finally, my own research uncovered a handful of drug sites that do indeed tack on hidden fees that may not be seen until your credit card is actually charged and which may never be explained.

Hidden Fees

In one of the test orders done for this book, I used a site that promised that the price you saw was the price you paid with no hidden charges. Comparing a particular drug at local prices with those at online venues such as drugstore.com, this medication seemed like a fair bargain… at least right up to the point where I clicked Buy Now. The final price for the drug turned out to be nearly five times the originally listed price.

If you shop online for other goods besides prescription drugs, you know that there is usually a confirmation process by which you would be able to back out of an order. This site completely bypassed this safeguard. Instead, it delivered the low price quote, allowed you to order, allowed you to fill out the credit card and delivery information, and only once the order had been placed was the full amount of the cost revealed: just under $150 for a prescription listed at a very reasonable $35. Attempts to cancel the order received no response and the toll-free number listed for customer service was answered by someone citing a different company name who claimed to know nothing about an online drugstore site using that number.

By the consumer laws in place in most civilized countries, such hidden fees are completely illegal. Most sites, in fact, will at least state that fees may be attached to the order, especially when ordering from a site where no prior prescription is required, even if the final figure isn't always made available until relatively deep into the ordering process.

But there's another rub that comes with using these alternative "no prescription" sites for your drug needs: some may rely on your unwillingness to complain to authorities in cases where you suspect or know that what you're doing circumvents the normal rules. After all, some intrusive questions may be asked of you by such authorities and you may fear that you may be charged with something like "doctor shopping" or illegal possession of a controlled substance (depending on the medication you attempted to order or did receive).

Others companies, based in foreign countries, know that it will be difficult for a U.S. citizen to sue them successfully. The worst such sites may face is losing the ability to make sales in the United States, a ruling they can probably circumvent by setting up operation under a new name. This practice appears to be relatively common among fly-by-night and unauthorized drug retailers.

CHAPTER 9

For everyone who screams bloody murder when such hidden charges are applied, several others may just assume it as the cost of doing business this way. Many consumers, too, aren't going to call Bali or Belize or Pakistan long distance repeatedly to argue an extra charge.

Thankfully, the number of sites charging hidden fees appears to be relatively few. Of the hundreds of drug-selling sites reviewed for this book, I found just one chain of stores (whether or not they are a chain is actually unclear, but all use the same interface with the same text and pictures, although the sites themselves have different names and phone numbers) that always tacked on fees that well exceeded the cost of the prescription itself.

DOCUMENTING YOUR ORDER THROUGH SOFTWARE

The practice I used in preparing for this book and a technique I use with various types of online ordering may work for you too, both to remember order details and prices as well as to provide proof if you run into a problem later.

What I do is use screen capture software to take a digital image of each significant screen of information as I prepare and then place my order. This gives me a snapshot of the facts that were presented to me, what details I supplied through the ordering process, as well as a receipt for the order I can then print out and store in my computer.

You may already have screen capture software on your PC, but you can also locate a number of them available for download on the Internet. Good download sites for such tools include **www.download.com** and **www.tucows.com**. Screen capture programs come in both free forms and in shareware (meaning that you get to try the software for free over a period of time such as 30 days, and then register it for a fee once you decide you like how it works). One of the most popular and easy to use of these utilities is SnagIt.

Once you install the software and read its documentation, you may want to create a new folder—and name it for easy identification—where you can automatically store your screenshots for quick retrieval. Depending on the graphic file format your screen capture software uses, you can often open these captures directly in your Web browser when you want to review your order details or product prices.

Overcoming Ordering Problems

As mentioned elsewhere in this book, it's important that you pay close attention to the details of your order and seek prompt remedy when a problem is noticed, whether it's early on in the ordering process, your delivery has not arrived, you discover that you have received the wrong medication or in the wrong strength or amount, or someone else used your credit card to place the order without your authorization.

Fighting Overcharges and Non-Delivery

Since most online stores of any kind usually allow you to pay by credit card, understand that your credit card company may provide a valuable service to you if you encounter a problem such as being overcharged, never receiving delivery of your purchase, or otherwise not getting what you paid for (getting a different drug other than the one you ordered). This is protection not afforded you if you use an electronic check or personal check, cash on delivery (C.O.D.), or direct debit from your bank account.

Most credit card companies, particularly those offering "platinum" service, provide some purchase protection to their customers. They may go after a vendor who has not honored an order placed using their issued card. However, credit card companies require that you dispute a claim within a reasonable time after the fraud or non-delivery is recognized. This is usually a period between 30 and 90 days, with 60 days being the most common deadline. When you order from a site that discloses that it may take several weeks for your order to be delivered, you could find yourself bumping up against a deadline because 30 to 45 days may have already passed from the time the online drugstore charged your card and the time at which you realize the order is simply not going to arrive. Keep track of the time!

Also, although you can call your credit card company using the 800 number available on your bill—as well as often on the back of the card itself—it may be best to file your complaint in writing. It may be extremely helpful if you provide a copy of the bill and a full statement about what has gone wrong, including any salient facts. This not only facilitates the matter for your credit card company, but it also helps you organize your material before too much time passes and your memory fades.

However, appreciate the fact that while your finance company may intervene on your behalf, it probably won't be willing to go to bat for you if there is any indication you're involved in an illegal practice. For example, a woman I know who worked for one of the major credit companies told me about a customer that repeatedly reported online drug sites for fraud, for sending the wrong medication or less than that ordered, and for non-delivery. A check of the customer's records allegedly revealed that she was buying copious amounts of dozens of different drugs from discount foreign sites and, according to the credit account representative, the customer admitted she was obtaining these drugs to resell them to others at a profit. The reselling of such drugs is strictly illegal. In fact, federal laws specifically prohibit the transfer of controlled substances from one person to another, regardless of whether money changes hands.

At the point that this information was disclosed, the credit card company cancelled the customer's card and refused to further assist her in obtaining refunds. It was unclear, however, whether the customer was reported to the police or federal authorities.

Now, this is a more extreme circumstance than you would normally find. It's unlikely that your credit card company is going to question you over a one-time charge dispute for normal orders. If you're not doing anything wrong, there is really no reason to fear.

The normal process for handling problems is as follows:

1. First, try to get satisfaction directly through the site where you placed your order. As I indicated elsewhere, some sites may ask you to wait 30 days for delivery before a supposedly shipped order is considered lost and then reshipped.

2. If you're concerned because the order has not been received and now you question the legitimacy of the business itself, ask the company to refund your money rather than ship a replacement order.

3. If the site/business agrees to refund your money and you paid by credit card, check with your finance company to be sure a refund has been applied to your account.

4. Should you not get a response or get no satisfaction from the site, then contact your credit card company.

What about situations in which a substantial amount of money is involved? Say, for instance, that you order a foreign-sourced drug you need and buy in a quantity that costs $300 or more. Here, too, you probably want to follow the procedure just listed. Although you can call the police or the district attorney's or state's fraud office or even a private attorney, you face two issues. Local authorities have little jurisdiction over a sale actually transacted in Tobago or Spain, and your first concern is apt to be recouping your financial loss. It may make no sense to involve a private attorney if the legal fees would exceed the amount you originally paid.

TIP

If the online pharmacy is part of the VIPPS network mentioned in Chapter 2, you may want to register a complaint with them. See Chapter 2 for details.

Dealing with a Bad Order

You must check your order as soon as it arrives to be sure you received the right drug, in the proper strength, and of the correct amount. The greatest concern here is not one of cost but of the risk(s) inherent in taking the wrong prescription, especially with medications that either have life-threatening complications or can endanger your life if not taken regularly.

Remember when I talked about the documenting your online order through the use of screen capture software? If you have a digital camera available, you can also document the order delivery, the images of which may help you prove your case if you need to contact the online drugstore because of a problem like the wrong drug or the wrong quantity.

In test orders conducted for this book, for example, I received one order for a completely different drug than the one ordered, one in a different strength than ordered (but with instructions for taking the dose that applied to the originally ordered strength rather than the strength received, which could have resulted in an overdose), and four different orders where the number of pills received was not the exact amount ordered. In fact, pill count appeared to be rather sloppy in some cases. An order for 90 pills in one case resulted in a delivery of 81 pills; in another, I received 96 pills in a 90-count order. One seems like a rip-off whereas the other sounds like a bounty. In any case, pill count should be correct.

During the test order process, I developed a system for documenting orders as they were received that works like this:

1. Take a picture of the package unopened when it first arrives (digital cameras work great for this, because you can take 3–4 pictures to get a better one).
2. Open the package, remove all materials (the bottle and any packing instructions, for example), place the materials on top of the package, and shoot another picture of this.
3. Take a third image of the actual prescription label and then of any accompanying literature.
4. Shoot another image of the bottle unopened to reflect how full the bottle appears to be (this only works if the bottle is at least partially transparent).

5. Open the bottle or packaging, carefully dump the contents into a bowl or onto a plate or other flat surface, and take another image.

6. Count the pills (I actually did three separate counts to be certain).

7. Shoot pictures of both the front and back of one pill (to document any drug imprint codes).

8. Transfer the images from the digital camera into my PC where they are stored in a specially created and named folder for later retrieval.

In the case of an incorrect pill count, this process isn't proof positive. The drug seller could always argue that you removed pills (assuming that you might not report an overage to your advantage) before you performed the count.

But a reputable company will usually try to satisfy its customers and make good on any shortfall. This is usually done through a pro-rated refund based on the number of pills missing in the order, since most laws prohibit sending you a fully fresh order or just sending the pills missing from the initial delivery.

Where this process might be invaluable, however, is in documenting a situation in which the wrong drug itself was shipped or the order arrived damaged (one test order arrived with many smashed tablets and lots of powder and fragments). A great beauty with digital cameras, of course, is that not only can you get immediate pictures you could simply send via email to the drug seller as proof, but also that there is relatively little cost involved in shooting several different pictures to document an order.

Even when there is no dispute and no problem with the order, you may someday have use for the information yourself. For instance, you could review images or screen captures to remind yourself of a dosage or drug name you have long since forgotten.

When Your Child Uses Your Credit Card to Order Drugs

What's your recourse if your child orders drugs online using your credit card? Unfortunately, this happens more and more frequently today.

If you find out about it soon enough thereafter, you may be able to cancel the order and obtain a refund directly from the pharmacy site. Legally, children are not recognized as valid parties to a contract until they reach the age of 18, which is why you often see even normal online vendors specify that a person must be 18 or over to purchase a product or a service.

Yet what you do beyond this really depends on how much control you want to exercise over the situation. For instance, you can call your credit card company, explain the situation, and ask that the charge be vacated. However, credit card companies when faced with this scenario often behave in one of two ways: either hold you responsible for what appears to them to be your implicit approval for such use or suggest that, in order to remove the charge from your card, they may require that you file fraud charges for the improper use of your card. Although this might teach your child a lesson in responsibility, it's probably also going to add to your headaches rather than curb them.

"But that's not fair," you say. "The site never should have sold medication to a legal minor!"

True, but it's unlikely that your child supplied his or her true age when placing the order. Almost all sites at least request the birth year for customers requesting a prescription. Often enough, children use the approximate birth year for their parents, knowing that some secure transaction sites actually try to match up the birth date to the legal owner of the credit card; if there's a discrepancy, the prospective customer either receives a message stating that the billing information cannot be processed as provided or an invitation to call the pharmacy's order line to resolve the problem.

In practice, however, I've yet to find a site that expressly double-checks to be sure that the person placing the order is a legal adult. Some sites will tell you that they require proof of identity and age when you place the order, but I have not seen one that actually carries through. In one test order, I gave a birth date that was just shy of age 18 and encountered no problem in completing the order.

While this is a reckless and downright dangerous practice, you may not know any of this has occurred until either a) you receive a bill with a credit charge you don't recall making or b) a medical or legal emergency arises out of your child obtaining the medication.

You'll learn more about this in Chapter 12, "Are Your Kids Pharming?" but know now that your best bet is to be proactive; keep your credit and debit information out of the hands of your children (and do not store that data on a computer where a child or anyone else has access). You should also review your credit card bills carefully each month, as well as monitor what packages come into your home.

Chapter 10
Identifying What You Really Get

Many of the warnings about using online pharmacies—especially foreign ones—often center around claims that you may not receive the drug you order. But you don't need a drug wholesaler in search of high profits to get the wrong drug.

Mistakes happen. You make them. I make them. Pharmacists and doctors make them, too. When they happen with medication you need, the result can be a lot worse than simple inconvenience.

We hear about the horrible ones, where a young mother is accidentally given synthetic heroin in place of another prescription drug and dies quickly because the right dosage for her prescription was a lethal dose of painkiller that stopped her breathing. Yet most errors are simple and non–life threatening: the wrong number of pills, a mistyped label, or a missing sticker to advise you to take a pill with meals.

Medication mix-ups happen everywhere, every day. Even though serious mistakes usually account for just a tiny fraction of the number of prescription orders filled each day in pharmacies and hospitals around the globe, people still get hurt or ill. Some die. One mistake is all it takes.

More issues develop beyond the immediate potential risk to you if you get and begin to take the wrong drug. Getting the wrong drug—whether or not it's a potentially fatal situation—can really shake your trust. You don't know these medications like a pharmacist does and you may feel you have no choice but to depend on this professional to get it right.

Although the information in this chapter is designed to help you check and identify the exact medications you get from an online order, they apply equally as well to those you get from your corner drugstore. Whether I shop through a regular pharmacy or through a virtual one, I check to be as sure as I can that what I ordered is what I receive. I count the number of pills or capsules, double- and triple-check the label, and when it's a new drug I'm unfamiliar with, I go online to verify that the medication is the one ordered and presented in the dosage my doctor specified. A few times, I've spotted small problems or drug conflicts a doctor or pharmacist has not.

In the old days, checking medication was much tougher for mere mortals to do. You needed access to a huge book called the *Physician's Desk Reference* (PDR) to look up your drugs. You also had to operate on pure faith when a drug you were given was too new to be listed (the PDR is re-issued every year, but lots of new drugs and variations on old ones can come on the market in the intervening time).

But the old days are over. The Internet offers you a number of ways to check your medications *and* learn more about what you take than your doctor or pharmacist has time to discuss. So whether you're buying new drugs online and need to check your orders or you simply want to know what's in the drugs you take and what effects it can have, this chapter shows you exactly how to do that.

The Range of Experience

Did you realize that 64% of Americans use at least one prescription drug on a regular basis? That's an astounding number because it means that nearly every U.S. household is affected by drug prices and policies. It also tells us that we take prescriptions at a record rate compared to people in other industrialized countries.

When you have approximately 190 million Americans (roughly 64% of the current 290+ million U.S. population) taking at least one drug, imagine how many trips to the drugstore, bottles, and refills this involves. Then realize that many people take more than one drug; the older we get, the more prescriptions we tend to take. It's not unusual today to see someone over age 60 taking five or more different drugs each day.

This hit home for me last year when I went from a lifetime of almost never taking any medications to regularly needing three or more on a daily basis, two of which I may need to take for the rest of my time on this planet. It also bothered me a bit because having worked in a hospital, I knew that medication errors happen just like mistakes happen anywhere else. Like a small percentage of Americans, I've already been on the receiving end of a drug error that could have been a disaster or a tragedy.

Next time you go into your local pharmacy, notice how extremely busy the folks behind the prescription counter are. I live in a rural area and the closest pharmacy, while small in comparison to some, is always one of the most active places around. Three or four pharmacists move deftly about filling orders and making follow-up calls to confirm drug orders while a half dozen clerks rush back and forth and field incoming calls. For all that busyness, however, I've never found one single problem with any of the dozens of orders they've filled and refilled for me.

Computers have helped pharmacists—and by extension, us—a great deal because special software now checks for drug interactions and other concerns that medical professionals once had to identify all by themselves. Where once we had to depend on our local pharmacist to keep track of all the information about us (my allergy to this, your bad reaction to that) in his or her head, software can now track this in a way that helps even pharmacists we've never met before give us medication that should treat or cure us without causing a nasty interaction with something else we take.

But consider for a moment the level of accuracy that is required, added to the sometimes thousands of pills a single pharmacist may handle in a single hectic workday. Most of us are very pleased when we can get through a workday without making too many blunders. Efficiency experts tell us that a very good workplace still produces mistakes in about five percent in everything we do. Yet most of us don't have someone's health at stake when we make an error.

What You Need to Check

To protect yourself and those you may care for, there are some smart steps you should take whenever you receive a new prescription or a refill. Although it sounds like a lot of detail work, it usually doesn't take too long, especially once you are familiar with the process you need to follow. Remember that this information applies equally well to real-time pharmacy orders as it does to online orders.

Once you get your medication, follow these steps:

1. Check the package before you open it. If it's a delivery, check to be sure it's from the pharmacy you ordered from and that it is indeed addressed to you. Mistakes happen with deliveries, too.

2. If you have a digital camera handy, you might want to take a picture of the package contents, especially if it looks like it's been previously opened.

3. Check the label using the information you'll read in this chapter. Look to be sure your name is listed, and read the usage instructions.

4. If the medication is in pill or capsule form, open the container and count to make certain you received the correct amount. If it's incorrect, you may want to contact the pharmacy immediately.

5. If you've taken the medication before, look to be sure the appearance of the pills or capsules is the same. If it isn't, use the tools in this chapter to try to locate information about the drug online so you can verify it's the right drug. If you can't verify the drug immediately, you may not want to take it until you can. Contact your doctor or pharmacy.

6. If the medication appears to be heat damaged, broken, or the container has a high concentration of dust of the same color as the pills, you should contact the pharmacy immediately.

7. Read the documentation that accompanies the medication, if any. Use the resources in this chapter to find information about possible side effects and interactions with other drugs, and to check dosage amounts.

The following sections take a closer look at some of these steps, starting with the all-important drug label.

Look at the Label

Once you receive your prescription, you want to look very closely at the label before you ever open the container. But have you ever closely examined a drug label before? An amazing amount of information is stored there.

Figure 10.1 shows a prescription drug label.

Figure 10.1
A prescription drug
label with all its detail.

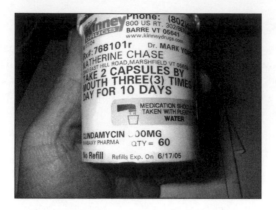

Medicine labels usually include the following details:

▶ Name, address, and phone number of the pharmacy that filled your order

▶ Name or initials of the pharmacist who processed the order

▶ Name of the doctor who prescribed it

▶ Date the prescription was filled

▶ Your name (and often your address)

▶ Directions for use

▶ Name of the specific drug (this frequently includes the manufacturer, too) and unit size (for example, 10 oz or 50MG)

▶ Quantity of medicine

▶ Refill information (may include the date it was first filled along with number of refills remaining and any refill expiration date)

▶ Recommendation or caution stickers such as "Take this with meals," "May cause drowsiness," "May cause dizziness," or "Do NOT drink alcoholic beverages when taking this medication"; these labels may vary by region or chain store used and may be quite conservative in nature

▶ When a drug is a controlled medication, a sticker should be attached stating that the drug is dangerous unless taken as directed and that federal law prohibits the transfer of this drug to anyone else.

Label details are usually quite exact, and information found there typically appears just as it's stored in the pharmacy's database. It's how the information will be reported to your insurance company, how it will appear to anyone else at the pharmacy checking your record, and where appropriate, to any state or federal agencies that may track certain types of prescriptions. That last part sounds ominous but in truth, it's not like every federal agency gets a printout of exactly what you buy each time you fill a prescription. Some agencies track the overall number of orders sold for certain types of pills, such as narcotic pain medication.

If you spot a mistake on the label, you should report it immediately to the pharmacy, even if your order is otherwise accurate (meaning that you have the right medication in the correct number and dosage). Even seemingly inconsequential issues can come back to haunt you later.

For example, perhaps your name is spelled wrong on the label or it has your maiden name if you're now married. That may not seem like a big deal, but it's always possible that the pharmacy has managed to create two records for you: one with your correct name and one with a typo or former name. Having the name wrong could affect whether the drug is properly paid for through your health insurance and can also create confusion later on when you try to refill the medication or transfer it.

UNDERSTANDING YOUR LABEL

While certain information is required by law (both federal and state) to appear on a medication label, how those details get presented can vary widely between different pharmacies and different geographical areas.

If you have trouble understanding what everything on a specific label means, one great resource to check—besides asking the pharmacist—is the pharmacy's Web site. Many drugstores and drug chains offer a guide to the contents of the labels they use, which can be found in either printed material available at the pharmacy itself (ask for it) or by visiting the store or chain's Web site.

Figure 10.2 shows a refill page for my local drugstore, which is part of the Kinney Drugs chain, that shows important information on the label that I'll need to note when I call in or order a refill online. If I move to other parts of Kinney's Web site, I can find additional details. If you still have questions after checking the Web site, call the pharmacy and ask. If the clerk can't help, ask to speak to a pharmacist or the manager. A good pharmacy encourages questions and tries to help you get the best answers, another point that differentiates them from some drug dispensaries online.

Figure 10.2
Identifying parts of your drug label.

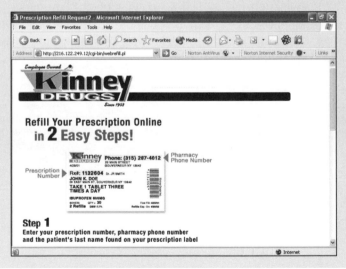

Expiration Date

Beginning in the late 1970s, manufacturers of products ranging from food and medicine to personal hygiene and car batteries began to provide expiration dates. Over the years, more products have been added to the list of those requiring expiration dates. Even your bottle of soda today bears an expiration date.

With prescription drugs, the expiration date is always printed on the medication a pharmacy receives from its supplier, along with specifics about the batch in which it was manufactured by a particular factory. If you buy medication in bulk or get it from a doctor as a sample, you should be able to locate the manufacturing as well as the expiration date on the package. Often, this does not appear on a standard prescription label. But some pharmacies go the extra distance to provide you with the expiration date as well so you have some idea of when you should toss any leftovers. Others don't.

If your bottle doesn't have the expiration date of the drug itself listed, you can usually check this online and then use the date the prescription was (re)filled as your reference date.

Don't confuse the refill expiration date—the day on which you can no longer obtain refills for that drug so a new prescription order is needed—with the actual expiration date for the medication itself. The two dates could differ by years. Your doctor may write a prescription for a particular medication that you can refill for up to a year before you have to get a new prescription order. But the actual expiration date of the drug itself may be up to three, four, or more years from the time it was manufactured.

A consumer study done several years ago tells us that medicine cabinets across America are chock-full of truly ancient drugs. That's bad news for a few reasons. First, the more drugs you have lying around (even when stored in a medicine cabinet) can increase the risk that children may be able to get to them. But more important, these drugs can lose their potency as they pass their expiration date. Some, if stored incorrectly, could lose their effectiveness even sooner.

Try not to think of the expiration date as a guideline you can safely ignore as you might that quart of milk that usually lasts a few days past its last sale date. The aforementioned loss of potency is a big issue; you don't want to negate the possible effects of drug therapy by relying on outdated drugs. But in rare cases, you might experience a reaction to the way a particular drug has broken down with time.

TIP

Make it a policy to clean your medicine cabinet(s) of expired or "won't be used" drugs on a regular basis. Extend this to over-the-counter medications, which often have an expiration date stamped either on the package (as shown in Figure 10.3), the bottle, the cap, or the blister pack. If you have kids or anyone else around who you suspect might go after a cache of pills dumped in the wastebasket, you can always flush them down the toilet or dissolve them in water first.

Figure 10.3
Look for the expiration date on over-the-counter medicine, too.

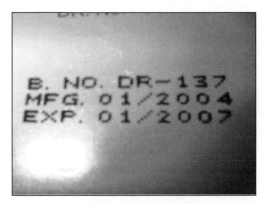

STORE THEM WISELY

Obviously, medical compounds of any type, from vitamins to antacids to prescription drugs, should be treated as potentially toxic material and kept safely out of the reach of children. Like the old joke goes, the child-protective caps on many products seem to be best opened by kids with nimble fingers.

But don't stop there in your efforts to store your medications wisely. A few commonsense measures can help you prevent problems and keep your drugs viable.

First, there's a good reason why most medications are packaged for you in an amber bottle. This coloration helps reduce the amount of direct light that can reach the contents of the package. Too much exposure to direct light can make some medical compounds break down faster.

But despite the amber bottle (and some pharmacies today use clear plastic), it's still smart to store your medications—plus vitamins and other non-prescription supplements—away from sun-drenched windowsills, tables, or desktops. Heat is an issue, too, so avoid storing meds in a car or other spot that can really warm up because liquid formulas can turn quickly and some capsules will dissolve, leaving just powder or tiny pellets.

Wherever possible, don't transfer a drug from its original container. If you do, try to transfer the prescription label with it. Whatever you do, don't mix two or more medications together in a container.

Documentation

Depending on how you receive your prescription drugs, you may receive documentation along with it spelling out the chemical composition of the drug, both common and unusual side effects, what foods or drugs you should avoid or consult your doctor before using in conjunction with this prescription, and other important details, such as what to do in the event of an accidental overdose.

If you receive a sample from your doctor or buy medication in bulk (where the pharmacy may literally just stick its own label on a manufacturer's bottle), this often comes in the form of a piece of paper or booklet called the drug package insert. Some pharmacies also issue their own documentation that they'll usually include in your prescription package along with your medication (see Figure 10.4 for an example).

Figure 10.4
An example of a pharmacy's own documentation sheet for a particular drug.

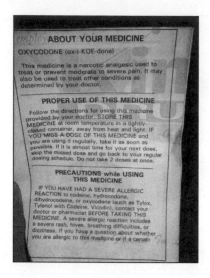

If you want more information about a drug you receive, you can use many of the resources discussed in this chapter, along with a service provided by a site called Drug Information Network that lets you look up patient drug medication package inserts (see Figure 10.5). To look through these, visit **http://www.druginfonet.com/index.php?pageID=patient.htm**. You can also click on its Manufacturers Information link to get names, addresses, and contact details for all major drug companies, organized alphabetically (see Figure 10.6).

With access to the Internet, you also have many more options for checking information from a wide range of different sources (some even in plain English so you can understand them without a medical or chemistry degree).

The Drug Information Network is just one resource for researching your medications. Other strong choices include (but are by no means limited to) the following:

Figure 10.5
Use Web sites to look up patient information on the drugs you take.

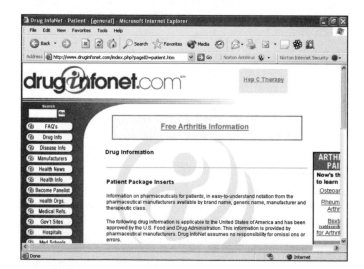

Figure 10.6
Look up an address to contact a drug manufacturer.

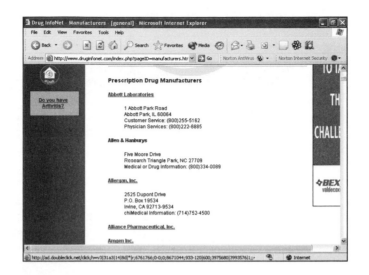

► Drugs.com

► RxList.com

► WebMD.com

You will get a better look at these other sites as we go through this chapter because many let you check everything from normal dose ranges to side effects to potential drug interactions. Also, a drug manufacturer's Web site or your pharmacy's Web site may offer important details and drug checking tools that you can use even before you fill your order. Figure 10.7 shows the Drug Advisor Tool on the Eckerd pharmacy chain Web site at **www.eckerd.com**, and Figure 10.8 displays information from the Eli Lilly (drug manufacturer) Web site about programs to help patients obtain drugs they can't afford.

Figure 10.7
Eckerd's Drug Advisor Tool helps you research your medications.

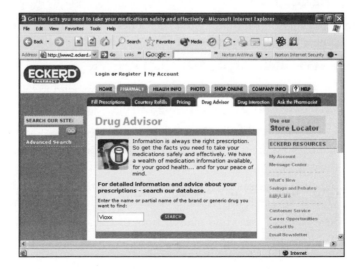

Figure 10.8
Drug manufacturer sites also offer information both on drugs and drug programs for low-income people or senior citizens.

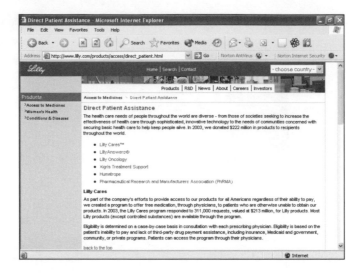

NOTE

Drug manufacturer sites often provide information about and links to special programs they offer to help those on limited incomes get drugs, like those mentioned in Chapter 1. Some sites also provide links to research studies for new medicines being developed.

Dosage Level

Your prescription should spell out exactly how much of the medication you are supposed to take in a single dose at usually specified intervals. Yet it doesn't hurt to double-check the dosage information, not only that contained on the medicine bottle or accompanying documentation, but also through another source.

Remember the sites I mentioned in the previous section on checking your drug documentation? Many of those same sites allow you to look up dosage details as well.

Follow these steps to try this using the RxList.com Web site:

1. Open your Web browser (be sure you're connected to the Internet).
2. Go to **www.rxlist.com** (see Figure 10.9).
3. Click Advanced Search.
4. Type in the name of the drug (brand name or generic) you want to check. Click Search.
5. When your drug search results come up in the browser, locate the listing for your exact medication and click the link listed for it as shown in Figure 10.10.
6. Review the dosage information from the page that opens once you click the link in Step 5 (see Figure 10.11).

Figure 10.9
RxList.com is one of several Web-based information resource sites to help you check drugs.

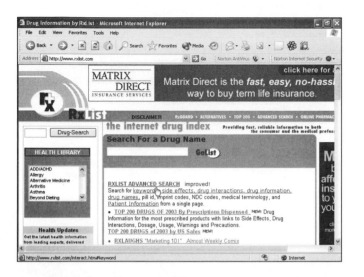

Figure 10.10
Find your exact drug from the listed results.

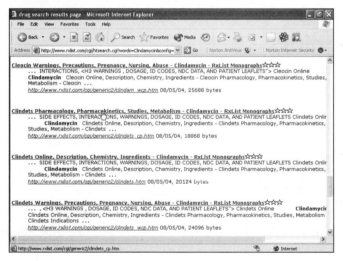

Don't close your browser window yet. You'll want it open to the same page for the next section, "Knowing the Possible Side Effects, Precautions, and Warnings."

If you find slightly different information listed under the dosage recommendations found on these drug resource Web sites, don't decide to change your dosage without talking to the doctor who prescribed this for you. If the dose is significantly different, contact the prescribing doctor immediately before you take the first dose just to rule out a mistake. As you now know, doctors often base their prescription order on a number of factors, including your weight, your specific symptoms and/or lab test results, your overall health, and even your diet (since someone eating a very small amount of food could be impacted more by a higher dosage of some types of drugs than someone who eats robustly).

Figure 10.11
Dosage information for
the drug Clindamycin
made by Ranbazy
Pharmaceuticals.

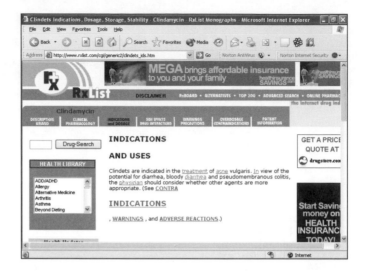

Knowing the Possible Side Effects, Precautions, and Warnings

Have you ever listened to those prescription drug ads that run on TV and radio during the dinner hour? They always show people having a great time—smiling, affectionate, warm, active, showing a lust for life—and those aren't just the erectile dysfunction drug ads either.

Yet sometime after you've gotten lost in the sheer bliss these folks are experiencing, comes a rapid list of nasty potential side effects, such as your hair will fall out, your teeth will turn green, and you may start inexplicably doing cartwheels in the middle of your office during a financial audit. Okay, not quite that strange, but some of the direness of the side effects listed—if you pay attention—can almost make you forget why you thought you wanted the drug in the first place.

But all kidding aside, almost any drug has the potential for producing unwanted symptoms or results in some small percentage of the people who take it. Small, hopefully, because these drugs get tested before they go to market. A full 999 people might take a standard dose of decongestant and get just the results they would expect: better breathing once you clear your head. Yet for every 1,000 people, one person reports feeling mild to moderate nausea.

The term "side effects" tends to be treated like a catch basket for any type of non-standard symptom experienced after taking a drug. But what's in the basket tends to divide out between what may be a real problem rooted in the drug itself and other factors, such as effects caused not so much by one drug, but the interaction of multiple drugs or compounds in your system at any given time. This is known as drug interaction.

Beyond what's in the drug itself, our bodies and our state of health play a big role in how we're able to process the drugs we take. So if we're extremely run down, malnourished or dehydrated (since many of us stop consuming enough nutrition and fluids when we begin to feel ill), anemic, or have very little fat storage in our bodies, we may be far more sensitive to the chemicals contained within a drug than we would when we're operating normally.

Ever take an antihistamine when you're really overtaxed by allergy symptoms and have it hit you far more strongly (you feel sleepy or spacey) than it has before? That's the same basic principle.

Finally, not all side effects are minor annoyances. Some can impair your ability to work or to drive, whether you can breastfeed a child or should avoid becoming pregnant, and whether you can eat a normal diet. Although many symptoms of drug side effects will diminish over the period of time you're taking the drug as your body learns better how to process it, you do infrequently see the results of side effects cause problems that last well beyond the point you stop taking the drug. This is partially because some medication stays stored in parts of the body such as fat cells or the liver for a period of time, whereas others flush out of your system very rapidly. Even less frequently, permanent changes can occur that may be the result of actual damage. How your body tends to process drugs through your kidneys and/or liver, what other medications you may be taking, and a number of other factors also come into play in terms of what side effects—if any—you may experience.

TIP

If you become concerned after reading a list of possible side effects for a drug you are taking, talk with your doctor. Medical professionals may be able to help you reduce your risk of experiencing side effects, such as by suggesting you avoid certain foods or always take your medicine with meals.

CAUTION

The degree of side effects—if any—you experience can be exaggerated if you fluctuate your dosages. This is especially true if you always take the maximum dosage (or more) or you take your medication more frequently than is recommended.

THE WHY OF DRUG SIDE EFFECTS

People sometimes ask why any drugs are allowed to get into the marketplace for use if they cause side effects in even just a tiny number of the people who take them. But consider the alternative.

If a drug company tested every new drug endlessly for many years before it was approved by the FDA and sent to drugstores and hospitals, we would probably pay far more for our drugs than we do now. We would also likely see drug manufacturers less interested in new drug development. Without drug research and development, patients with today's untreatable or incurable conditions and illnesses can't hope for help tomorrow.

There's also the reality of a situation where some drugs, just in the way they need to act within the human body, are treated by our bodies as a toxin. Some cancer specialists will tell you that chemotherapy is "scheduled poisoning," where the objective is to give just enough of the poison to kill the tumor but not enough to kill the patient. But if you're a cancer patient faced with the possibility of hair loss, anemia, and nausea, you may be very willing to assume these possible effects to kill the tumor or at least get it under control.

Locating the Side Effects for Your Drugs

Some medication, especially that provided in its original manufacturer's packaging, usually has printed material with it that spells out the possible side effects of the drug along with additional advice about what foods or other medications you may want to avoid while using the drug. But you won't normally see this information on a prescription bottle itself.

This information should be contained in the documentation discussed earlier in this chapter. Go back to glance at Figure 10.5 to again see an example of a page listing possible interactions and side effects provided by the pharmacy.

There are additional ways you can learn about the type of symptoms to watch for whenever you take a new drug for the first time. Don't be afraid to ask your doctor, who can offer a perspective from his or her experience in prescribing this medication for others. Bricks-and-mortar pharmacists also are good resources to ask, and online drugstores frequently offer information pages on each of the drugs they sell that spell out side effects and warnings.

You can use the same sources already discussed for checking a drug's identity and dosage to look up the side effect potential. This is also true for drug interactions covered in Chapter 3.

Let's see how to do this with the RxList site. If you kept the page open from the steps listed in the previous section, look at the window displaying the information about dosage. Notice that Dosage is one of the major categories available near the top of the page (refer to Figure 10.11). Click the Side Effects Drug Interactions Category title and you see a page like that shown in Figure 10.12 that displays the side effects reported for this drug. Now click the Warnings Precautions Category title and you see any notes of concern listed, as shown in Figure 10.13.

Figure 10.12
Side effects reported for a particular drug.

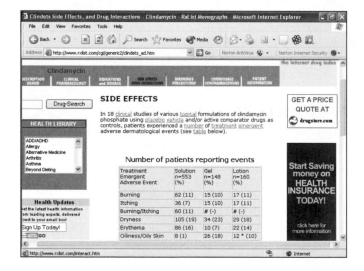

Figure 10.13
Read through the
warnings, interactions,
and precautions for
each drug you take.

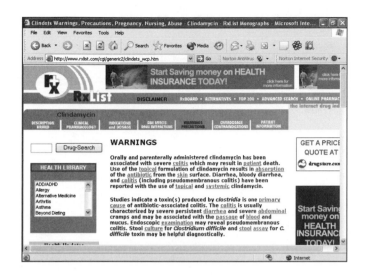

However, if you want to start a new search, follow these steps:

1. Open your Web browser and type in **http://www.rxlist.com**.

2. From the RxList site, click Advanced Search.

3. In the search window at the top of the page, type in the name of the drug you want to check (see Figure 10.14). Click Search.

4. From the results page, look for the best listing for the drug you're trying to research. For this search, I used Protonix, a drug used to treat acid reflux disease. Under the Side Effects/Interaction column, click the link provided (usually CheckRX) as shown in Figure 10.15.

5. You may then see a page listing topics that match the drug you're looking for. Click the listing that best matches what you're looking for (such as Warnings or Side Effects).

6. A final page opens with your results as shown in Figure 10.16, where you can see what the commonly reported adverse reactions are along with other details.

Now let's briefly look at another side effect/interaction checking tool, this one located at Drugs.com. Its Drug Interaction Checker allows you to search for and add both prescribed drugs and over-the-counter medications to a drug list (see Figure 10.17), and then get information about the ways in which this combination of drugs may interact with one another.

To use this tool, go to **www.drugs.com** and click the link marked Drug Interaction Checker. Instructions there show you exactly how to find and add each of the drugs you take to a master list and then how to run the check for interactions between them.

Figure 10.14
Use RxList.com's
Advanced search
feature to check a drug's
details.

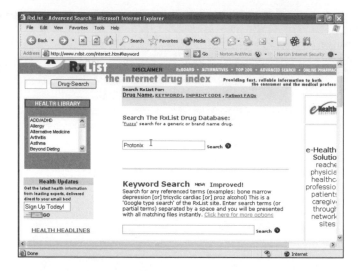

Figure 10.15
Click under Side
Effects/Interactions to
search for listings that
match your drug.

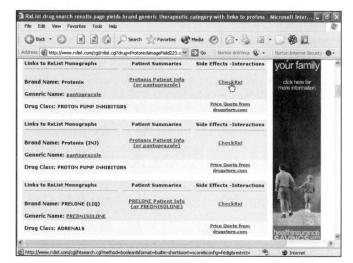

Checking What Your Drug Looks Like Against Drug Reference Sites

If you're getting a prescription for the first time or if you're trying a generic version instead of a name brand, you may have no idea what the drug is supposed to look like. This makes it awfully tough to know for sure that you got the correct drug before you take the first dose.

Even though some online pharmacies may show a picture of a pill or capsule next to many of the drugs on their site, I've noticed they aren't always good about using a photograph of the right pill or capsule. So you might buy something that on the Web site looks like a medium-sized, round white tablet only to receive a bottle of clear capsules containing multi-colored beads. Should you take them on faith?

Statistically, the odds are with you that it's indeed the right medication. But let me show you how to check for yourself to be certain.

Figure 10.16
A page opens showing the most commonly reported side effects (usually listed for both the drug in question as well as a placebo used as a control).

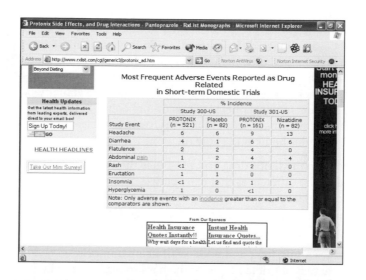

Figure 10.17
Drugs.com's Drug Interaction Checker lets you create and check your unique combination of medications for possible problems.

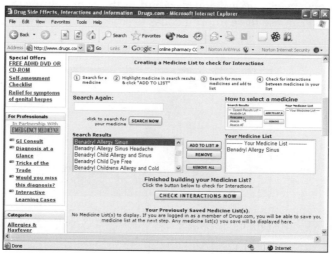

If you're at a standard pharmacy, I recommend you check your package before you ever leave the store. That doesn't mean you have to plunk yourself down next to the counter and begin inspecting and counting each one, but at least eyeball the contents and ask questions if something doesn't look quite right based on what you were expecting. When shopping online, you can't really do that until the order is delivered.

Once you get your medication to your home or office, you can use the Internet in various ways to verify that a drug is what you believe it should be. You can access the aforementioned *Physician's Desk Reference* online through **www.drugs.com** (more about this shortly). Other sources such as RxList.com and WebMD.com have tools to help you identify your pills. If you happen to have access to a recent edition of the PDR (hospitals, doctors' offices, pharmacies, and libraries usually have them), you can look up the drug there by name and then check the appearance through the images in the book.

Drugs: Using Appearance and Imprint Codes as Identifiers

You've no doubt seen enough different medication in your lifetime to realize not everything is a plump round tablet. In fact, drug manufacturers have strategically produced drugs with very unique colors and shapes both to grab your eye and help uniquely identify their product from others. Some of these are so elaborate and cool that there are actually people who collect samples much as others might collect stamps or rare coins. A former colleague's father, for example, taught in a pharmacy school for many years and has a rather extensive collection of fancy pills and capsules he likes to show off.

When you need to verify that a drug you receive is the drug you ordered, one tool to help you do this is found in the differences that exist between one pill and another—its size, shape, color, logo (the sometimes fancy graphic drug manufacturers may add to a pill), and its drug imprint code (the way many drugs are marked with letters and/or numbers to identify the manufacturer and the pill type).

Figure 10.18 shows a pill, front and back, with its own imprinted code (one side, DAN, the other side, 5513). The actual imprinted type can be hard to read even when you're eyeballing it closely, so you may need a magnifying glass and/or the right lighting to distinguish what is printed there. You can use these imprint codes to search for identifying information about the drug.

Figure 10.18
A pill with imprint codes on both sides.

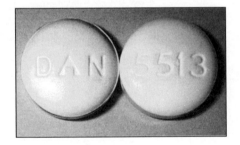

Using the Pill Identification Wizard

While many of the Web resources discussed in this chapter allow you to verify your drugs in one way or another, Drugs.com's Pill Identification Wizard can make the task easier by stepping you through the entire process while you're looking at the pill you want to identify.

Before I show you this wizard, let me note that you can also use the search tool on the Drugs.com page shown in Figure 10.19 to search for a drug by name and then drill down to a description of what that medication should look like. You may want to use this method when you have a pretty good idea of what the drug should be, but fall back on the full Pill Identification Wizard when you're simply not sure.

To use the full-blown wizard, have your pill or capsule handy and then follow these steps:

1. Open your Web browser and go to **http://www.drugs.com/pill_identification_drug_picture.html**, which opens the page you see in Figure 10.19.

2. Click the blue underlined link labeled "pill identifier" or click the Pill Identification tab.

3. When the wizard opens, read the user agreement and click I Agree.

4. From the next page that opens (see Figure 10.20), read and perform the steps listed there for identifying a pill. You can try one of three different ways to search:

    ▶ Select a drug form and shape and click Next.

    ▶ Type the drug imprint code into the box labeled Text Imprint and click Search Now.

    ▶ Type in the name of the drug, if you know it, and click Search Now.

5. Follow directions through until you're able to identify the drug.

Figure 10.19
Use the entry page for the Pill Identification Wizard to search by drug name or manufacturer.

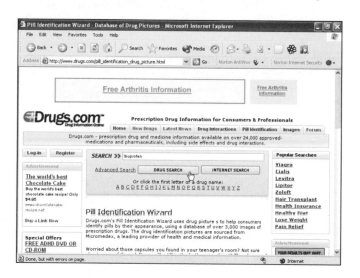

Figure 10.20
Your drug search
lookup options for
identification.

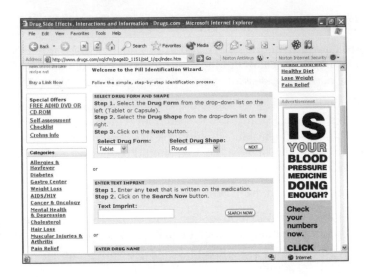

Let's go through a practice session, starting with one of the pills with an imprint code I showed you back in Figure 10.18:

1. Open the Pill Identification Wizard.

2. Go to the section marked Enter Text Imprint. In the Text Imprint box, type in the imprint for the two pills DAN 5513 (see Figure 10.21). Click Search Now.

3. Your search results appear in the next browser window displayed. But if you look at Figure 10.22, you'll see we struck out. So notice the suggestion on this page to try the search again, but only use part of the imprinted text.

4. Click the link to Re-start the Pill Identification Wizard and repeat Step 2, but type either **DAN** or **5513** and then click Search Now.

5. The Search results window opens telling us again no luck (and no, I'm not sending you on a wild goose chase; I want you to see how you may have to try different methods to locate what you need). Click again on the Re-Start Pill Identification Wizard link.

6. This time, we'll try a different method. When I ordered this pill as part of a test order, I requested Carisoprodol, the generic form of Soma, a muscle relaxant. So we'll try searching under the drug name. Click in the dialog box below Drug Name and type **Carisoprodol** as shown in Figure 10.23. Click Search Now.

7. When the search results page opens, scan down through the list of drugs and their images. Bingo! The last row of pills (front and back of the same pill) shows an exact match for the drug (see Figure 10.24). We've identified it. Mystery solved.

Figure 10.21
Type in the drug import code found on the drug you want to verify.

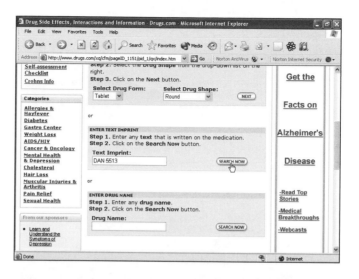

Figure 10.22
When your search results draw a blank, check the tips or recommendations offered and try again by refining or expanding your search.

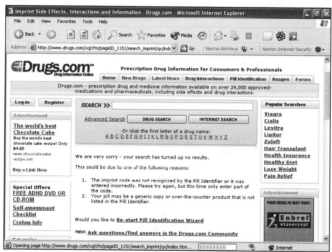

What happens if you find a very close but not a fully exact match? This really depends on what is different about the drug you find through the search and the one you're staring at in your hand. Tiny variations can be expected, particularly if different batches of pills are manufactured in different plants using a slightly different color or manufacturing process. Other small changes can result just through poor packaging and rough treatment during shipping. Even a small issue like differences in lighting can affect the overall perception of color.

If you're concerned, immediately contact the pharmacy where you ordered the drug to report your findings. It's wise to do this before you take any. The pharmacy may be able to fully explain the difference to your satisfaction so you can go ahead and take them.

The possibility also exists that what you have is a counterfeit. Let's explore this next.

Figure 10.23
Type in the name of the drug that you ordered and click Search Now.

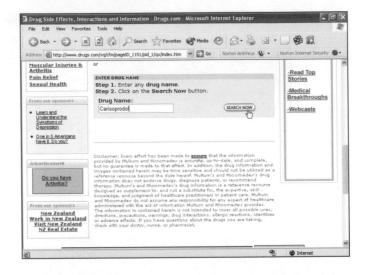

Figure 10.24
Scan the list and images of the pills shown; here we have an exact match.

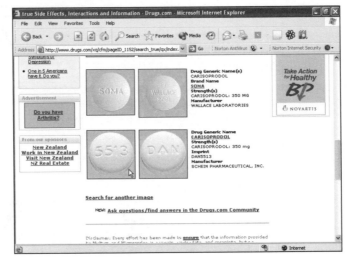

NOTE

Don't be discouraged if you can't verify your drug on the first pass. In verifying the drugs received from my test orders, I sometimes had to try two or three different resources to find exactly what I got. If you can't find what you need through Drugs.com, try RxList, WebMD, or one of the others.

Is It a Counterfeit Drug?

Just as not all illegal drug dealers work from a dimly lit corner or in a park full of bored teenagers, not all prescription drugs are exactly what the labels say they are.

The problem of counterfeit drugs started a very long time before the Internet ever came into being. Almost as long as people who sold medical preparations realized there was money to be made doing it, we've had people who came up with some kind of knock-off version they could pass off as the real deal. Once upon a time, that was an herbal elixir; today it's Viagra, Xanax, and Phentermine.

But with many Americans taking three or more prescription drugs and frequently encouraged by ads to ask their doctors for new ones, demand for prescription drugs is on the rise. Attracted by the lucrative profits available even among drugs that only *look* legitimate, it's estimated that the counterfeit drug trade may be operating at record high levels. It's hard to say that, however, because we can only count the fakes we catch.

Counterfeits show up virtually anywhere you would find their legitimate counterparts and many others besides. For example, in 2000 and 2001, the FDA joined state and local law enforcement agencies in California and elsewhere to put a dent in the sales of fake Viagra tablets sold at flea markets, along with imported foreign drugs that are not allowed under U.S. law. But for all the raids and arrests, you can still find both counterfeit and illegally obtained real products sold openly at flea markets and other large public venues where people may sell out of boxes or the back of a car.

Before you think, "Hey, that's OK. I wouldn't buy drugs from someone's car trunk," this fact doesn't mean you're immune. Counterfeit drugs are winding up in the inventory of legitimate pharmacies and hospitals everywhere. Although most pharmacies work hard to be sure their supply comes from a trusted source, more and more are seeing these less-than-fabulous fakes; others aren't finding them until after they start unwittingly passing them along to customers.

We're also no doubt seeing more trade in counterfeits among some online drugstores, including very legitimate pharmacies that just happen to receive a shipment of counterfeit drugs. But not all of this may be accidental. If a site is already breaking U.S. laws by supplying drugs outside of an FDA-approved manner, it's also within the range of possibility some percentage of them may try to improve profits by using lower-cost counterfeits. Also, U.S. laws rarely apply outside our jurisdiction and many of the drugs seen in test orders appear to have been manufactured or distributed through a foreign source.

Not All Counterfeits Are Created Equally

The term "counterfeit drug" is actually sort of a catch basket for any pill not manufactured by the company of record or as a recognized type of generic drug. But the category can include everything from pills that are little more than sugar, starch, and artificial coloring to formulas that are "budget" versions or "recipe variations" on a particular drug manufacturer's patent that may be somewhat to very similar to the drug they mimic.

The problems occur with the differences. Some counterfeits may contain a very different dosage amount for the primary ingredient; a dose that may be either higher or lower than that offered by the real drug. Others may contain secondary or filler ingredients that are harmful. Yet others may be contaminated: there was recently a case where a Mexican factory was shut down many months after it began to turn out counterfeit drugs manufactured with ingredients tainted both by mouse and rat droppings as well as by unclean water used in the production process. In cases like this, you might get sick and have no idea what is causing it.

Obviously, you're in trouble if you really need the proper medication and all you have is a fake. Spotting that fake before you ingest it can be tough.

Think about it. Take Viagra, a well-known and popular drug you always hear described as "the little blue pill." But do you have any idea what shape a Viagra pill comes in or how the logo on the pill should appear? If not, how would you identify that the little blue pills you ordered off the Internet are indeed Viagra and not a rip-off?

In one of the counterfeit drug busts that has been televised, the resources needed to turn out a fake that can pass as the real drug among non-professionals were pretty low-tech. The alleged counterfeit salespeople ordered blank blue pills of the rough size and shape of Viagra tablets from a Mexican manufacturer. Then they used a simple hand stamp to imprint their version of the Viagra logo onto the pills before they sold them as the real deal for perhaps as much as $3–$10 per pill.

The FDA's Plan to Combat Counterfeits

To deal with the increasing problem of counterfeit drugs, the FDA has announced a new initiative designed to help track particular drugs from the moment they're produced by a manufacturer until they end up in your medicine cabinet. The goal is to try to identify fakes that are introduced into the system somewhere in between the factory and your home.

Unfortunately for you, part of the reporting system the government will depend upon for reporting fakes is you and your ability to identify a good pill from a knock-off version. This new FDA initiative asks both pharmacists and consumers to watch for and promptly report the following things:

> ► Unexplained differences in pill size or shape from previous batches
> ► Pills that may seem more powdery, chipped, or of a varying color from what you usually see
> ► A different taste when taking the medication
> ► A change in effectiveness of the drug

The problem is that a very busy pharmacist who knows what many of these drugs should look like might not always spot a fake. Some of the variations with counterfeits are so slight that they could easily escape even a trained eye.

Passing the responsibility along to the consumer to catch those counterfeits seems both kind of late in the process and unreliable. We often don't faithfully remember the exact shape and color of pills we take each and every day. Unless we have leftover drugs from a previous batch to use as a comparison, we might not notice anything is up until after we suspect that we're not getting the same effects from the drug. With some drugs, that could take days or weeks to determine.

TIP

To report a possible counterfeit, you can contact both the pharmacy that prepared your order as well as use contact links found on the FDA's Web site at **www.fda.gov**. You should also set the pills aside for safekeeping (I would not suggest taking them until you can be sure they aren't fakes).

With a life-saving drug such as one to try to stop a heart attack or end an asthma attack, you could realize the difference a lot faster but with much more risk.

About Foreign Version Substitutions

You may also find that when ordering a particular medication, what you receive may actually be a foreign version of that drug.

How do you tell? Well, if the package instructions are all or mostly in a non-English language or the package is stamped from a foreign country, you have a strong clue.

Another clue is when you can't find the drug you received listed in any of the U.S. product drug references. Here's an example: Say you order a specific antibiotic over the Internet. When you get your order and check it, you find red gelatin capsules. You go to one of the drug lookup references cited in this chapter, search on the name of the drug you ordered, and discover that you can't locate any variety of this medicine that appears as a red gelatin capsule.

How do you proceed? The first thing to do is to look closer at the capsule. Does it contain any printing on it that might tell you what it is? Check the documentation, too. Hypothetically, let's say the capsule has one stamp that reads "KAL" and another that reads "1164." You check your drug references again and still can't find anything based on that imprint code.

So try this:

1. Open your Web browser.
2. Go to a major Web search engine such as Google.com, Lycos.com, or Yahoo.com.
3. In the Search window, type **KAL 1164**.
4. Click Search.

From this, you may be able to find some reference somewhere on the globe that identifies this capsule as an antibiotic manufactured in India. Yet you may not be able to find any information

CHECKING ON FOREIGN VERSIONS

In a test order for Xanax (the original, non-generic anti-anxiety drug), I received a generic, Netherlands-manufactured form (alprazolam) instead.

When I went to look up the drug using some of the methods I've provided in this chapter, I couldn't find it. I had to go to a Dutch Web site with a reference to the drug, then translate the site into English to find yet another reference to a site where I could confirm that the pills I got were actually the Dutch generic.

In another test order, I ordered what an online drugstore called OxyContin, a powerful, time-released opiod-based painkiller that is widely abused. When I received the order, the documentation—which was very crudely printed—identified the drug as "South Asian OxyContin" made in Lahore, Pakistan. The other information was entirely (I assume) in Pakistani, a language I can't read.

After a couple of hours of checking, I learned that it was not OxyContin at all but a drug that was mostly acetaminophen (the essential ingredient in Tylenol) combined with a tiny amount of codeine. There is almost no comparison between these two drugs: the codeine-acetaminophen pill would be fine for mild pain, but OxyContin is usually prescribed to those with severe pain. To even begin to get the same analgesic effects as OxyContin, you would need to take so many of the foreign version that you would likely have a toxic reaction to the high dosage of acetaminophen.

that compares this drug with the one you ordered. If this happens, you need to contact the pharmacy immediately. Don't take any of the medication assuming it's a trustworthy substitute because you simply don't have enough information to assume this.

Your Avenue of Recourse if You Don't Get What You Ordered

The very first step you should take (beyond not taking the wrong pills) once you discover that the drug(s) you received is not what you ordered is to contact the pharmacy that handled your order. At the very least, you want them to know. But you also probably want to see what must be done to return this order either for the correct medication or (if you no longer feel as comfortable dealing with this pharmacy) a complete refund so you can get your meds elsewhere.

Whether you call or email, be sure to have identifying information about your order handy, such as the date you placed the order and your order number. While the pharmacy may be able to look up your order just from your name and telephone number, being equipped with these details yourself increases the likelihood that you can get the problem resolved in one phone call. Also have a pen and paper handy so you can take notes. Write down what the person on the line tells you the pharmacy will do to rectify the situation, along with any other details you don't want to have to struggle to remember later in the event the pharmacy doesn't make good on providing an adequate solution.

If the pharmacy tries to tell you that it cannot refund your money or send a corrected order to you, ask to speak to the manager or customer-support supervisor. If you don't get satisfaction, ask for the name and address where you can contact the head of the pharmacy, then follow through with a fax or letter to file a formal complaint.

Should you have reason to suspect that the pharmacy is not operating in good faith, you can report online pharmacies using the link to the FDA reporting tool noted in Chapter 2. If the pharmacy is a member of the VIPPS network, use the VIPPS reporting link also noted in Chapter 2 to report your situation. But if the pharmacy in question is a regular drugstore, you can also report them to your state health department as well as to the state board of pharmacy.

Also, contact your credit card company and identify the transaction and the amount of the purchase to inform them that you consider this charge in dispute, giving them the reasons why. You need to do this as soon as possible after you discover the problem with your order since many credit card companies limit dispute claims to between 60 and 90 days from the time of the charge.

CHAPTER 10

Chapter 11
Getting Refills and Transferring Prescriptions

If you're satisfied with your first experience with an online apothecary, you may be very happy to continue using them. You could even be so convinced, in fact, that you want to move your prescription from your local drugstore to your preferred cyber shop. This is referred to as prescription transfer.

What you see both with refills and prescriptions can make your life a lot easier. But they can also present some complications, particularly when you're working with a pharmacy you don't know well yet.

Read on and you'll see that my experience with test orders shows two key points: that refills and transfers can be iffy with less than fully legitimate cyber pharmacies, and that some of these drug dispensaries aren't very careful about making sure no one is ordering inappropriate amounts. As you can imagine, this makes it even more important to use real vs. fly-by-night online pharmacies.

Yet whether you are trying to make a full move to electronic ordering or plan to continue shopping locally for some of your needed drugs, this chapter offers some helpful information about checking refill details and transferring a prescription from one drugstore to another.

What You Need to Know

Besides the intriguing and not altogether uncontroversial ways the Internet offers people access to drugs and medical information, the Web provides express assistance for easing and even automating the process by which you can get refills and move your prescriptions from one pharmacy to another. Some of these are advantageous even if you're still doing most of your medication shopping in a traditional bricks-and-mortar drugstore.

With both refills and prescription transfers, you can see important differences in how an online pharmacy operating according to state and federal medication laws handles these routine matters versus what some of the non-standard cyber shops do. In fact, before you place your first order anywhere online, you probably want to check first to see what that electronic drugstore says about refills and transfers. If it doesn't say anything, you should wonder why because neither of these is an exotic request. You'll find out more about this issue in the next section.

Also, just as when you're ordering a drug for delivery for the first time, you have to be sure you order your refill with enough time to allow the order to arrive before you exhaust your current supply. This usually means a buffer of no less than four and perhaps as many as seven or more business days before your supply runs out. Some pharmacies allow you to set up automated refills to ship automatically around the same time every few weeks or months; others alert you automatically when it's time to order.

The Legitimate Versus the Not

Once you hit the issue of refills (and transfers, as you'll learn later in this chapter), you see a big dent in the idea that using a "no prescription needed" online drugstore is always easier than going through your regular doctor. That's because many of the pharmacies offering you a drug based on a limited consultation usually just give you a single filling of that medication. You don't get refills, so you have to go all the way through the process again like you're placing a fresh order. This is a problem when you need a medicine you use regularly. You'll likely pay far less long-term going through your regular physician to do this even if that doctor requires follow-up visits.

There are exceptions to this, of course. Several sites, including the one shown in Figure 11.1, offer a 3-month, 6-month, or 12-month refill offer from the time you place your first order. Check each online drugstore's Frequently Asked Questions (FAQs) page to see if it addresses refills (it should).

If you don't see the word "refill" mentioned anywhere on the site, don't be too surprised, especially if you already questioned whether the site is strictly legal. You have to consider that some of the sites selling drugs without a standard prescription aren't necessarily looking for your long-term business because they aren't sure how long they'll be open. A standard pharmacy—online or local—has much more of an incentive to keep prices reasonable to try to ensure your repeat business.

Figure 11.1
Check a pharmacy's
FAQ page for refill
details.

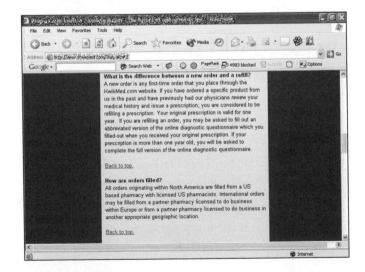

NO SAFEGUARDS

In doing test orders for this book, I saw one critical and potentially life-threatening difference when ordering certain drugs from less than legitimate sites: The safeguards in place to prevent someone from obtaining too many refills of controlled substance drugs aren't always in place.

Here's an example I saw repeated a few separate times. In one of the test orders, I requested a 90-count bottle of Norco, a version of the pain reliever Hydrocodone. Despite not having a prescription for it, the pharmacy supposedly reviewed my record and issued the medication.

But what was of even more concern was that within 2–3 days of placing and receiving that order, I received a refill offer by email from the same pharmacy suggesting it was time to reorder. A few days later, another refill offer came. Now, my prescription dosage—as set forth by whatever doctor approved the prescription—indicated I should take no more than four pills a day, so a 60-count bottle should last at least two weeks. I shouldn't have been offered a refill so soon.

Just to try this out, I decided to see what would happen if I tried to place a refill for it before my existing order should have run out. To my surprise, there was no problem, even though less than a week had passed. I didn't try this more than once, so it's hard to tell whether repeated refill requests would have resulted in the pharmacy deciding I was ordering too much and stopping it. But no legitimate pharmacy comes chasing after you to refill drugs, particularly controlled-access drugs that can be easily abused.

Later in this book, when I discuss kids and pharming and what to watch for when you and people you care for are shopping online, you'll understand how easily this kind of no-checks system can allow people to get access to large volumes of dangerous medication, potentially leading to bigger problems than just a huge pharmacy bill.

BEWARE OF EXTRA REMINDERS

When dealing with a new online pharmacy, watch your email box for refill reminders and then look closely at who sent them.

In test orders, a few of the drugs I bought through various online Web sites generated refill reminder notices to my email within a week of ordering. But of more concern was the fact that I often received these refill notices from pharmacies *other* than the store where I placed my order.

This can happen for a number of reasons, none of them great from a consumer perspective. These not-so-nifty possibilities include:

- ▶ Spyware hidden on my PC is reporting back to some company that I'm looking at online pharmacies, and also that I'm ordering a drug, so competitors learn and send me refill offers (see Chapter 8).
- ▶ The order was placed on an unsecured server or where someone can get access to the information so it can be reported to competitors.
- ▶ The online pharmacy is selling information about orders to other parties, violating any privacy they promised me.
- ▶ The pharmacy is part of a group of drugstores all sharing the same customer information and now I'll be hounded by all of them.

If you run into this when you order, contact the pharmacy where you placed your order and request an explanation. If they can't provide a good one—and after you check your PC for spy- or adware that may be snooping—consider using a different pharmacy with better privacy policies.

Refill Aids

Automation and simplicity is the name of the game when obtaining refills, and pharmacies of all types generally go the extra distance to make it a snap—or a click—to get a fresh order of your medicine. Many pharmacy services, for example, like the one for Eckerd drugstores shown in Figure 11.2, offer you automated reminders when it's time to refill your order to keep you from running out. Some call you; others leave you email. With some very automated programs, the pharmacy can automatically prepare and even ship your refill when it's time without any effort needed on your part.

You can use your Web browser to return to a cyber pharmacy to order your refill directly. But you can also use the Web to reorder a medicine using your local pharmacy's online refill form so that your order can be waiting for you when you next visit the store.

Whatever type of refill you're looking for, always be sure to check your last medicine bottle both to get the prescription number (Rx#) needed to obtain the refill and to be sure the label specifies it can be refilled. If it doesn't, you normally need to at least phone your physician to call in a fresh order; certain drugs may require you pick up a signed prescription and deliver it to the pharmacy either in person, or via fax or mail for online orders.

Some pharmacies are happy to call a physician directly to ask if the prescription can be renewed without any intervening steps by you. But if you need the medication quickly, you'll want to be sure the renewal order is in place rather than take the chance that the pharmacy will simply hold your request until you contact them directly.

Through an Online-Only Pharmacy

When you're dealing with an online-only pharmacy, these can be the easiest refills of all. Remember the account you likely had to set up to place your initial order and then used the user name (or your email address) and password to check your order status? That same information can be used to let you log in and order a refill based on your past order number. Figure 11.3 shows the login screen when selecting refill from a cyber pharmacy named—easily enough—CyberPharmacy.com.

Figure 11.2
Eckerd's automated refill reminder service alerts you and them when it's time to reorder.

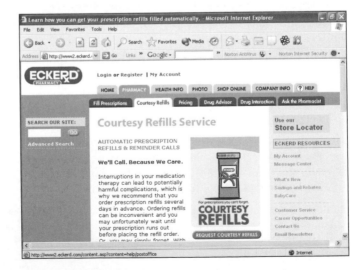

Figure 11.3
Log in using the
account name and/or
email address plus the
password you set up
when you first placed
your online
prescription.

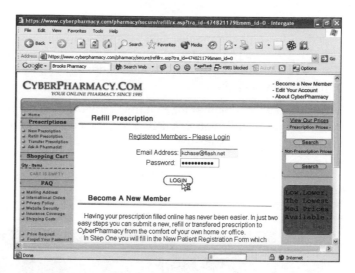

Of course, you'll see some variation between virtual drugstores. One of my favorites allows me to log in using my account name and password, then simply click to check any of the drugs I get through them to immediately begin to process the refill request for delivery. Since credit card details and any applicable insurance gets added to the account information when the account is created, it doesn't need to be provided all over again when it's time to refill.

Other pharmacies may handle this more like traditional pharmacies that use an online refill form (covered in the next section). With these, you probably still need to sign in using your account or email address, then type the prescription number listed on your medicine bottle. If all your previous details were saved to your account information, you usually get the option to choose to use your existing information (including the credit card where order should be billed and your shipping address) or to edit your details to specify a new credit card or different shipping address.

Online Refill Requests for Standard Pickup

Even if you continue to get most of your prescriptions through a regular bricks-and-mortar pharmacy, you'll find that many such pharmacies today offer an online refill service where you provide the prescription number and when you want to pick it up, and then click. This can be faster than calling and waiting on hold with the pharmacy's direct line or by punching in all the buttons when you call a special automated refill request line.

Let's look at how to do this. For this example, lets use Brooks Pharmacy (at **www.brooks-rx.com**), the fourth largest drugstore chain in the country.

1. Go to the pharmacy or pharmacy chain's Web site.
2. Click Pharmacy Services from the main page.
3. Locate and click the Refill option (see Figure 11.4).
4. If needed, click the Refill Request link (different sites may require extra clicks).

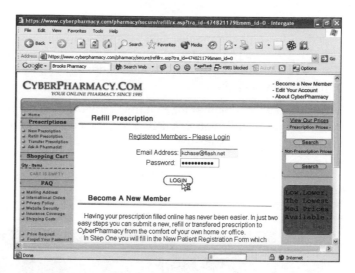

5. Fill in your details as shown in Figure 11.5. This usually includes your name and address, phone number, and your prescription number (listed as Rx#) on the label. You also provide the pharmacy location where you want to pick up the prescription (or specify delivery if they offer that option too). Review your details and click Submit.

To check on the status of a refill request for an online-only order, go back to the site or click the status link provided in your confirmation email to check your account (or click Order Status) from your cyber pharmacy site to view details.

Figure 11.4
Visit the drug store's Web site and choose Pharmacy or Pharmacy Services.

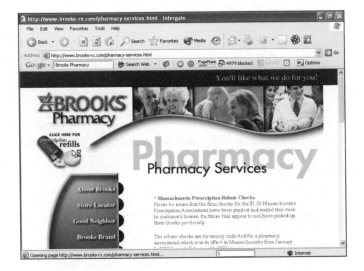

Figure 11.5
Fill in your name, prescription number, and other details, then review before you click Submit.

Look at the Prices Again

Don't assume that the low price you were able to get for a medication the first time you placed your order will be the same when you refill it. Some pharmacies of all types may offer discount incentives with your first order to get you to try them only to enforce a more standard price once you're a customer.

For this, use the price-checking techniques discussed in Chapter 9. If you find a new pharmacy with much better prices, you may be able to transfer your prescription from the original.

Also, let's take a quick look at an additional resource not covered back in Chapter 9, but mentioned briefly in Chapter 7—PharmacyChecker.com—because I found this fast and helpful in analyzing prices from a number of different pharmacies at once. PharmacyChecker also offers a customer rating system for each of the pharmacies that come up when you search on price and availability of a medication. It includes Canadian and other foreign pharmacies in its searches along with prices from U.S. drugstores.

Let me take you through an example where you'll see I'm looking for prices and pharmacies for the popular drug Keflex, an antibiotic.

Follow these steps:

1. Connect to the Internet, open your Web browser, and go to **http://www.pharmacychecker.com**.

2. Click in the dialog box next to Enter product name (as shown in Figure 11.6), type the name of the medication you want to check, and then click Go. Notice that you can also select a drug from a list of common medications or search by a medicine through alphabetical lists.

3. You may see an additional screen asking you whether you want the generic or brand name. Click on your preference.

4. Next, you see a listing sorted by different drug strengths, such as 5 or 10 mg, or 250 or 500 mg. Select your preference and click on the View Prices listing corresponding to that listing (see Figure 11.7).

5. A list then appears like that shown in Figure 11.8 that tells you what pharmacies offer this (and some of these may be a mix of cyber and brick-and-mortar pharmacies), along with the price, extra fees, shipping time, consumer ratings, and even what country the drugstore is located in. Click on your choice to go to that pharmacy and learn more.

Since new consumer resources go online all that time, you may be able to find other good tools like PharmacyChecker.com by the time you read this.

Figure 11.6
Type in the name of the drug you want to check for or select it from an alphabetical list.

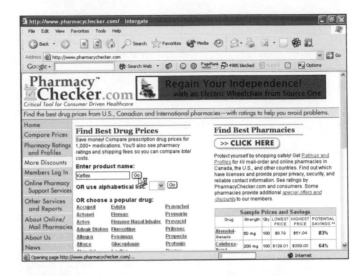

Figure 11.7
Narrow down your choices by selecting a drug strength.

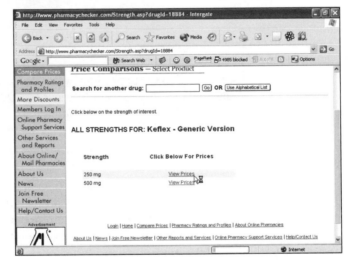

What Can't Be Simply Refilled

State and federal laws come into play with certain drugs that prevent them from being refilled. Each time you need the medication, the doctor must write a fresh prescription just like it's a brand new one.

In fact, when you're dealing with a bricks-and-mortar pharmacy, you may have to physically go into the doctor's office to pick it up and then drive it over to the pharmacy, since specific drugs like serious painkillers can't be ordered over the phone or by fax because the opportunity for abuse can be so high. However, online pharmacies will probably require direct contact with your doctor—where they receive a signed prescription form—and may not accept a slip you send yourself.

Figure 11.8
PharmacyChecker breaks down the details for you; just click on a link to visit that pharmacy.

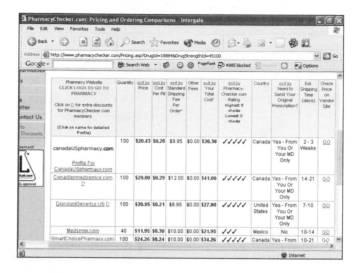

Issues with Easy Automated Refill

One of the big benefits with online pharmacies is that many really try to make it as simple as possible for you to get your medication refills. Use the account name and password you created when you first used the service, and you can order your refill without having to fill out the same information you originally provided. Who wouldn't like saving time and keystrokes?

However, if you're someone who shops carefully for prescriptions based on the best price, using an automated refill service isn't wise unless the pharmacy has an option in place to verify any price increase with you before the order is shipped and billed. These refill services tend to lock you into the current prevailing price until you notice a raise in price and stop the service.

A few chain pharmacies I saw with automated refill services allow you to opt-in (meaning you have to specify you want them to do this) to notify you by phone or email if they have to substitute a different manufacturer's drug or there's a price increase. But not every pharmacy offers this, so you have to check. If you don't mind the extra work, you can simply sign up for an automated refill service, but continue to check for pharmacies with a better price on the drug so that you can stop the refill from one pharmacy and transfer your prescription to another.

The Process of Prescription Transfers

When you want a different pharmacy to take over the processing of your prescriptions from your current pharmacy, you need to request a prescription transfer. Many if not most drugstores require that transfer requests come in writing, although many accept an online form you submit (like the one shown in Figure 11.9) as virtually the same as filling out a physical form and signing it. This is true for both standard and online-only drugstores.

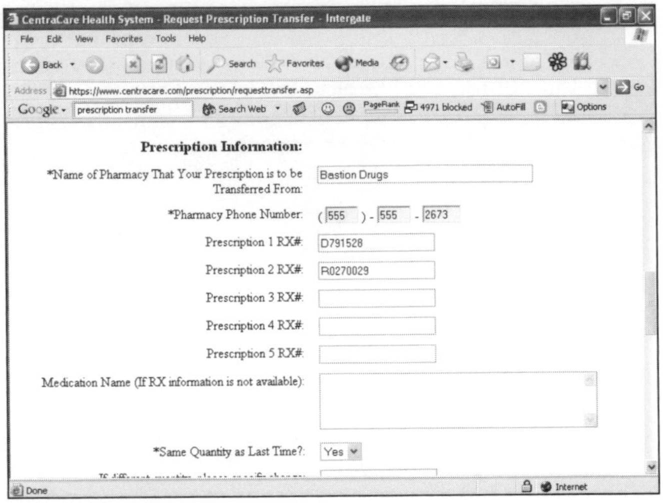

Figure 11.9
Fill out the online form
to transfer your existing
prescriptions to a new
pharmacy, cyber or not.

Here's what usually happens:

1. You choose a different pharmacy.

2. You contact that pharmacy—by phone or through online form—and request a prescription transfer.

3. You provide the name of the pharmacy where the prescription is currently being serviced, along with the name and prescription ID number (often listed as the Rx#) of the drug(s) you want to transfer.

4. The new pharmacy contacts the original pharmacy and obtains a copy of your prescription(s).

5. The original pharmacy may contact you directly to verify that you want to make this transfer (not all pharmacies do this).

6. The new pharmacy prepares your refills when requested.

Transfers of prescriptions from one pharmacy to another don't always occur seamlessly. Each pharmacy—real or virtual—may have slightly different ways of handling it and it's usually smart to check up on your order until you're sure the transfer is complete and your order is being processed by the new pharmacy.

Your best results are apt to be between two drug stores in the same pharmacy chain because most have a system for orderly transfers, but that won't usually be the case when you're shopping online.

This raises another difference between using a legitimate versus a drug-dispensing-only pharmacy online. If you get a prescription generated by a medical consultation using a "no prescription needed" pharmacy, even when the order allows for refills, you probably can't get them to transfer your prescription to another pharmacy. Some make this very clear when you place your first order, stating that you can get your refills for the drug nowhere else but on this same pharmacy site. Others may not spell this out until or unless you try to transfer the prescription.

If you have serious problems in transferring a prescription for any reason, your easiest route may be to simply call your physician and ask for a new prescription so you can get started with the new pharmacy. Cyber pharmacies like Drugstore.com will even contact the doctor for you, as needed.

However, if you run into an issue where a pharmacy refuses to transfer your prescription to another pharmacy, contact your state pharmacy board. Refusal to transfer a prescription can be a violation of practice, which can result in action taken against a pharmacist or pharmacy that willfully refuses.

You can usually find the phone number for your state pharmacy board by doing a Web search or by calling the reference desk at the local library.

TIP

Try to plan ahead when you want to transfer prescriptions from one pharmacy to another because you don't want to run out of your existing medication before you get the refill. Expect a prescription transfer to add at least a day or two (a few specify as long as 10 days) to the time it takes the new pharmacy to deliver—or with a physical drugstore, pick up—your order.

CHAPTER 11

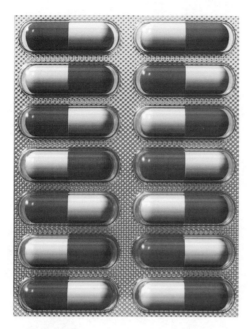

Part V

Perils, Penalties, and the Practice of Pharming

Are your kids pharming? If you don't know what this term means, there is probably a good chance your teenagers do— and you should, too.

This final part of the book looks beyond the actual online prescription ordering process to important topics like the practice among teens of trying to lay their hands on whatever drugs they can for weekend fun. While they may start with your family medicine cabinet, many of them are going online to find their drugs or buying them from friends who do.

There's also a discussion of the fake pills often being mixed in the drug supply and questions about the quality of foreign drugs vs. the issues with our piggy-backing on the Canadian health care system looking for cheaper prices.

Chapter 12
Are Your Kids Pharming?

No. The title of this chapter is not spelled incorrectly. If you haven't heard about pharming, you should pay attention to this chapter. If you have kids, they may have heard of it. To many parents' great surprise, many kids are participating in this sometimes group, sometimes solo activity. Not all of those kids are screw-ups, either. Many pull good grades, are active in extracurricular activities, behave at home, and still play Russian roulette with their friends on the weekend.

There are actually two kinds of pharming. One is used in the science field to refer to the wedding of agriculture with pharmaceuticals: genetically engineered livestock, for example. The other refers to what kids and adults do to come up with an effective "altered consciousness" cocktail from whatever they can find in the family medicine cabinet, the local drugstore, and the online shopping venues that sell chemicals and more.

Pharming usually involves more than one drug or drug type. In fact, at some pharming parties, kids contribute whatever pills and potions they can find into a big hat or a wastebasket to share among everyone present. One week the cocktail might be a mix of laxatives, prescription cough medicine, and Ritalin borrowed from someone's little brother, while another week might offer a combination of painkillers, diet pills, sedatives, and even the added bonus of hallucinogenic mushrooms.

While such pharming parties used to be confined to whatever drugs and substance they could find easily around home or local stores, the great rise in access to a slew of different drugs on the Internet gives them far more selection. With this increased selection comes a subset of kids who buy meds online only to sell them at a modest-to-considerable profit to their schoolmates and friends. Kids then buy and trade pills and capsules at lunch time much as an earlier generation might have traded bubblegum cards.

This chapter is all about pharming, including some of the signs you can watch for in your own children or those you may work with. Yet understand that this type of drug misuse and abuse isn't strictly limited to teenagers. Some of the same signals and behavior we see in the young, we also find in adults, both young and mature. Senior citizens, for example, are misusing drugs at a record rate and they, too, are taking advantage of some of the Internet's broad access to obtain the prescriptions they want.

What the Studies Tell Us

One of the vexing things about studies is that you can almost always find one to support or deny your position, and it's fairly easy to spin statistics a certain way for effect. But drug studies, in particular, can be notoriously prone to error because you have to depend on the truthfulness of the participants. Some people (kids included) may view reporting drug use as something cool so they may say they use when they either don't or don't use to the degree that they indicate. Others, however, know that the topic of drugs brings with it a stigma and won't divulge to anyone that they use.

With that in mind, let's discuss some of the studies out there. One tells us that prescription drug use among all Americans is at record levels. Children as young as pre-school may regularly take as many as two different prescription medicines each day, and senior citizens can take an average of 11 drugs every day. As a society, we're very accustomed to taking our medicine, and we learn fairly early in life that it's OK to take whatever a doctor prescribes for us.

Where studies can begin to divide in results is on how our early exposure to taking drugs of any type may lay the groundwork for our willingness to use drugs—prescription and not—later in life.

The National Household Survey on Drug Abuse (shown in Figure 12.1) offers statistics showing that illegal drug use among 12–17 year-olds has been dropping every year for the last several years, yet researchers haven't explained why. It would be nice to believe that kids are getting the message that drug abuse complicates rather than frees your life. Yet other studies suggest that the rate at which we're prescribing drugs to children to treat conditions such as hyperactivity and depression, among others, is rising sharply. Early use of prescription drugs has been known to factor into a person's decision later to abuse drugs, because these people get the message that "there's a pill to treat anything."

Talk to some kids about the situation, and they say they've just switched drugs from marijuana and alcohol to products from Watson, Merck, and Pfizer.

Figure 12.1
One of the many drugs available without too many questions.

Several youths between the age of 14 and 20 who contacted me or were willing to be interviewed for this book said that it's very tough for them to buy alcohol and cigarettes but much easier for them to acquire prescription drugs, including codeine-based cough formulas, serious pain medications like Fentanyl and OxyContin, and diet drugs no longer sold in the U.S.

"Go online and in 15 minutes, I can find you a place that sells E," reported one, referring to Ecstasy, the popular club drug. Figure 12.2 shows some Web search results for Ecstasy. But he said it's faster if you want an erectile dysfunction drug like Viagra or Levitra or a sleeping pill such as Ambien. He tells me he's purchased online at least a half dozen times with no hassle, but he usually just gets his supply from schoolmates and friends.

Another said he began ordering online with his parents' consent. He was playing varsity football and wanted to try a bulk-up pill being advertised that other students were using as part of their weight training. Now he lets his folks think he's still getting the bulk-up pill when he's actually ordering Levitra for himself and codeine to share among friends.

Several kids admitted to using Ritalin and Adderall, the drugs often prescribed to children to treat hyperactivity, as a form of "speed" to help them get through study sessions, big games, and all-night parties. These can be ordered online, as shown in Figure 12.3, or raided from the family medicine cabinet when another child in the family is using the drug under doctor's prescription.

Four out of every five kids arrested are found to be under the influence of some type of drug (alcohol, illegal substance, or misused prescription) at the time of their arrest according to a report by the National Center on Alcohol and Substance Abuse at Columbia University (its Web site is shown in Figure 12.4). Although some two million of the 2.4 million kids show this inclination toward substance abuse, fewer than 70,000 each year will receive actual treatment for this.

Figure 12.2
An abundance of sites offering to help you find Ecstasy.

Figure 12.3
Online drugstores offering "hassle-free" Ritalin and similar drugs abound.

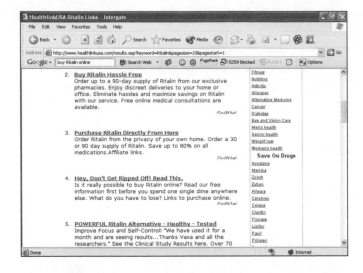

Figure 12.4
You can visit the National Center's Web site to learn more.

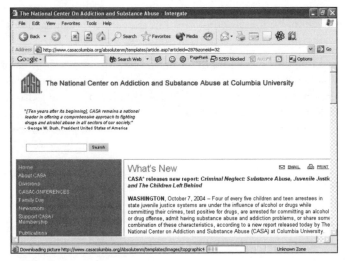

TIP
The National Household Survey on Drug Abuse is now known as the National Survey on Drug Use and Health. Visit **http://www.oas.samhsa.gov/nhsda.htm#New** to get more information.

NOTE
It's estimated that every year, about four million Americans outright abuse prescription drugs, while far more occasionally misuse them. Prescription drug abuse accounts for more than 30% of all diagnosed cases of addiction in the U.S.

"THE RISK WAS THE FUN"

"Jude378" was one of a half dozen people logged into a public Internet chat room called "PharmPhun" one afternoon. Those "talking" were sharing their stories about pharming.

Although she denies doing it currently, Jude says pharming parties were a big part of her last two years of high school. The kids she hung around with would never think of buying pot or taking illegal pills, but they had heard of pharming from other students at school and then began their own parties.

Her group couldn't even wait until the weekend. Every Thursday evening, between six and ten high school juniors and seniors would congregate in a bedroom or a family room at one student's house to place that week's snare of pharmaceuticals in an old back pack. Most weeks the selection wasn't very big—cold medicine and stimulants. But other weeks the grab bag was enhanced because one of the kids' father was a doctor who frequently brought medical samples home to store; the son would take some and add it to the drug kitty.

Each teen would "draw" his or her drugs from the strange grab bag. The rules were that everyone reached in at least three different times and that each took whatever they grabbed; also, every one had to begin taking their stash during their next-to-last period on Friday so they were feeling something by the time school ended.

Over the weekend, Jude says, the teens would call or get together and compare notes on the experience the drugs were giving them. A couple of times, she admits, she and others got very ill or scared from the reaction they were getting. Only one boy, she says, had to go to the ER after consuming beer along with Tylenol with codeine tablets.

"But the risk was part of the fun," she adds. "It was also funny because our parents were so glad to see us hanging around home when we couldn't even get up because we were stoned out of our minds. Nobody ever seemed to figure anything out even when prescription bottles disappeared."

Why Kids Choose Online Venues for Their Highs

Kids are smart. They don't want to have to work any harder than they must to get what they want.

If their easiest stimulation or buzz was available on the street corner closest to their homes, that's where they would flock. Yet one of the effects on the War on Drugs is that illegal drugs are a bit less available, at least in many good neighborhoods.

But these kids are usually already online, using the Internet for sometimes hours each day. They browse faster and harder than adults, and are apt to dig up a number of sites that offer information about drug use, even when parental control utilities to restrict Web access are used.

To them, the process of ordering drugs or chemicals over the Web is just a slight inconvenience that is otherwise anonymous. If they tried to perpetrate a scam at the local drugstore, their parents and likely the police would be called. That's not the case with some of the fly-by-night Web drugstores that allow anyone—without proof of age or need—to order powerful medication (like the site shown in Figure 12.5) without a prescription or doctor's check.

Figure 12.5
Some kids find shopping for drugs online the easiest way to do it.

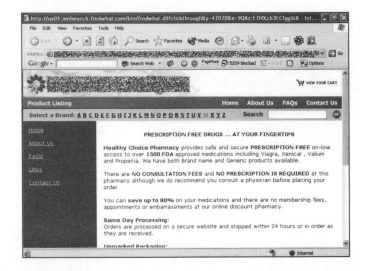

"THERE OUGHT TO BE A LAW..."

Believe it or not, there is not a single law on the books in the United States that specifically requires drug-selling Web sites to disclose anything to you except the basics of your actual order transaction. They don't have to tell you who they are, where they actually operate from, who the doctors are that write prescriptions on those sites where they take orders without prior prescription, or anything about the pharmacy that dispenses your order. That's extra frightening if you try to avoid seeing your doctor and depend instead on "no prescription needed" sites because you're placing your trust in an entity you don't know.

As you'll see in Chapter 8, many sites that promote themselves as U.S.-based actually operate in a foreign country. There are also those that are registered in a different nation to place them outside U.S. law enforcement jurisdiction, but are actually run from a warehouse in New York or somebody else's garage in Florida or Cuba.

However, there are laws covering lies and misstatements on medical sales Web sites like online pharmacies. The FDA and/or the Federal Trade Commission (FTC) can take action against an online pharmacy purporting to offer an unproven "miracle" cure, or says its selling a diet drug when it is actually selling you a salt tablet. Considering the abundance of sites you can visit daily that violate these laws and the overall low number of prosecutions the federal government undertakes, some online drugstores may not be too worried about getting shut down by making fraudulent statements.

"IF THIS STUFF ISN'T LEGAL, I COULDN'T BUY IT, RIGHT?"

"Marden" says she's been buying drugs online using an older sister's credit card for about 18 months. But unlike many who do it, Marden insists her motives are purely profit-oriented.

Identifying herself as a college junior in school in the Virginia area, her parents hit financial problems that made it difficult for them to even cover the tuition, let alone Marden's out-of-pocket living expenses off campus. A friend of hers suggested the idea of reselling drugs purchased off the Internet as a way to have a steady flow of cash; they knew a couple of other people who were doing it.

Once or twice a month, Marden reports she buys 90–100 pills each of a male impotency drug, Ritalin, a popular sleeping pill, and alprazolam (generic Xanax, an anti-anxiety tablet) from two or three different off-shore pharmacies. She then sells them each for between two and three times the price she pays.

Her customers are other students or young adults already working who frequent the clubs Marden visits on weekends. She says club goers are always looking to see what's available and no one's ever experienced a problem from anything she sold to them. She also says she draws the line at selling the popular club drug, Ecstasy, because she knows it's illegal and that some have been harmed by taking it.

"This isn't like selling other kinds of drugs like street drugs," she insists. "These are real medical drugs. I refuse to sell anybody more than two-three pills because I don't want anybody getting addicted or hurting themselves. If this stuff isn't legal, I couldn't buy it. Right?"

THE FUN THAT ENDED

I heard of "Perry" through a friend of a friend of a friend after the story of what had happened began to circulate.

Perry had been part of a group of friends that liked to experiment with drugs. Starting in junior high, the school pals had begun to borrow cold medicine out of their parents' medicine cabinets; eventually, they graduated to shoplifting three-to-six packages at a time out of local drugstores, supplemented with whatever new pill or potion a parent added to the drug cabinet at home.

Then one of the boys in the group discovered a foreign Web site offering all types of controlled access drugs including painkillers like Darvon, Vicodin, and Percodan and serious muscle relaxants. After talking it over, the group decided it was time to upgrade their recreational weekend arsenal to include these prescription drugs.

Before long, a few weeks' worth of medication meant for someone experiencing truly life-debilitating levels of pain would be consumed by the boys in a single weekend. As Perry later told his mother, it was just a great deal easier to go online and purchase mind-altering drugs than it would be taking the risk of going out to purchase marijuana or methamphetamines.

At first, the boys were usually able to find sites willing to ship their orders cash-on-delivery (COD). Then they found it tougher to find sites willing to sell without a credit card and without requiring the person ordering to show a picture ID proving he or she was over 21 before the delivery service handed over the pills.

Continued

Perry, whom his parents considered a very responsible 17-year-old, happened to be the only one with access to his own credit card. He became the person in his group who always ordered the drugs and after a short time, he realized he could pay for his own self-medication by charging his friends a handling fee. His parents asked no questions when Perry suddenly began to handle his own credit card, making payments himself; they thought it was just a sign of increasing maturity. Who would complain when their son was still pulling good grades and seemed to have some money of his own?

Then one weekend, one of the group members became ill after taking several different types of prescription medication. Thankfully, even though the other boys panicked and scattered, Perry had the presence of mind to get his friend to an emergency room where he told the medical personnel what the boy had taken. With that information, the doctor could pump the boy's stomach and neutralize the effects of the drugs before his breathing shut down.

While the boy in question made a full recovery, the parents of all the boys ended up having to sit down and look at the situation so they could stop it. Perry's parents were very upset to learn that their son's credit card bill clearly spelled out the online pharmacy charges. Had they seen it before, they might have been able to put an end to the "lost" weekends before near tragedy resulted. Tipped by this, other parents began to review their own credit card statements and discovered some unexplained charges from other online pharmacies.

How Kids Work the System

Kids are Internet-savvy; they know how to communicate information quickly and effectively—at least, when they want to do so. When teens finds a site that makes it very easy for them to order a desirable drug without a hassle, they're able to get the word out quickly to friends and strangers. Finding a "deal" offers a certain amount of credibility for some kids, and they want others to know what they score.

Teens and young adults also visit the abundance of global Web sites that offer information about drugs and drug experiences like the one shown in Figure 12.6. They're pretty easy to find using virtually any Web search engine. The same youths who won't look up what's on TV that night are happy to spend hours performing this kind of research.

Access to a credit or debit card helps for shopping online. It's important to remember that older teens are often targeted for credit card offers and it can be tempting to let them apply with the assumption that it will help train them to use financial resources. But many sites allow them to shop even without a credit card or debit card. With access to cash, kids can send a money order or personal check, or use one of the sites offering cash-on-delivery (COD) shipment.

Over-the-Counter Dangers

Never overlook the potential for abuse of easy-to-buy over-the-counter drugs. Kids and adults of all ages use these drugs as convenient legal ways to escape either into drowsiness or to enjoy a buzz. Drug treatment specialists know this and tend to be suspicious of someone who is constantly self-treating with non-prescription medications.

Ask any drugstore clerk and they'll happily relate a story about a guy or girl who comes in once each week to buy a large quantity of cold medicine, store-shelf sleeping pills, or something else that no one normally needs to purchase each week.

Figure 12.6
Teens use a variety of online resources to research drug types to look for to give them an optimum experience.

However, most over-the-counter use flies beneath the radar. While the store clerk may notice, many stores don't limit the quantity of such medications they sell, although some now restrict the amount of cold medicine sold to no more than three packages at one time since it's also used in the manufacture of methamphetamines.

It's also hard to measure since many people shoplift their over-the-counter drug supplies. A few pharmacy managers I spoke with said that as much as 50% of their stolen inventory gets lifted from within their "cough-and-cold" aisles. One was quick to note that it's not just teens doing the shoplifting either; he says he's seen a distinct rise in senior citizens taking merchandise without paying for it.

Keep in mind also that herbal preparations are usually sold over the counter and aren't subject to the same regulations as prescription medication even when the herb or herb combination does a similar job. While many of us may hear about an herbal medicine that produces some wild side effect that we can't imagine anyone wanting to experience, those can be the exact reports that interest teens and young adults. Many Web message boards and Web sites like that shown in Figure 12.7 discuss herb-based formulas that can produce comparable hallucinogenic or sedative or other effects as more restricted drugs.

Prescriptions

The same range of prescription drugs available to you is effectively available for your kids. While legitimate pharmacies may require that the customer be 18 years or older to order, not even every good pharmacy necessarily requires a photo ID to receive delivery of a drug order. Unfortunately, there are many "no prescription needed" stores that will sell to anyone who's willing to say they're of legal age without any proof.

The news media has even reported on cases where kids gave their actual ages (sometimes under age 16) and still received heavy-duty drugs that would not normally be prescribed to non-adults.

Figure 12.7
Other people comment
on their herbal ecstasy
experience.

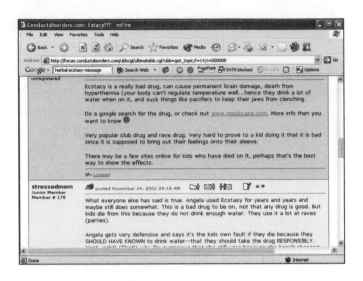

Figure 12.8 shows a site that allows kids to purchase Hydrocodone, a pain medication, without requiring a credit or debit card to do so.

Popular online purchases by children include the aforementioned Ritalin (Figure 12.9 shows a "hassle free" Ritalin order site), pain medications ranging from those with small amounts of codeine to OxyContin and Fentanyl, both similar to heroin and morphine in their effects on the body and mind, male impotency drugs, birth control pills, and diet medication.

Figure 12.8
Many sites don't even
require a person to have
a credit card to order.

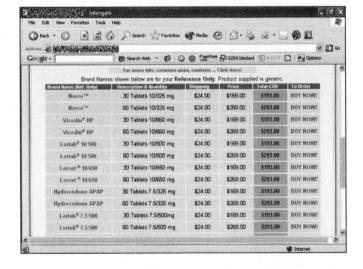

Figure 12.9
One of the sites offering Ritalin without a prior prescription.

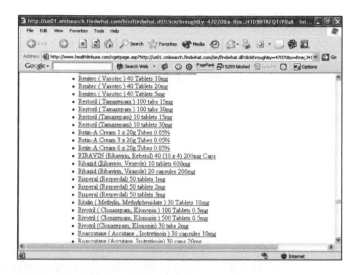

THE ON-CAMPUS DRUGSTORE

"Jon" says the only exposure he had to drugs before he hit his college campus last year was a few joints shared among friends. But that all changed when he arrived at what he describes to be a Christian-oriented four-year university that his parents chose because it seemed like a safe choice from bad influences.

Almost immediately upon arrival for his freshman year, Jon says, drugs were everywhere. But not the kind—alcohol and pot—that he expected. Instead, classmates and dorm residence assistants always seem to have a supply of "uppers and downers" students can buy for $3–$10 a pop.

During exam weeks, Jon says, Ritalin and other stimulants are very popular among students who buy them so they can cram. He admits he has used Ritalin for this purpose but says he does so largely because everyone else does during these make-or-break test periods. He compares it to athletes who feel compelled to use contraband drugs to improve their performance because they are up against so many who do.

Jon insists that he and many other students he knows who take stimulants—and then downers like sleeping pills and sedatives to crash after the big test is over—would never consider going out to buy illegal drugs, adding their intent is to do better in their schoolwork rather than to get high.

Chemical Supply Companies

Remember the chemical supply companies mentioned in the beginning of this book? These can also be popular online stores for those looking for a cheap high or other psychological side effect. Such sites often sell compounds inexpensively with far fewer questions and less overall hassle than an online pharmacy.

What to Watch For

Are there signals you should look for in determining whether your child—or someone else you care for—may be using or abusing drugs? Certainly, but the experts warn that you need to be careful in making assumptions too quickly or in discounting the possibility because the person in question doesn't happen to show all the warning signs.

The government, for its part, has been running an "anti-drug" campaign for the last several years. The focus in its advertising is often on parents, encouraging them to be aware of what their kids are doing and to constantly drive home the message that drugs are bad. Literature advises parents to fight the potential for drug use or abuse by:

- ▶ Spending quality time with their children
- ▶ Regularly telling their kids that they are loved
- ▶ Being involved in their kids' daily lives
- ▶ Setting a good example for problem solving and conflict resolution, while avoiding bad examples that may pass along the message that escaping with a pill or a drink or a cigarette is acceptable
- ▶ Encouraging children to be involved in extra-curricular and community activities
- ▶ Taking the time to listen to as well as talk to their kids
- ▶ Providing their kids with clear, consistent rules and expectations
- ▶ Knowing where their children are and who they are with
- ▶ Rewarding their kids for positive behavior and setting clear punishments for poor behavior

It's also wise to become knowledgeable about the topic, which changes as kids' interests change. Use Web search engines to find new articles on pharming, such as the one shown in Figure 12.10 from the Hartford Advocate.

Figure 12.10
Learn more about pharming and how kids do it.

Before we take a look at some of the warning signs, here's a list of Web-based resources where you can learn more about drugs, drug addiction, and specific issues related to teens and drugs:

▶ American Council for Drug Education at **http://www.acde.org/**

▶ Government family prevention guide at **family.samhsa.gov/get/**

▶ National Center on Alcohol and Substance Abuse at Columbia University at **http://www.casacolumbia.org**

▶ Parents, the Anti-Drug at **http://www.theantidrug.com**

▶ Partnership for a Drug-Free America at **http://www.drugfreeamerica.org**

Physical Evidence

Now let's look at some of the physical evidence that may tip you off to a child or loved one misusing drugs. These include:

▶ Medications—prescription and over-the-counter—disappearing from home medicine cabinets

▶ Unexplained drug bottles and packages showing up in the trash

▶ Unexplained and/or frequent deliveries (not all will be clearly marked pharmaceuticals or that they are from a drugstore)

▶ Sudden change in behavior—attitude, daily routine, school grades, demand for privacy, or appearance—that seems to have no apparent cause

▶ A child or young adult who seems to have large amounts of cash—or expresses a need for such money—for no obvious reason

Access to Credit or Debit Cards

Many teenagers today have access to a credit or debit card—theirs or one borrowed from a parent or caregiver—long before they turn 18.

Although both credit and debit cards can be used as valuable tools in helping a child develop financial skills and independence, they can also be abused. Some teens get quite creative in covering their charges, too—they've been known to change the billing address on an account to go somewhere other than to home, to suddenly try to take over the paying of their own bills, and even to report fraudulent use of a card when they've used it to buy drugs.

Everyone needs to check their credit and checking account statements carefully each month and to call the card company when they notice an unexplained charge. Parents need to monitor their children's accounts as well and be prepared to question charges.

TIP

Not every online pharmacy charge appears clearly marked as a drug purchase. Many use names that disguise the nature of the charge, much like telephone sexually oriented services do.

CHAPTER 12

How They Can Get Stolen Credit Card Information

You might think of stolen credit card trading as the work of organized crime. But in truth, almost every day you can find an Internet chat room or Web site chat room where young people are exchanging stolen credit card details and other financial information.

In talking with some of the self-described crackers, they say it's often easier to use a credit card stolen in one part of the country to purchase goods or services in another part. This is often useful, they say, in throwing off bank fraud detectives investigating credit misuse. A teen or adult who wants to disguise their theft of a credit card may trade it for a credit card stolen elsewhere to make it less likely the theft can be traced back to them.

Physical and Behavioral Symptoms

There are certain physical and behavioral symptoms that tend to accompany drug overuse and abuse. These include:

> ▶ Significant change in grades or overall school performance
>
> ▶ Unexplained absences from school or after-school job or activities
>
> ▶ Withdrawal from social activities and functions; quitting membership in organizations
>
> ▶ Marked change in appearance (teens and adults may appear to "let themselves go," slowly abandoning good hygiene) or symptoms such as chronic sleepiness, red eyes, poor attention, and weight loss or gain
>
> ▶ Loss of motivation

Unfortunately, many of these symptoms or states can be seen in adolescents and young adults, absent any drug use.

However, it's also important to appreciate that not every child or adult in the throws of drug influence or addiction is going to seem like the stereotype of someone who stumbles about with red eyes rambling incoherently. Many teens and adults feel they have control over their drug use and may take a particular drug or drug combination just to support their busy, active lifestyles. Some may be able to cover their physical and behavioral symptoms for months or years before someone suspects there's a problem.

Playing Computer Detective

Our PCs keep a remarkable history of the places we've been, the files we've looked at or downloaded, and the stores in which we've shopped. Some savvy parents are using this history to play computer detective to try to figure out what their kids are doing online. Some go the extra step of adding spyware to their child's PC to snoop on everything the child does while sitting at the keyboard.

However, kids often know the Internet and the software available for it far better than their parents. They find and download utilities that help purge their Web browsing evidence before anyone can go in to check. Give them ten minutes and they can usually download and install a tool to kill spyware snoops or to wipe their Web browser history clean.

It may be wiser to keep home computers in general access rooms in your home. This step makes it easier for you to monitor what your kids are doing as well as makes it harder for them to hide information from you.

You also may want to turn off features like the AutoComplete feature in Microsoft Internet Explorer (available if you open the Tools menu, select Options, choose the Content tab, and click AutoComplete as shown in Figure 12.11; click to uncheck options here to turn it off). AutoComplete stores numbers and phrases you type frequently, like your street address or credit card number, so it can recall these when you begin to type them again. But it's also the way some kids get access to their parents' credit card numbers and expiration dates.

Also exercise control over your wallet. Don't leave credit cards or debit cards or large amounts of cash available to your kids or their friends.

Monitoring the Mail/Parcel Delivery

The simple act of monitoring your mail and parcel delivery can sometimes dramatically reduce the chance your child—or someone else you take care of—will receive a drug delivery from an online pharmacy or chemical supply firm.

One mother of a college freshman who began to abuse diet drugs ordered online said she immediately took steps to remove her daughter's access to credit cards. But she didn't stop the supply entirely until she contacted her mailman and delivery companies to insist that all packages be redirected to her business rather than delivered to her home. Just restricting her daughter's access to credit, she said, simply drove her daughter to find sites that offered these drugs cash-on-delivery.

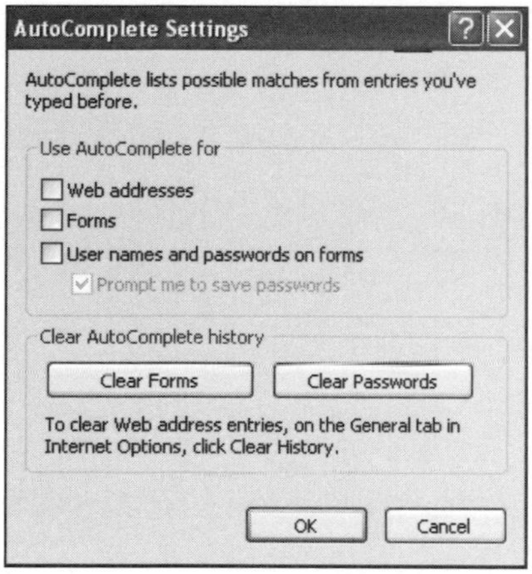

Figure 12.11
Turn off AutoComplete and other convenience features that may offer private details to kids.

CHAPTER 12

IT'S NOT JUST KIDS

Don't believe that it's just kids and young adults abusing drugs of all kinds. Stop and consider that loneliness and depression often play a factor in drug overuse and abuse and it's easier to understand that many older adults have become psychologically dependent on a variety of medications, including alcohol, illegal drugs, and prescriptions.

This seems especially true for older adults who have become caregivers again to their grandchildren or even great-grandchildren or to their sick adult children. The stress of caretaking combined with restrictions on earning capability and their own declining health can short-circuit otherwise sound judgment and lead these people to begin using medication to escape the situation, however briefly.

Also, because older Americans tend to take a number of different drugs at any one time, combined with the fact that they often see more than one doctor can make it somewhat easier for them to obtain controlled substances from multiple sources.

Yet drug abuse presents a special problem in senior adults. Drugs we take as we age last far longer in our bodies than they do when we're much younger. This can lead more rapidly to toxic drug levels as well as to physical dependence on a drug. Because older Americans often take so many prescriptions, the possibility of dangerous drug interaction is also much higher.

Chapter 13
Avoiding a Prescription for Disaster

Just one order screw-up—whether you accidentally order the wrong drug or a pharmacy sends you the wrong one—is all that differentiates an Rx for success from a prescription for disaster.

If you're considering or already starting to order your medication online, it's important you begin to develop a game plan for how you do this that not only gets you the prescriptions you need, but also protects your wallet, your overall security, and your health.

This chapter brings together the many positive aspects and pitfalls already covered in earlier parts of the book with additional concerns in putting together a regular system for ordering your drugs and refills quickly, effectively, and with the emphasis on your health and safety.

Remember, most Americans who have shopped online for their prescriptions liked the process and would do so again. Not every virtual drugstore out there offers counterfeit drugs or is only concerned with how many products they sell. I've covered a lot of the problems you may encounter, but that's only because I want you to be able to steer clear of them since there are plenty of drugstore shopping choices that offer you service and safety and don't cut corners at your possible expense.

Doing Your Homework

Use the research you've already done to guide your online purchases. This includes reviewing your pharmacy log—if you took my suggestion to start one—to determine which pharmacies sound like good matches for you. You should also investigate any recommendations you received from your doctor or medical support staff, your friends, family members, and co-workers.

However, If you haven't yet done much exploring, get busy using some of the resources I've provided you.

Then jot down your questions. Next, commit yourself to the goal of getting these questions answered by an online pharmacy before you give them your business.

Consulting a Professional

I don't mean to sound like a CD stuck playing the same track over and over again, but involving your doctor and other medical professionals is much safer than trying to treat yourself. This is especially true when you believe you have a serious illness, but self-medication of any type can be fraught with errors and health risks.

Prescribed medication isn't available without a doctor's order for good reason: it's deemed best used under the supervision of a trained physician. Even if you order online using a drugstore that provides medications based on a Web-form consultation, you should inform your doctor of what drugs you take and what dosage you take. If you don't have a doctor, you should find one. If you're financially strapped, check out the options that might be available in your area such as a clinic, wellness programs at your local hospital, or statewide programs that can help. You shouldn't go it alone.

Watching Where and What You Order

The type of pharmacy you order from can matter a great deal. Ads insisting a drugstore is "no hassle" and "really easy to order from" doesn't necessarily mean it's a good place to get your medication.

Use the tools I showed you in Chapters 7 and 8 to find good online drugstores that offer the following:

- ▶ Good and prompt service
- ▶ Order tracking
- ▶ Adequate security and privacy measures to make certain your confidential information stays that way
- ▶ A way to contact the pharmacist to ask questions as needed
- ▶ Competitive pricing
- ▶ A way to interact with your doctor as needed
- ▶ Proper controls in place to catch potential drug interactions with other medications you take
- ▶ Proper coverage for your health or pharmacy insurance

Remember, if you have a prescription filled by one pharmacy and don't like how you or your order were handled, don't use that pharmacy for your refill. Contact your doctor to write a fresh prescription for a new pharmacy or locate a new pharmacy and have your existing prescription transferred to it. Legitimate pharmacies like Drugstore.com, CVS.com (shown in Figure 13.1), and others are happy to handle the details necessary to transfer your orders for you.

Figure 13.1
CVS.com's prescription
transfer request form.

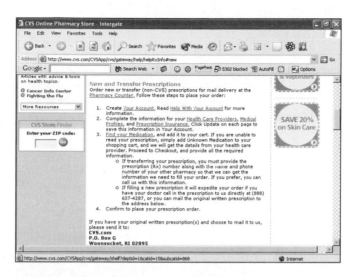

BEING CAREFUL: THE VIOXX RECALL

As this book is going to press, the FDA has issued a voluntary recall of the anti-inflammatory drug Vioxx, due to reports that as many as 27,000 American deaths may be linked to use of this medication. However, in the aftermath, many news reports have centered on the fact that both the manufacturer and the government may have been aware of the increased risk from this drug for months or years before the recall was issued. Many doctors interviewed said they had stopped prescribing the drug some months before the recall because they were hearing buzz.

Yet a surprising element of the Vioxx story is how it's played online. You might think that after a voluntary recall is announced, it would be pretty hard to obtain the drug. Right?

Actually, with the Internet, you're wrong. Although most legitimate online pharmacies pulled their Vioxx links immediately, there seemed to be a rise in the overall number of drug-dispensing shops that offered the drug for sale. Notably, some of the sites that had not offered the drug before began to advertise it once the recall went into effect.

There's a two-pronged explanation for this, both elements of which are also somewhat surprising. For one, some drugstores apparently made the decision that they might increase their orders if they made Vioxx available when so many other stores (virtual and otherwise) were suspending sales. Many long-time Vioxx users wanted to continue taking the drug, commonly used to treat the symptoms and pain of osteo- and rheumatoid arthritis, despite reports it was linked to progression of heart disease. Figure 13.2 shows one of these sites where you could order the drug without a prescription several weeks after the recall began.

Because the recall was voluntary the FDA only asked, rather than required, drugstores to stop selling it to consumers. Technically, sites still selling it are not breaking the law, however much we might question a person's decision to begin or continue on the medication or a "no prescription needed" drugstore allowing people to request it from an authorizing physician. But only one of about 35 sites I found still selling it bore any kind of notice of the recall or the concerns surrounding it.

Figure 13.2
A drugstore selling Vioxx after the FDA recall began.

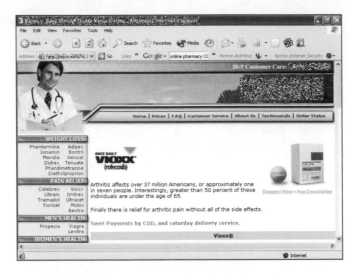

But the truly strange side of the online Vioxx phenomenon was the appearance of some Web sites advertising in places such as Craig's List (shown in Figure 13.3) that suggested consumers could take advantage of class action lawsuits against Vioxx's manufacturer (Merck) if they found a drugstore still dispensing it and could order a supply. This site even offers to send you a list of online pharmacies where you can buy it.

Other Issues Raised by the Vioxx Recall

Before we move on, there are a couple of other issues raised by the Vioxx recall that are worthy of note.

First, if the media had not covered the Vioxx recall story so extensively, would we have known about the recall? In fact, both food and drug products are recalled by the FDA on at least a somewhat regular basis but unless you check the FDA Web site or unless news outlets choose to

Figure 13.3
One of the Vioxx class action sites.

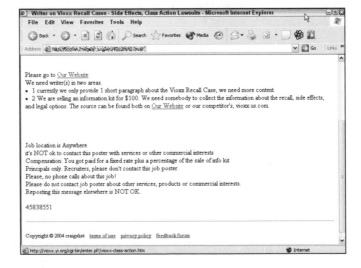

cover the story, you're not apt to know what medicines you take that may be affected. For example, as a relatively new user of Vioxx shortly before the recall, certainly no one called me to be sure I would discontinue taking the drug.

This represents a risk for everyone, but those who choose to self prescribe drugs for themselves likely expose themselves to more danger because they're not apt to know that the medical community has concerns about a particular drug before it's recalled. As you've already seen, you can still purchase Vioxx online on many pharmacy sites that won't tell you it's been associated with heart attacks and death.

Another concern affects everyone and that has to do with how well the FDA serves to protect the interests of consumers. Charges have been levied by the public at large as well as some experts that the FDA should have issued a recall on Vioxx long before it did and that the agency was more worried about the possible harm to the manufacturer than it was about the patients taking the drug. Critics say this is not unusual operating procedure for the FDA.

In light of Congressional hearings over the matter, some are recommending that a whole separate organization be created to look at approved drugs more from a consumer safety perspective. How far this will go remains to be seen, but already, some states have created their own drug safety boards to look at claims of problems with various types of medication.

Checking Your Order

Check every prescription order you get, regardless of whether it comes from an online source like the one shown in Figure 13.4 or your corner drugstore. Be sure that the drug's appearance and any imprint codes (see Figure 13.5 for the logo and drug imprint code for Viagra as an example) match that for the medication you expected. If you have any previous medication of the same type left, use this to check your new order against—but that only works if it's the same brand or generic as before.

Figure 13.4
Be sure to check your order thoroughly.

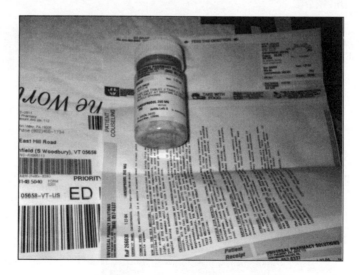

CHAPTER 13

Figure 13.5
Viagra front and back
with imprint code.

If the drug appears to be the wrong one or something appears "off" about the order (wrong drug count, the medication looks old, capsules have started to dissolve, or you question whether it's a counterfeit), contact the pharmacy immediately. Do not take the medication unless the pharmacist can assure you that you have the correct medication.

Should you continue to have doubts, consider doing something a little uncommon and taking the drug to the local pharmacy to try to verify. The pharmacist on duty should be able to tell at least by appearance whether the drug matches other drugs in their own inventory.

NOTE

Refer to Chapter 10, "Identifying What You Really Get," for details about identifying your medicine once you receive it.

Review the Instructions

Don't read your drug label (see Figure 13.6) just once. Memorize it. A phenomenal number of drug-related problems and health emergencies are caused simply because we don't follow the directions on the bottle.

Figure 13.6
Read your label.

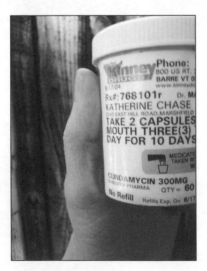

Look for any warning labels. These may advise you to avoid certain activities or other medications or alcohol while taking the drug or tell you to take the medication with water or milk or meals. Then follow those directions.

Most prescriptions advise you not to double up on the dosage if you miss a dose. If you don't catch the missed dose soon after it's due, proceed along to take your next dose at the scheduled time. Any variance from this should be noted in the accompanying literature for your prescription (see Figure 13.7). Check for any paperwork with the order or within the medication package.

Watch Yourself

If this is your first time taking a new medication, pay particularly close attention to how you feel. Call your doctor or contact an emergency center if you experience anything out of the ordinary, such as difficulty breathing, sudden onset of pain or swelling, or something else that may signal an allergic or other reaction.

Should you notice symptoms that are bothersome but don't rise to the level of an immediate crisis, make a note of your experience and then gauge your continued reaction. Provide this information to your doctor.

Understand, too, that not all drugs produce side effects immediately. Some only give you problems after you've built up a level of the medication in your system over time. However, most allergic reactions and serious problems are seen within the first 24 hours of taking a new medication.

Figure 13.7
Look for accompanying
literature or
instructions.

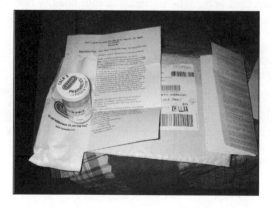

Looking for Credit Card Theft, Fraud, and Hidden Charges

Remember to review your credit cards and debit cards carefully for the first few months after you begin to use a new online pharmacy. Specifically, you want to be sure you are free from the following:

▶ Hidden or extra charges beyond what you thought you would pay

▶ Unauthorized use of your card to charge another order such as an automatic refill you didn't sign to get; but your credit card information could also be used by someone else who obtained it from the pharmacy or by snooping on your PC to get it

▶ Surprise "monthly" fees because a pharmacy or drug-ordering group has assessed a membership you did not specifically agree to participate in

If you're the parent of a teenager or live with someone you suspect may be using drugs, it's smart to check your statements, too, to be sure that your credit or debit card hasn't been "borrowed" to pay for medication. Teens and young adults have been known to make a parent's card available to friends as well.

Caregivers of elderly and otherwise incapacitated adults are urged to review financial statements for the people for whom they care to spot whether drugs are being ordered or charged beyond those you might expect to see. Senior citizens are often seen as "easy targets" for "miracle" potions and scams that add unexplained extra fees onto orders. Also, many adult children spot a parent's pattern of self-medication before the patient's doctor simply because they've investigated strange charges made to a credit or debit card or drawn against a checking account.

NOTE

When you're shopping online for medications, be careful which cards you use for payment. Many of today's debit cards—usually featuring MasterCard or Visa logos—allow you to use these cards just like a credit card for making purchases. You can use them for online pharmacies, too. However, you don't have nearly the same protections in place when using a debit card that you have with a credit card—you may be liable for more costs if someone uses your information fraudulently, especially if you don't report a problem promptly.

Using Online Resources to Verify Information

Take advantage of other online resources shared in this book to double-check details. This should include:

▶ Pricing—use the many online sites like CVS.com (see Figure 13.8), Drugstore.com, Pharmacywatch.com and others to find that day's going price for the medication you're ordering so you can be sure you aren't paying large fees

▶ Dosages and drug interactions—remember sites like Drugs.com (shown in Figure 13.9) and RxList.com that let you look up information about normal doses and possible drug interactions

▶ Side effects—the same sites that let you research dosages and drug interactions usually spell out possible side effects and warning signs to watch for

Figure 13.8
Checking for pricing on drugs at CVS.com.

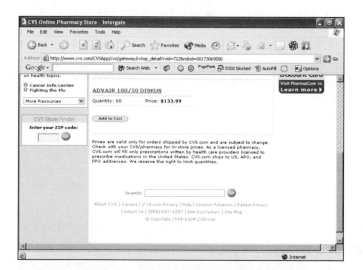

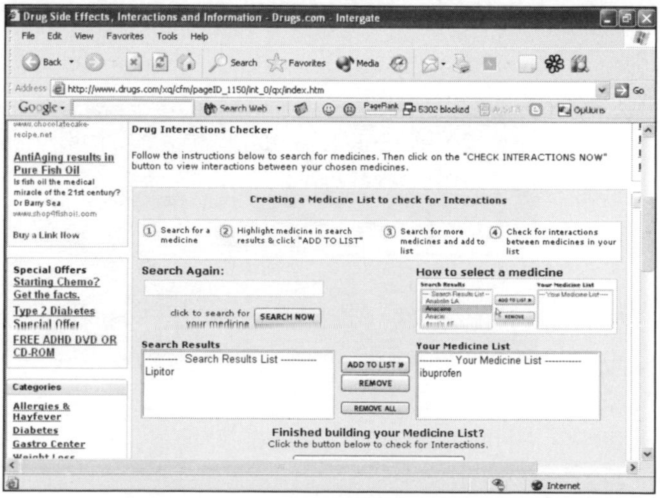

Figure 13.9
Researching normal dosages and possible drug interactions at Drugs.com.

Documenting What You Take in the Event of Emergency

Medical emergencies are bad times to rely on either memory or your ability to speak for yourself. You may not be thinking clearly or be unable to respond to questions.

Because of this, make sure your doctor and family members, along with anyone else who may live or work with you, know what medications you take. Even then, consider typing up (or printing neatly) a list of all your medications and their dosage requirements—similar to that shown in Figure 13.10—which you then can keep in your wallet or purse where those looking for a medical warning card or insurance information might look.

Ten Warning Signs You're in Trouble from Self-Prescription

Understand that just having one or more of these warning signs isn't, by itself, proof that you have a drug dependence issue. But because almost all of these signs can definitely represent some risk to your health and well-being, you need to consider them, especially when you're practicing self-treatment.

Also, appreciate the fact that you run into real problems with prescription medications other than just the ones we commonly hear about, like opiate-like painkillers, highly sedative sleeping pills, and anti-anxiety drugs like Xanax and Ativan. People can develop psychological dependence on just about anything we associate with making us feel better than we do without it.

1. You're ordering as much for psychological need as symptom correction or relief.

Are you ordering a medication because you need it or because you can't face the prospect of a day in which you don't take the drug? If your answer is the latter, you may be headed for a problem.

Figure 13.10
Make a list of your medicines for emergencies.

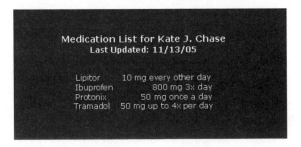

Medication List for Kate J. Chase
Last Updated: 11/13/05

Lipitor   10 mg every other day
Ibuprofen   800 mg 3x day
Protonix   50 mg once a day
Tramadol   50 mg up to 4x per day

Unfortunately, too few of us realize we have a psychological attachment to a particular medication until we're too far into the dependence. This can be a very poor time to be able to sort out the issue for yourself. It's like a catch-22 situation where those who can still think objectively about the situation probably aren't into full-fledged addiction, yet once addiction strikes, they're less likely to see the problem for what it is.

Talk with your doctor. He or she may be able to find an alternative treatment that is less addictive or be better able monitor your usage.

Don't just go "cold turkey" and decide to tough it out either. Many of the drugs that cause us to form a dependence belong to medication categories for which the dosage should be slowly reduced over time rather than stopped abruptly, to reduce your risk of experiencing severe withdrawal symptoms or precipitate a health emergency. Your doctor can step you through a slow but steady withdrawal and suggest ways to make withdrawal symptoms more tolerable.

2. You aren't paying attention to drug interactions.

The issue of drug interactions is more important with each additional drug, prescription or not, that you take. The matter grows to critical status when you're using online pharmacies to self-treat medical conditions, especially when you're using different drugstores and not letting one doctor/pharmacist know what another has provided to you.

3. You're fudging your answers.

While it's almost human nature to fill out a form of any kind with a mind toward manipulating the results you want (meaning we conveniently leave out unflattering information on a job form or embarrassing details on a loan application), there is a legitimate medical concern when you begin doing it to get a specific prescription.

One of the behaviors addiction specialists report in patients who abuse substances is a point at which these people begin to lie about their need and use of a particular substance. This can appear as

> ▶ Lying to family members about the frequency with which we take medication
>
> ▶ Fudging answers on online pharmacy medical consultation forms or to our doctors
>
> ▶ Filling prescriptions at different pharmacies to hide how frequently we fill or refill the drug
>
> ▶ Failing to tell bosses, co-workers, teachers, or parents about a problem from the medication that may interfere with our ability to properly work, learn, or perform basic tasks

4. You're mixing alcohol with your medications.

As you've learned in earlier chapters, alcohol and various drugs do not mix well together. Even a single alcoholic drink (one beer, one shot of hard liquor, or one glass of wine) can either reduce or exacerbate the effects of some medications, with some producing a dramatic and even potentially fatal reaction.

5. You're setting your own dosages.

The basic idea with dosages is to get the right level to combat the problem without creating new ones. Taking too little may do nothing; taking too much can expose you to serious health risks.

The exact right dose for you may be quite different than it would be for another person, even one of similar height, weight, and general health. Finding a satisfactory dosage level is an issue that even doctors, with all their advanced training, can find difficult and time-consuming.

Whether you're taking a medication your doctor prescribed or you're using an Internet pharmacy that lets you request a drug through an online consultation, you should not adjust your dose without speaking with the doctor who authorized the prescription.

As I'm writing this book, the makers of Tylenol have begun to air an effective commercial in which one of the company heads states that she knows that many people are not taking Tylenol as recommended. She finishes by saying that if you aren't going to take Tylenol as directed, she would prefer you didn't take it at all. Your own doctor is likely to tell you something very similar about all the medications you take.

6. You find yourself hording medication.

When you need to take a medication on a daily basis, it's natural to become concerned if you face a situation where you may not have access to the drugs you need. You realize that most drugs aren't meant to be started and stopped frequently and that consistency is important.

However, one of the symptoms addiction experts see with people who have developed an unhealthy relationship with their medications is the practice of hording, where you invest considerable time and effort into always being sure you have a supply available to you above and beyond what's necessary. Unfortunately, not all medications store well for weeks or months at a time. Also, most doctors aren't very happy with the idea of patients having large supplies of drugs on hand because of the potential risks.

If you find yourself panicking when you don't have large amounts of a drug available to you, talk to your medical professional. Your doctor may be able to help you find a middle ground between securing your needed supply and compulsive hording.

7. You're ordering drugs to self-treat the side effects of other self-prescribed medication.

Even medical experts run the risk of prescribing a drug that produces side effects that may require a second or third drug to control. But the situation becomes more serious when we do it as part of self-treatment since we don't have nearly the background or chemical knowledge to try to juggle a roster of drugs. The risk potential for drug interaction increases substantially as does the possibility you can do yourself damage.

8. You're ignoring warnings to monitor drug levels.

Some drugs are meant to be used only in conjunction with regular testing, such as blood tests, to evaluate the effect the medication is having on your body and blood chemistry. Anti-cholesterol and asthma drugs, diabetes and thyroid treatments, some types of antidepressants, and many cardiac medications are examples of prescriptions that usually require careful monitoring by your doctor along with regular testing.

9. You're routinely spending much more money than necessary to obtain your medication.

Probably few of us would say that prescription drugs are generally cheap. Without good health or pharmacy insurance co-pays, it's not unusual to spend $50, $100, or more on a single bottle of anything from antibiotics to antidepressants to cancer- and cholesterol-fighting drugs.

While it's one thing to be willing to spend a little more for convenience, it's another to routinely use the far more expensive "no prescription needed" sites to fill and refill routine medications. Even those who consider it cheaper to buy a one-time drug through these venues rather than pay for the cost of a doctor's visit won't find it cost-effective to shop regularly through such sites for medication taken daily.

10. You're willing to take unnecessary risks to get your medication.

If you're regularly shopping through sites you know operate at less than full legitimacy, you're no doubt taking unnecessary risks to obtain your medication. You may have doubts about the authenticity of the drugs you get from these pharmacies and whether you're making a big mistake.

At some point you need to ask yourself, "How much is too much risk?" Yet perhaps a more important question to pose to yourself is, "What does it mean that I'm willing to take such risks to use this medication?"

As you learned in Chapter 2, "Big Brother Watches, But How Much?" a number of agencies are involved in trying to fight illegal drugstores and improper drug importations. Although the focus has usually been on the commercial offenders—doctors who write huge numbers of prescriptions for patients they treat in no other way and operators of "no prescription needed" drug sites—little prevents local, state, and federal agencies upon reversing course to go after the people who knowingly use such services to obtain drugs they couldn't get otherwise.

A much more immediate concern, however, is your health. If you're getting drugs through questionable pharmacies, it's probably because you're not seeing a doctor regularly or feel you can't ask for a particular medication, or you already know that your physician won't prescribe what you feel you need. This raises the question of whether you should be self-treating with a drug your doctor does not feel you should take. If you think your doctor is wrong, consider consulting with a different physician.

Chapter 14
Border Skirmishes: Special Issues in Drug Importation and More

Probably one of the very reasons you picked up this book was not only to learn how to avoid online scams when shopping for pharmaceuticals, but also because you're concerned about the future in the face of prescription drug prices that have jumped sharply in the last few years. A week rarely passes when some aspect of prescription drugs—their price, their availability, and their safety—fails to make headlines and news programs across the country.

Many view Canada with its cheaper pricing as the solution to our steep drug costs. But is it? Canada set several standards to get its citizens much more affordable drug prices, not the least of which is negotiating with prescription suppliers for the best price.

Although drug price ceilings are something many American citizens say they want and need, our elected officials and planners do not seem to be moving in this direction. The new U.S. Medicare prescription drug benefit, already in place in the form of prescription drug cards but not due to take full effect until 2006, specifically prohibits the government-sponsored program from negotiating for best prices at the same time the U.S. government is taking steps to try to reduce the number of citizens who head north for better bargains.

If that seems a little confusing and contradictory to you, it probably should. Perhaps a more intelligent long-term approach for the U.S. isn't in tapping into Canada's drug supply, but in finding ways we can achieve affordable drug pricing here at home.

A retired doctor wrote to me, "No American should have to go outside the country to be able to pay a reasonable price for a medication he/she needs and it seems short-sighted to think that the current system can or will work forever. We can't keep putting off a solution and that solution isn't piggy backing on Canadian health care when we refuse to allow that system here."

As you read this final chapter, understand that this is a diverse topic with many, many extenuating factors and considerations. This chapter is intended to give you some important background information on a topic near and dear to most of us. It is not meant to be a definitive or exhaustive analysis of a fairly complex, multifaceted subject. Still, you should know some of the basics because we're all living with the problems, including the confusing rules and regulations and competing interests.

But if you're feeling torn trying to deal with all this, you're not alone. Polls suggest that the average American tends to feel caught in the middle between wanting a much more workable, proactive system and being concerned about how something like the universal health care plan first touted by Hilary Rodham Clinton in the early 1990s would work. It's easy to divide the players up into good guys and bad guys, but it doesn't help one bit in moving us toward a system that makes sense while still respecting that we operate in a free market economy.

The one certainty in all of this is that there are no easy answers for how we proceed in a way that keeps drug manufacturers earning enough profit to continue making our needed medications, while still trying to keep critical drugs affordable to those who need it. With this in mind, let's look at some of the thorny issues that go into creating our current problems.

DIFFERING OPINIONS ON UNIVERSAL HEALTH CARE

As an example of how conflicted we can be on the subject of health care, just appreciate how divided we tend to be on the issue of some nationalized health program such as ones that Canada, England, and many other industrialized nations offer. Some would say that what we absolutely need to do is provide universal health care. Others would argue vehemently that this is the absolute wrong way to go and that the very last thing we should do is place the important nature of our health care in the hands of the government.

Recently, I happened to do an informal poll on this subject that I made available through one of the Web sites I manage. While the majority of people voting in the poll indicated they definitely would like to see some "available-to-everyone" health plan, many also stated that they would like it only if it were not managed by the U.S. government. In another poll, most respondents stated they did not believe that the current presidential plan for a medical savings account, where individuals and families could contribute money each year tax-free to cover health expenses, would in any way help them. Many Americans lived paycheck-to-paycheck even in the booming economy of the 1990s and have seen their ability to save any money in today's less lucrative economy sharply curtailed as salaries froze or decreased and health insurance premiums rose along with conditions they might not cover.

Yet some national polls suggest that the issue of health care doesn't necessarily divide along political party lines as it once did. Republicans, Democrats, and Independents alike recognize that we're experiencing a health care crisis in this country that is affecting more and more Americans who go without health insurance through work.

A new tax plan reportedly being discussed by the White House at the time this book goes to press recommends eliminating the tax deduction employers receive for paying part of the health insurance costs for their workers. This is likely to increase the number of people who go without any type of coverage, since insurance premiums are rising sharply at a time when the average worker income is not.

This is bad news because illness affects the entire U.S. economy in the form of unpaid bills, more involvement by courts to resolve those unpaid debts, lost worker productivity, infection and disease spreading more rapidly, and a host of other things that make us pour more of our attention into problem-repair than preventing problems in the first place. Even if you and your family have proper health care coverage, you can still be affected in the form of higher taxes, fewer services provided without upfront proof of ability to pay, more illness moving through the workplace and schools, and other ripple effects.

On the issue of unpaid hospital bills, there's another wrinkle. Making a bad situation worse, uninsured people are charged a much higher rate by many health care facilities. Health insurance companies negotiate for lower prices for their members, while those not covered are charged full price. An illness or emergency that might result in $4,000–$5,000 billed to your insurer could cost you between $10,000 and $20,000 directly without insurance. That's a huge difference. The result is that many hospitals are now in the courts, placing liens on homes and personal property, seeking wage garnishments, and other financial judgments trying to get paid.

An Overview of the Issues in Drug Prices and Importing Cheaper Drugs

Now let's look at some of the important specific issues, including the much-debated price difference between drugs here at home and those found in places like Canada. We'll look at what makes the Canadian system different, as well as some initiatives we're seeing here where cities, states, and groups are rebelling against U.S. attempts to limit drug importation by actively purchasing from Canadian pharmacies and making resources available for its employees and citizens to do so.

Why the Price Difference for the Same Drug?

Americans pay the highest per-pill drug prices on average than any other people in the world. Now, if you factor in the relative prosperity of the U.S. compared with several other countries, this softens the impact slightly. For example, a drug may be far cheaper in parts of Africa or Eastern Europe, but once you compare that price against a citizen's ability to afford it, we tend to come out better.

A recent Congressional study reported that prescription drugs purchased by U.S. citizens in or through Canadian pharmacies can reduce the price paid by as much as 80%. This means that a drug that may cost you about $100 per month here in the U.S. can be had for as little as $20 if you simply head over the border. Of course, this savings can vary by product and by pharmacy. Figure 14.1 shows the price lookup on CVS.com for Celebrex, the non-steroidal pain reliever, where I can buy 30 100-mg capsules for $56.59. Figure 14.2, comparatively, shows the price for the same product at a Canadian pharmacy (chosen at random) where I can pay less than $72.15 for more than three times the amount (100 caplets), a price difference per pill of more than one dollar.

For the average senior who may regularly take 11 different prescription-only medications—not to mention over-the-counter drugs—on a daily basis, this is a huge consideration. To older adults on a fixed income who are faced with drug-only costs that can run many hundreds of dollars each month, even a 25%–50% average reduction in drug cost can mean the difference between being able to take their medication as directed (rather than splitting pills to make the order last longer) or being able to afford to eat as well as medicate.

Now, to play devil's advocate here, those dozen or so drugs a senior citizen may take are likely there not just to help them today but to extend their life—both qualitatively and quantitatively

Figure 14.1
A price check at CVS.com for the drug Celebrex (prices as of 11/11/04).

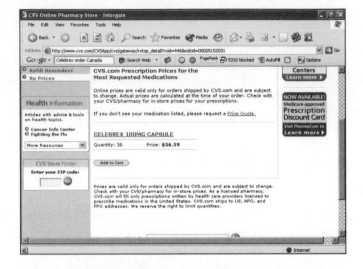

Figure 14.2
The same drug price lookup via a Canadian pharmacy (price as of 11/11/04).

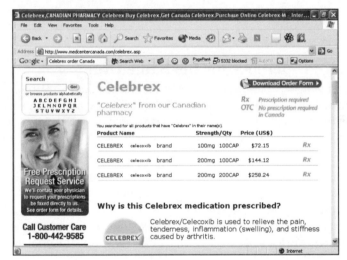

(quality and duration)—in ways that will help them enjoy themselves more and continue their productivity. So it's a blessing that these drugs—many of which were developed in the last two decades—exist.

Yet as valuable as this is, why do we see what can amount to a huge price (as much as 80%) difference? As I wrote earlier in this book, Canada has two strong factors working to its benefit, at least with regard to drug pricing. First, it offers nationalized health care. Although the system is far from perfect, it provides at least basic care at a reasonably affordable price to all of its citizens. But second and more importantly, Canada places price ceilings on the drugs it buys; when manufacturers want to sell to Canada, they need to meet Canada's price.

Now, we use the price model to some degree here in the U.S. Health insurance companies, hospitals and hospital corporations, medical firms, and others in the business of keeping people healthy negotiate for better rates than what a mere mortal walking in off the street to fill a prescription without any health insurance will pay.

But the prices aren't just different between the U.S. and Canada. The same drugs sold here may fetch very differing prices throughout the world. Drug companies sometimes make reduced-cost shipments available to poorer nations, for example, or in response to a particular health crisis. Different countries may have arrangements similar to Canada for negotiating better prices.

Yet even this doesn't necessarily account for all the variation in price, and this often leads to charges that the American health care system is poorly designed with a fair amount of fat and other excess built into it. Critics charge that the influence exerted by rich pharmaceutical companies that often contribute generously to political campaigns helps inflate drug prices here. Pharmaceutical manufacturers will tell you that the U.S. pays the costs of research and development—as well as extensive marketing.

How Canada's Order System Works

To the benefit of Americans seeking better pricing, there's nothing in Canadian law that forbids selling drugs outside the country. While we're just hearing about the push to go north for cheaper medications, some Americans—especially those living in border states from Maine and Vermont to Washington—have been taking advantage of the price differential for a number of years.

Canadian laws allow a foreign prescription to be filled once a Canadian physician signs off, verifying that it is a valid prescription, which in turn allows any pharmacy to fill the order and either hand it to a waiting U.S. resident or ship it to the U.S. It's slightly more involved than that; technically, Canada sees this as converting a U.S. prescription into a Canadian one.

Unlike U.S. law, which tries to make sure a physician sees a patient before recommending a prescription, the Canadian system accepts on good faith that an American doctor has already taken care of that detail. However, the Canadian government, the Canadian pharmacy association, and Canadian doctors are quick to point out that their physicians don't just rubber stamp any prescription form. They may make phone calls to the U.S doctor to verify the information, look at possible drug interactions when a person is filling more than one prescription, and otherwise try to protect patients in getting the right medications.

The chink in the otherwise smooth-running system can occur once the drug actually enters the U.S. For consumers, Customs agents and border guards usually allow personal supplies to pass through. Bulk shipments are a different matter.

When U.S.-based hospitals and medical organizations buy large shipments from Canada, their orders are much more likely to be seized by authorities here in the U.S. There was a recent exception to this, however. During the flu vaccine shortage in the autumn of 2004, a 400-vaccine shipment from Canada bound for a West Coast physician's office was first confiscated and then allowed to continue on its journey, something the U.S. has not usually allowed.

Changes Looming?

Recently there has been some discussion in Canada, principally surrounding the health minister (the equivalent of our Health and Human Services Secretary), about proposed changes to the Canadian Food and Drug Act. These changes, as discussed, could require a Canadian physician to actually examine a U.S. patient before a prescription can be filled through a Canadian pharmacy.

If these changes make it into law, it would seriously impact the ability to do mail-order prescription drug delivery because a patient would need to physically see the Canadian doctor. It's also likely to add both time and much higher costs, including travel to and from the country. How that would balance out against the bargain of Canadian drug prices is unclear. It's likely to cut down on the number of Americans crossing the border.

In a previous chapter, I also mentioned that some Canadian pharmacies are making it policy not to sell drugs to Americans, feeling that doing so ultimately endangers Canadian citizens' continued access to reasonably priced medications. Right now, however, there remain a number of pharmacy and pharmacy chains in the country very willing to sell and ship drugs into the U.S.

Groups, Cities, and States in Rebellion

In August 2004, the state of Vermont filed the first-in-the-nation lawsuit against the FDA charging that the federal agency was acting improperly in trying to block access to cheaper Canadian drugs for its citizens. The lawsuit was in response to the FDA's denial of a plan by the state to import drugs from Canadian sources to reduce medication costs for Vermont state employees.

Yet Vermont is just one of a number of states, municipalities, and organizations that are looking to cut costs for their employees and/or citizens by looking across the border. Figure 14.3 shows a drug savings site operated by the state of Wisconsin, and Figure 14.4 shows a very similar site operated by the state of Minnesota, both with an eye toward importing cheaper drugs from Canada. Rhode Island, considering a move toward letting its citizens order through Canada, also offers a site, shown in Figure 14.5.

Figure 14.3
The state of Wisconsin's drug savings site for state residents.

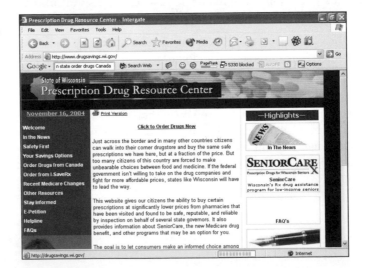

Figure 14.4
Minnesota also offers a "drug connection" for its residents to prescription drug savings.

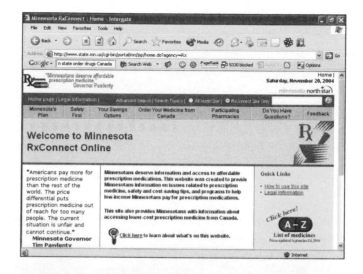

Figure 14.5
The state of Rhode Island provides links and additional information through a state-sponsored Web site.

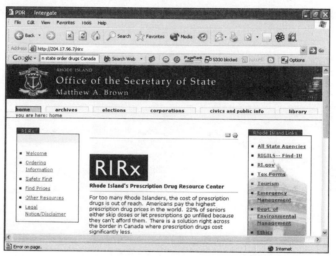

Most of these programs steer people toward ordering from Canada, either directly or as a group order placed by the site with a Canadian pharmacy. Others also look beyond to Europe and other regions of the world that offer good pricing and a reliable, reputable supply of pharmaceuticals.

CHAPTER 14

A FEW FACTS ABOUT "OVER THE BORDER" PRESCRIPTIONS

If you decide to try your luck ordering from a Canadian pharmacy, there are a few things to keep in mind.

First, you can't fill prescriptions for friends or family members this way. The person placing the order—either by physically going to a Canadian pharmacy or using a Canadian-based Web site—must be the person for whom the prescription was written.

Legitimate Canadian pharmacies do not provide drugs via online consultation only. In my research, Canada was the only country in which I found no cyber-pharmacies offering drugs without a prior written prescription. Two that did which advertised themselves as Canadian pharmacies actually operated outside Canada—one registered in Florida and the other in Tobago. While this isn't a definitive study (since new pharmacies come and go rapidly and I looked at no more than 300–400 sites), it was notable because I found so many supposed American pharmacies offering this service, while finding none in Canada (which made me wonder what Canada is doing so differently that may reduce the number of charlatans and pill vendors from setting up shop).

Also, as mentioned earlier in this book, some drugs cannot be purchased or shipped, including narcotic pain relievers. Some people also have trouble filling orders for Ritalin and other controlled substances. This is true even though other cyber-pharmacies, like that shown in Figure 14.6, make it ridiculously easy to buy these potent medications. This is because Canada tends to follow the rules and at least appears to have successfully limited the number of people setting up bogus online drugstores.

Figure 14.6
While cyber-pharmacies make controlled substances too easy to get, Canadian pharmacies do not.

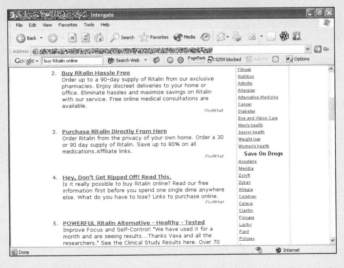

You can get no more than a 90-day "personal supply" of any medication you buy. Also, purchases made from Canadian pharmacies are usually *not* going to be covered by U.S. health care plans offering prescription drug benefits. There are exceptions to this. Additionally, there are unions, groups, and employee programs that help connect you to Canadian pharmacies as part of your health coverage. For example, the community of Pittsfield offers the Pittsfield Rx Direct site shown in Figure 14.7, where Pittsfield employees and retirees can order drugs through Canadian pharmacies through the municipal entity.

Figure 14.7
Pittsfield's Rx Direct
Canadian pharmacy
order site for municipal
employees and retirees.

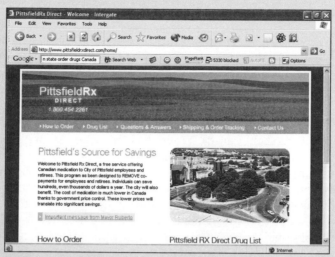

If you're crossing the border with your drugs after filling the order, it's probably best to come clean about what you've gotten. However, you should inform the border officials that you have recently visited your physician and that you had your prescription filled at a Canadian pharmacy. On the Canadian side of the border, that's no problem. On the U.S. side, it's possible that you may be asked additional questions, but there are few if any reports of border officials confiscating personal supplies of legitimate prescription drugs. Technically speaking, however, you are violating U.S. law.

For more information about ordering from or visiting a Canadian pharmacy, U.S. Rep. Bernie Sanders (I-VT) makes a press packet available that actually contains great information for consumers, as shown in Figure 14.8. You can find this at **http://bernie.house.gov/prescriptions/RX_Info_Packet.html**.

Figure 14.8
Rep. Bernie Sanders'
Canadian drug ordering
information page on the
Web.

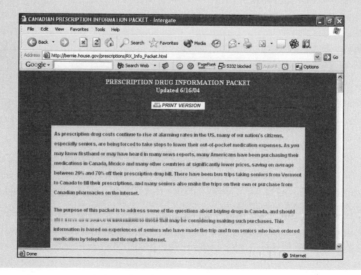

NOTE

It's estimated that between 22% and 35% of all senior citizens in the U.S. either go completely without needed medication or cut their directed dosage to try to make a month's supply stretch. There are no figures available on younger Americans who may not be able to afford their prescriptions.

Why Canada (or Mexico) Isn't the Answer

Consider a few facts about Canada. While the U.S. population will soon swell to over 300 million people, Canada has just an estimated 32.5 million people as of July 2004, making it slightly less than a tenth the size of the U.S. in population. Canada's health care is nationalized, with the government picking up roughly 30%–40% of the health care costs of its population and the provinces and municipalities picking up much of the rest. Its health care is also more preventative in scope (trying to catch problems before they develop into larger illnesses) and Canadian citizens on average consume less prescription medication than their U.S. counterparts.

How exactly does a smaller nation such as Canada then assume the burden of the costs of supplying cheaper pharmaceuticals to a population the size of the U.S., even if only a small—but growing—number of U.S. citizens take advantage of its more competitive drug prices?

It's not so easy to pass off the argument by saying that since U.S. residents pay the going price in Canada, Canada is unharmed by the practice. In fact, the Canadian health care system is picking up the costs of administering a program that its southern neighbors are now tapping into. Just the extra paperwork and additional monitoring involved in the Canadian system to process foreign orders places a financial burden on the country as a whole.

But that's not where the burden and impact ends for our neighbor to the north. Canada operates on the threat—both real and anticipated—of drug companies cutting its supply to try to curb the practice of re-importing American drugs sold to Canada at cheaper prices than those same drugs fetch here. In response, some Canadian pharmacies have banded together to refuse to serve U.S. customers, at least in part because of how the practice may affect their future ability to do business.

The health minister of Canada went on record in November 2004 stating that his country "cannot be the drug store for the United States," referring to the fact that many U.S. consumers—and even whole states—are heading across the border to purchase lower-price prescription drugs.

Reported by the Associated Press, "It is difficult for me to conceive of how a small country like Canada could meet the prescription drug needs of approximately 280 million Americans without putting our own supply at serious risk," Health Minister Ujjal Dosanjh said in prepared text for a speech at Harvard Medical School.

With Mexico, the situation is quite different. Like Canada, Mexico usually enjoys much lower prices than the U.S. when it comes to prescription drugs. But unlike Canada, it has no nationalized health care. In fact, a good portion of the population there is dramatically underserved by any type of health care. As Mexico continues to progress, this is slowly changing.

However, when it comes to Mexican pharmacies, don't expect many of the same controls you see with U.S. and Canadian pharmacies. There are many legitimate pharmacies there, but they're not recognized in the same way their North American counterparts are. There also tends to be far more difficulty in bringing any type of medication across the border, and getting controlled substances in Mexico to carry across can land you in jail on either side.

Several of the Mexican pharmacies I looked at for this book require a certified check or money order rather than credit cards. Most require some type of existing prescription or some way to guarantee that you actually have a legitimate need for the drugs you order. Then there are those at the other end of the spectrum that appear to largely serve as prescription drug tunnels to the U.S. with few questions asked.

"I've ordered from Canada and I've ordered from Mexico," reported one woman veteran cyber-prescription shopper who lives in the Southwest. "It's night and day. When I order from Canada, I always get exactly what I expect. With Mexican pharmacies, the quality of the product changes with each order. I pay less than here, but I can't always use what I get there because sometimes it's a totally bogus product sold as a name brand."

Special Conditions: Foreign Countries Creating Their Own Versions

U.S. patent laws, including those covering pharmaceuticals, don't usually have much if any clout outside the United States. Although there are certain international laws that apply in various parts of the world, it can be extremely difficult to keep something developed here from being copied widely beyond the borders by manufacturers located around the world.

India is a case in point as a country that is known to produce its own versions of popular American drugs. But its versions aren't necessarily exact duplicates of the ingredients, and they may not be made to the same standards. As a country with a huge and growing population and extremely crowded cities, potable water and sustained, affordable electricity has been an issue there. It's an issue that can potentially translate into lesser standards for water quality and the overall sterile nature of the process.

This doesn't mean drugs made in India won't be as good as American drugs. But they certainly may be different. Most of us don't want to send our drugs out for lab analysis before we take them to be sure that they are exactly what we expect them to be.

India is by no means the only country where contaminated water or other factors may affect quality. Nor are all of the drugs affected necessarily foreign-only brands.

For more than two decades, many American drug and research companies have begun to close factories here to have the actual production of their products done somewhere else. Statistically speaking, one almost has to expect that some drugs sold by American companies that are manufactured outside the U.S. are made in countries where the standards may change considerably over what might be acceptable within the U.S.'s border. Years ago, a friend of mine worked for a major drug research and developer; part of her job was to oversee the move of production facilities from New England to Mexico. At the time, she stated that it was a grave headache trying to be sure the Mexican facilities kept their water purification system in perfect working order since the local water supply was badly polluted. More than once, she admitted, the water cleaning system had broken down and against orders, supervisors hooked up to the public water system without any filtering.

The Risk of Imports

In overruling the law passed by Congress in 2003 that allowed the re-importation of drugs by American citizens for personal use only, the FDA and the U.S. government said they could not guarantee the safety of drugs not manufactured and sold under their express control. A few officials even suggested that terrorists might wage an attack on the U.S. by contaminating foreign medicine bound for the U.S.

Some of their concern is understandable once you appreciate the fact that not every country has strong protections in place to be sure that drugs are manufactured under sterile, exacting conditions and that counterfeit or contaminated drugs can't make it out to unsuspecting customers. As one veteran online shopper said, "I've gotten orders from countries where I'd be worried about eating a sandwich. Getting my heart drugs from them is scary."

But what about Canada, one of our two closest neighbors and the source of all the new interest about cheaper drugs? Canada isn't exactly a third world country; it's an industrialized nation with strong laws and standards in place to oversee prescription drug manufacturing as well as proper distribution to those who need it.

In fact, many—not all—of the drugs currently purchased in Canada by U.S. customers are the same as we can buy here, made by the same manufacturers and sold by the same people. The difference is that Canada's price ceilings reduce the price Canada pays, and some of these savings get passed to U.S. customers who order drugs that are then re-imported back into this country.

The Validity of the Risk Weighed Against the Great Flu Vaccine Debacle of 2004

As autumn began to settle over the U.S. in late 2004 word came that more than half of the anticipated American supply of flu vaccine—manufactured by a British company called Chiron—would not be available because of contamination at the vaccine factory. This, following a bad start to the 2003 flu season in which several non-vaccinated children died after another flu vaccine shortage, sent people into a panic.

Suddenly, the chronically ill and the elderly went to stand in line for hours at some vaccination clinics only to be turned away to find a new line another day. Medical experts began to wonder whether the panic was causing people to needlessly exhaust themselves or expose themselves to the kinds of germs that come together when hundreds of strangers gather in close proximity under stressful conditions.

While the FDA told people not to be concerned, public consensus was not very positive after it was learned that everyone in Congress was allowed to get the flu shots that were rationed in the rest of the country. There were also questions flying about why the FDA, which had all but guaranteed the smaller vaccine shortage of 2003 would not be repeated, didn't try harder to protect the U.S. vaccine supply. British and European officials, for example, had responded to news of the Chiron contamination much more briskly and already had alternative supplies on order before the U.S. began to act.

But in the middle of this controversy—which followed on the heels of renewed warnings from the U.S. Health and Human Services Secretary and the president about the safety of drugs imported from countries like Canada—came word that the U.S. could lay its hands on about 1.2 million vaccine doses: from a Canadian firm, ID Biomedical.

Exactly what makes Canadian drugs risky for consumers to buy but fine for the U.S. government to acquire when federal officials are in hot water is a bit sketchy. This decision drew laughs from some and sparked serious criticism from others. Why, after all, were the drugs that a senior citizen wants to buy at a better price in Quebec risky when U.S. officials snapped at the opportunity to buy a large supply of flu vaccine also made in Canada?

Dr. Erik Steele, an administrator at the Eastern Maine Medical Center put it this way in an article on rising drug costs that appeared in the *Bangor Daily News* (11/9/04):

"On the issue of rising prescription drug costs, it would be helpful if we could get [the current U.S. president] to act more like the CEO of America and less like the CEO of a pharmaceutical company. His administration has resisted… the re-importation of prescription drugs from Canada arguing those medications may not be safe. That argument is so thin you would be arrested for wearing it at the beach, as evidenced by the recent efforts of the administration to re-import influenza vaccines from Canada."

"The Little Guy" Versus "The Big Guys"

One criticism leveled again and again about U.S. drug prices centers around the perceived power and the overall clout exerted by drug companies among politicians to keep any ceilings from being imposed that could reduce costs to Americans who buy them. As I indicated in Chapters 1 and 2 of this book, drug associations are often generous contributors to political candidates and seem to get some additional input into policy because of this. I cited the Medicare prescription drug plan for seniors as one example of this.

But it's both difficult as well as not quite the point of this book (which has focused on ordering safely online) to try to determine how much influence drug companies actually exert. What may be more useful is if Americans are able to come together through discussions and effect changes in government focus that place the emphasis back on what's in the best interest of the American public as a whole.

In my area, for example, doctors, lawyers, hospital and insurance program administrators, along with members of the public have recently gathered together for discussions about what steps can be taken to change the system to make health insurance coverage as well as medical care itself more affordable for all citizens. What will ultimately come of this remains to be seen, but it's a start at analyzing the many problems and looking for a solution.

As a free market economy, the U.S. is guided by the principle that people producing a good product or service should be able to profit from their efforts. Any plan for the future really has to recognize that few people will be in the business of providing health care or medication if the costs outweigh the gain. But we also may need to move in a direction that protects Americans as medical consumers from paying inflated prices compared with the rest of the world, while also ensuring that doctors, drug companies, and other concerns are well compensated. The health of the nation may depend on this.

Index

INDEX

INDEX

X–Z